THE SOLDIER
KINGS
of
FRANCE

To Joyce

During our journeys together through the emptiness of time, you have filled the days with tenderness, joy and unrelenting love. We first came together on a moonlit night, pledging to share our lives as one. Stay with me into the barren future, bringing the soft touch of happiness on golden wings. For without you, my being becomes an empty time.

THE SOLDIER
KINGS
of
FRANCE

PHILIP J. POTTER

PEN & SWORD **HISTORY**

AN IMPRINT OF PEN & SWORD BOOKS LTD.
YORKSHIRE – PHILADELPHIA

First published in Great Britain in 2024 by
PEN AND SWORD HISTORY
An imprint of
Pen & Sword Books Ltd
Yorkshire – Philadelphia

ISBN 978 1 39904 706 7

Typeset in Times New Roman 11/13.5 by
SJmagic DESIGN SERVICES, India.
Printed and bound in the UK by CPI Group (UK) Ltd.

Pen & Sword Books Limited incorporates the imprints of Atlas, Archaeology,
Aviation, Discovery, Family History, Fiction, History, Maritime, Military,
After the Battle, Military Classics, Politics, Select, Transport, True Crime,
Air World, Frontline Publishing, Leo Cooper, Remember When,
Seaforth Publishing, The Praetorian Press, Wharncliffe Local History,
Wharncliffe Transport, Wharncliffe True Crime and White Owl.

For a complete list of Pen & Sword titles please contact
PEN & SWORD BOOKS LIMITED
George House, Units 12 & 13, Beevor Street, Off Pontefract Road,
Barnsley, South Yorkshire, S71 1HN, England
E-mail: enquiries@pen-and-sword.co.uk
Website: www.pen-and-sword.co.uk

or

PEN AND SWORD BOOKS
1950 Lawrence Rd, Havertown, PA 19083, USA
E-mail: uspen-and-sword@casematepublishers.com
Website: www.penandswordbooks.com

Contents

Preface

In the chronicles of ancient history, the western part of Europe which evolved into present-day France was first united in the third century BC by the warriors of the Celtic tribe. The Celts settled a large region bordered by the Atlantic Ocean in the west, the Rhine River to the east, Pyrenees mountains in the south and North Sea to the north. The tribesmen occupied the territory known as Gaul until the Romans moved north from Italy and slowly seized control of their lands, with Julius Caesar completing the conquest in 51 BC. The Romans ruled over Gaul for more than 200 years, until Germanic tribes from the east began their piecemeal occupation of the area. The Frankish tribe was part of the Germanic migration to the west, first appearing in Gaul around AD 250. The Franks slowly spread their presence over modern-day north-western France and Belgium, and by the mid-fifth century had become the dominant tribe. During the reign of King Clovis, the Merovingian branch of the Franks rose to prominence by defeating the southern tribesmen and uniting Gaul in 507 into a single kingdom called Francia. The name of current-day France was derived from the Latin name for the Kingdom of Francia.

Upon the death of Clovis in 511, his unified monarchy was divided among his four sons in accordance with Merovingian traditions. The fragmentation of the kingdom produced a long period of civil wars and unrest among the regional warlords, which steadily weakened Merovingian domination over Francia. The kings of this period came to be known as the 'do-nothing kings', increasingly coming under the dominion of the local magnates and high churchmen, who served as the mayors of the palace and held the reins of power. In 623, Dagobert succeeded to the throne of Austrasia – comprising parts of modern-day eastern France, western Germany and Belgium – and seized control from the mayor of the palace, ruling under his own authority. He launched an aggressive military campaign against independent monarchies in Francia, and by 629 had briefly reunited the Kingdom of the Franks created by Clovis.

Following the death of Dagobert in 639, the Kingdom of the Franks again became fragmented until Pippin II overran the rebellious regimes and reigned over the united demesne. When Pippin died in 714, his son, Charles Martel, was acknowledged as king by the nobles and clerics. During the reign of Charles, his armies advanced into the southern princedoms; by his death in 741, he had consolidated his power throughout most of the Frankish realm, passing a unified kingdom to his successors.

In keeping with Merovingian customs, Charles Martel divided his kingdom between his two sons, Pippin and Carloman. The brothers at first ruled together to quell the rebellious churchmen and nobles, with Pippin III solidifying his power over the fiefdoms of Neustria, Burgundy and Provence while his younger brother governed over Austrasia and Aquitaine. In 747, Pippin III outmanoeuvred Carloman, seizing his princedoms and forcing him into a monastery. Pippin, now holding the reins of power over the united Frankish kingdom and emboldened by his support from his nobles and churchmen, expanded his realm to the south.

With Pippin III ruling over the powerful and unified Francia kingdom, Pope Stephen II petitioned the king to intervene against the Lombardy tribe, which had attacked the papal lands in northern Italy. The Frankish king gave his pledge to support the papacy, and in June 753 was anointed as king by the pope in Rome. During the investiture ceremony, Pippin was acknowledged by the Church as the rightful sovereign of the Franks. The consecration of Pippin III was the first investiture of a king by a pope, establishing the precedent for rule by divine right in lieu of elective monarchy. The pontiff was deemed God's representative on Earth, and his anointment of Pippin was considered heaven's approval of his assumption of the Frankish crown. Fulfilling his pledge to Stephen, the Frankish king carried out two military campaigns against the northern Italian Lombards, securing the return of the papacy's conquered territories.

During his reign, Pippin III continued to aggressively expand his domain, ordering his troops across the Rhine to subdue the German Duchy of Bavaria, while also launching punitive attacks against the rebellious Aquitainians. When Pippin died in 768, his aggressive and martial initiatives had laid the foundation for the creation of an empire that would include the majority of Europe by his successor and son, Charlemagne.

Charlemagne and his younger brother, Carloman, reigned over the Frankish kingdom as co-kings. When Carloman died in 771, Charlemagne occupied his brother's eastern lands and ruled over a united realm. He resumed the policies of Pippin III and became the protector of the Holy See and the defender of his kingdom against incursions by rogue fiefdoms and mutinous warlords. While safeguarding his domain, Charlemagne overpowered the rebellious Lombards in northern Italy and attacked the

Saxons in Germany. He reached the height of power in December 800, when Pope Leo III anointed him emperor at St Peter's Basilica in Rome. At the time of his death on 29 January 814, Emperor Charlemagne's vast imperial sphere encompassed present-day France, Switzerland, Belgium, Italy, Germany, the Netherlands and parts of Spain and Austria. He founded an empire that was not seen again in Europe until the reign of Napoleon Bonaparte some 1,000 years later. The empire of Charlemagne was inherited by his son, Louis I the Pious, who held the crown for twenty-six years. Following the king's death, his empire was divided among his four sons, with Charles II seizing control of the lands of modern-day France.

Charles II

In June 840, with the death of the emperor of the Carolingians, Louis I, war soon erupted between his three surviving sons for possession of his vast empire. In 842, as the struggle continued inconclusively, the youngest son, Charles, negotiated an alliance with his half-brother, Louis, for their combined campaign against Lothar, who had earlier assumed the imperial throne of the Carolingian domain as the eldest son. The following year, Lothar was decisively defeated at the Battle of Fontenoy-en-Puisaye and forced to come to terms. Under the Treaty of Verdun, Charles was recognized as king of the western territory, which comprised most of modern-day north-western France, while Lothar claimed the middle realm and Louis the German was ceded the eastern lands of his father. During the following thirty-four years, through relentless campaigning, negotiations and alliances, Charles the Bald expanded his empire across current-day France and was acknowledged as King of Italy and Emperor of the once again reunited Carolingian Empire.

Charles was the first son of Louis I the Pious and his second wife, Judith, and was born on 13 June 823 at the royal castle in Frankfurt. He was associated to the ruling Carolingian dynasty through his father, who was the third son of the empire's ruler, Emperor Charlemagne. With the deaths of Louis' two older brothers, he became recognized as the sole inheritor of the Carolingian Empire. When Charlemagne died in January 814, Louis was uncontested in his succession to the Frankish throne, which included the majority of Western and Central Europe. Before the birth of his fourth son, Charles, the emperor had divided his lands among his sons Lothar, Pippin I of Aquitaine and Louis the German. To secure the future of his fourth son, Louis I made arrangements with his oldest child, Lothar, for Charles to receive part of his inheritance. Furthermore, Lothar agreed to become his half-brother's godfather and serve as his protector.

The young Charles was raised by caretakers in the women's quarters of the castle, and as he grew older routinely witnessed the grandeur of his father's court. He was present when Louis I met with foreign envoys, held meetings with his court officials and was entertained by travelling poets and minstrels. In 829, at the intervention of Judith, a scholarly monk from the monastic school at Fulda named Strabo was appointed Charles' personal tutor. Instructed by the monk, he learned to read and write in Latin and studied languages by reading the Bible and poetry. Under the influence of his mother and Strabo, Charles developed an interest in expanding his literary education and was well-schooled in both Latin and German. Later, as emperor, he created an enlightened court, sponsoring the expansion of scholarly pursuits.

While Judith attended to Charles' education, his military training as a feudal warlord was from an early age arranged by his father. He was instructed by veteran warriors in horsemanship and fighting with the sword, battle-axe and spear, growing fond of hunting and participating in physical activities. As Charles became older, he spent time in Emperor Louis I's court, gaining exposure to the art of kingship while witnessing the political and diplomatic skills required to rule the empire. He frequently campaigned with the emperor's army, attended the annual assembly of nobles and clerics and was closely connected to the imperial government, observing the emperor's interactions with his advisors and foreign visitors.

The three half-brothers of Charles, having earlier been granted separate kingdoms by their father, grew increasingly wary of their relationship with the emperor. Lothar was given the Middle Francia realm, Louis the German was transferred the eastern region of the empire and Pippin I was made King of Aquitaine. Lothar was the oldest son and was born in Bavaria in 795. He spent his early years at the court of his grandfather, Charlemagne, witnessing the governing of the empire. When his father became emperor, Lothar was sent to oversee Bavaria to gain experience in ruling the kingdom. Pippin I, the second son of Louis, being born in 797, was granted Aquitaine in July 814. Three years later he was proclaimed king of the realm, but remained subordinate to his older brother, who was heir to the imperial title of his father. Louis was born in 806 and was the third son of Louis the Pious. He too grew up at the court of Charlemagne, and at the age of 11 was made ruler of Bavaria in place of Lothar. In spite of the emperor's earlier division of his empire, in August 829 at Worms, the 6-year-old Charles was given the title of king and the territories of Alemannia in the eastern region of the empire, along with Alsace and parts of Burgundy in south-eastern modern-day France, which diminished parts of Lothar's lands. Initially, Charles' older brothers appeared to accept the grants of the territories, but after their half-brother visited the Alemannia area and was well-received by the local warlords, their concerns over the future allocations of the empire by the emperor began to grow. The flame of revolt was lit when Lothar accused his mother of adultery with Bernard of Septimania and suggested he was the father of Charles. As Lothar intensified his campaign against his father, Pippin I united with the rebels and led his army of Gascon and Neustrian troops toward Paris. Louis the German now joined his forces with Pippin I and moved against Louis I. The rebellious sons surrounded the emperor at Compiegne and opened negotiations with him. Lothar, who had earlier been exiled from his lands and sent to Italy, now also joined the rebels seeking to gain control over Francia. During talks with his two sons, Louis I pledged to transfer a larger share of the empire to Louis the German and Pippin I, prompting them to end their rebellion. When Lothar arrived from Italy, he attempted to call a council meeting, but the revolt had by then been resolved. He was pardoned by the emperor but sent back to Italy for his instigation of the revolt. In 832, Louis I the Pious again revised his empire's allotment, assigning Neustria to Pippin, while Louis the German and Charles received parts of the Frankish heartlands and Lothar was left with only his Italian kingdom.

In October, 832 Louis I the Pious once more amended his division of the empire among his children. He transferred Aquitaine from Pippin I to Charles, summoning his warlords and clerics to meet at Limoges to swear allegiance to their new king. While the emperor was securing the throne for his 9-year-old son, Pippin refused to accept the loss of his kingdom; after gathering his allies, he returned to Aquitaine and forced his father and younger brother to withdraw. From Le Mans, Louis I attempted to acquire Lothar's support, while Louis the German and Pippin I united against him. To gain the cooperation of Lothar, the Carolingian emperor agreed to transfer a larger part of his lands to him. However, the eldest son had greater goals for acquiring an extensive inheritance, and convinced Louis the German and Pippin I to join him against their father.

In June 833, at an assembly of magnates and bishops later known as the Field of Lies, Lothar and Pippin I seized the emperor and Charles, and with promises of large bribes combined with threats they convinced the Carolingian crown's supporters to defect to them. Charles was taken under guard to the monastery at Prum, while his father was escorted to Soissons. Following the dethronement of Louis I, the empire was divided among the three rebellious brothers, while Lothar assumed the imperial throne and ruled the realm.

To secure his assumption of power, Lothar forced his father to perform a public penance for his crimes against the Church and high magnates. When Louis I reached the Church of St Medard in Soissons, he confessed to his crimes of oath breaking, violations of the peace and the inability to control his adulterous wife. The allies of Lothar were generously rewarded for their participation in the rebellion, while Pippin I was granted the lands reclaimed from his father. Meanwhile, at Prum, Charles' education was resumed by the church's monks and he utilized the monastery's extensive library to continue his studies in religion, Latin and mathematics.

Lothar's attempts to hold the reins of power soon began to weaken. Infighting developed among the brothers, while many noblemen and high clerics expressed their disapproval at the humiliation Louis I was forced to undergo at the Church of St Medard. As his loyal vassals rallied to him, the emperor moved against his rebellious sons. By early 834, he was again acknowledged as emperor and reunited with Charles at the Abbey of St Denis. At the church, Charles witnessed the high clerics re-crown his father as emperor and dress him in the royal robes. Taking control of the empire, Louis I recreated his alliances of bishops and magnates to rule unchallenged. In September the same year, the great lords of the realm gathered in Blois to witness the rebellious Lothar and his supporters confess their disobedience, falling on their knees in front of the emperor. Lothar was sent back to Italy and forbidden to return to court without the permission of his father.

Charles remained with his father's court, continuing his education and preparations to rule part of the Carolingian Empire. He accompanied Louis I on his travels through the realm, learning to govern and defend the diverse regions. At the Christmas assembly at Aachen in 837, Louis the Pious transferred a large part of the Carolingian heartland to Charles, which would later become the centre of his empire. When Pippin died the following year, his Kingdom of Aquitaine was granted to Charles. With the transfer of these lands to their young half-brother, Lothar and Louis the German feared the loss of their inheritances and began plotting against Charles and their father, marking the beginning of Charles' fight for his birthright and principalities. Later in the year, when Louis the German was summoned to meet with the emperor in the present-day city of Nijmegen in the Netherlands, an argument soon erupted over the distribution of the imperial lands, Louis I retorting by depriving his son of all his properties with the exception of Bavaria, as hostilities again threatened to break out.

In June 838, Charles reached the age of majority when he became 15. At the summer assembly of warlords and churchmen at the town of Quierzy in present-day northern France, the emperor conferred on him the domains between the Loire and Seine. As part of the ceremony, Charles was given his sword and crown, signifying his independent assumption of power in his designated properties. He soon after travelled without his father to Le Mans to receive the oaths of fealty from his vassals. Despite being the youngest of his children, Louis I's grant of the region signalled Charles' special prominence and standing in the imperial family.

In 838, the 68-year-old Louis the Pious, under the influence of Judith, began planning for the future of Charles against his ambitious older brothers, who were eager to expand their territorial holdings and wealth. To protect his youngest son's inheritance, his father began plotting to bring him and Lothar together in an alliance against Louis the German. As the emperor manoeuvred against his second son in a bid to isolate him, Lothar of Italy made overtures to Louis the German to join him in a coalition against their father and Charles. When the German king refused the offer, the position of the emperor was greatly strengthened. With Lothar again isolated and his hold on Italy weakening, he was more receptive to his father's proposals to divide the empire with Charles. At Worms in 839, Louis I separated his imperial lands, ceding Charles the western part and Lothar the eastern lands. The division gave Charles the rich lands already granted to him, plus new territories to develop.

Soon after securing his inheritance, a faction of Aquitaine nobles loyal to Pippin I's successor, Pippin II, rose up in rebellion against the Frankish regime. When Charles received reports of the uprising, he hastened to Clermont and summoned his soldiers. From Clermont he moved north, establishing his base at Poitiers, while his father led another army south to attack the rebel castles held by Pippin II's followers. The campaign continued into the following year, Louis and his youngest son slowly reclaiming Aquitaine as Pippin II's men were forced to surrender. With Charles gaining the advantage, the emperor sent envoys to Pippin offering to negotiate a settlement. However, as Charles made his way to the agreed meeting site, news reached him of his father's death.

In the wake of Louis I the Pious' demise, his followers were compelled to choose a new overlord from the emperor's three surviving sons. Lothar was the oldest son and had a large following among the magnates and high churchmen, who quickly accepted his rule. After learning of his father's death, Charles sent envoys to Lothar, who was en route from Italy, reminding him of the previous year's division of the empire by Louis. As his support among the lords and clerics continued to grow, the oldest son now claimed the whole Carolingian Empire, ignoring Louis I's division of the realm. He held firm control over the territory east of the Meuse River in current-day western Germany, while Louis the German had the pledge of strong aid from the nobles and churchmen in Bavaria. While Charles' brothers had solidified the support of their allies, his position was weak in his designated lands in France. Indeed, when Lothar issued a call for his vassals to meet at Ingelheim, many of Charles' followers abandoned him to join his older brother. To protect his inheritance, he hastened north to Quierzy to bolster his support in August 840, leaving Judith to govern Aquitaine. As Charles was trying to enforce his northern rule, Count Pippin II of Breton and his troops moved against Judith, forcing her son to hurry back to Aquitaine. He fell on Pippin II with his loyal followers and put him to flight, ending the immediate danger to his kingdom.

After solidifying his rule, the Aquitainian king's position weakened when Lothar crossed the Meuse and marched west, causing his half-brother's remaining support to collapse. In October 840, Lothar advanced his army across the Seine, seeking to gain domination over all of Neustria. He had moved quickly to seize control of the western lands, which left his position exposed and vulnerable. In need of time to consolidate his gains, he agreed to a truce with Charles that lasted until May. As part of the agreement, Charles was to retain possession of Aquitaine, Provence and areas of Neustria. However, in spite of his treaty with Charles, Lothar actively solicited his brother's allies during the acknowledged period of peace.

During the ongoing truce, Charles worked to shore-up his support in Aquitaine, advancing his army against Pippin II's followers and first gaining control of Le Mans. The Breton count now agreed to abandon Lothar and join forces with Charles. By March 841, the Aquitanian king had gained new allies and strengthened his position against his oldest brother, allowing him to move north toward Paris to confront the magnates and bishops who had recently united with Lothar. He issued a declaration offering an amnesty to all who abandoned Lothar and came over to him. After reaching the outskirts of Paris, he rode to St Denis, offering thanks to God and asking for his protection.

While Charles was bolstering his powerbase in his Kingdom of Aquitaine, Lothar's forces defeated Louis the German in the Rhineland, pushing him back into Bavaria. With Louis weakened, Lothar sent envoys to his half-brother in Troyes, ordering him to advance no further. The two half-brothers spent the following six weeks manoeuvring against each other to gain the advantage for an attack. Charles' prospects for victory were enhanced by the arrival of Judith with reinforcements from the lords of Aquitaine, along with the arrival of Louis the German with a small army of veteran soldiers. On 21 June 841, the two armies of Charles and Louis faced off against their older brother near Fontenoy in central France. The next day, Lothar relocated his basecamp to Fontenoy-en-Puisaye and set up a defensive perimeter. The two half-brothers followed Lothar, keeping a safe distance. On 23 June, Charles and Louis sent envoys to Lothar to negotiate terms for a settlement. Charles offered to give up his claims to lands between the forest of Charbonniere and the Meuse, while Louis pledged to yield his rights to the region west of the Rhine. Lothar delayed giving an answer, pretending to consider the terms, but was merely stalling for time awaiting the arrival of Pippin II and his Aquitaine troops. When Pippin II reached the camp, Lothar swiftly broke off the talks and prepared for battle. With his army now reinforced, he was convinced he would achieve victory and believed his youngest brother would be tonsured by the Church and forbidden to ever rule.

As the sun rose on 25 June 841, the opposing armies hurriedly prepared for battle at Fontenoy in present-day Belgium. The battlefield was a flat expanse surrounded by numerous low hills. Charles and Louis deployed their army of 150,000 men on two separate knolls, and at the designated signal advanced against Lothar and his allies, the roaring battle cries of the men echoing across the valley. The infantry advanced in a tight formation, protected by a wall of shields against the waves of arrows from the enemy's archers. Armed with spears, swords and axes, the two kings' soldiers charged into their foe, while the cavalry rode into their flanks. The bloody and fierce man-to-man fighting raged for over six hours, with charges and counter-charges, until the mounted warriors of Charles and his brother finally crashed through the enemy lines and compelled them to flee. The brothers pursued the battered forces of Lothar and his allies, cutting down thousands. More than 40,000 men from the armies of Lothar and Pippin II were said to have been slaughtered at Fontenoy, which became the bloodiest and most destructive battle of the ninth century.

Fontenoy was a decisive victory for Charles, being considered as God's judgement confirming his rights to the Frankish kingdom of his father. The defeat of Lothar induced many of his indecisive counts and high clerics to pledge their fealty to Charles. The triumph secured Charles' sovereignty over the Western Frankish Kingdom and prevented its absorption by Lothar.

Although Lothar had been defeated at Fontenoy, he retained many supporters and was resolved to resume his quest for the Carolingian Empire. With their older brother still a dangerous threat, Charles and Louis pledged to resume their war against him until his surrender, agreeing to meet in Strasbourg in February 842 to renew their campaign. Despite his defeat at Fontenoy, Lothar continued to conspire, making new offers of friendship to Charles to break his alliance with Louis. However, the two allies remained firm in their belief that God was on their side and refused to answer their older brother's proposals. Lothar made a foray into western Francia to the Seine to shore up his support and negotiated with Pippin II and the Bretons for their friendship, while also again dispatching emissaries to Charles to break his pact with Louis and form a new alliance with him. His attempts to forge a new coalition ended in failure, as Charles continued to gain new followers.

On 14 February 842, King Charles II, Louis the German and their allies met at Strasbourg to forge a strategy to end the danger posed by their older brother. At the Strasbourg congress, before their gathered armies, the brothers swore an oath of mutual friendship and cooperation against Lothar. They told their soldiers that Lothar had rejected the judgement of God and was responsible for the relentless suffering of their people. Only through firm union could Lothar be compelled to accept the claims of his younger brothers. The nobles and high churchmen present at Strasbourg subsequently swore oaths to support their kings in order to secure peace.

Following their meeting at Strasbourg, the two kings sent envoys to Lothar seeking a peace agreement, but their eldest brother refused to negotiate and advanced his forces southwards from Aachen to challenge Charles and Louis. The German king then moved his army down the Rhine, meeting Charles at Koblenz on 18 March. With his brothers reinforced by new allies who had recently abandoned him, Lothar fell back to Aachen. After plundering the imperial treasury, he fled south, leaving the city and the Kingdom of the West Franks to his two brothers. To divide Francia, Louis and Charles each appointed twelve representatives to determine the boundaries of the two kingdoms. Shortly after the committee met, Lothar sent emissaries offering to negotiate with his brothers. When Charles and Louis proposed dividing the Francia into three realms, Lothar demanded the largest share. As the negotiations continued through the summer, Viking raiders attacked Charles' town of Quentovic near the Channel coast, forcing him to pay a large bribe to secure their withdrawal. Charles was also compelled to march against Pippin II, assailing him across the Loire River and putting him to flight. At the beginning of October, forty negotiators from each brother met at Koblenz to set the terms of a peace agreement. Mistrust between the two parties persisted, and to reduce the threat of violence, the mediators agreed to spend each night on opposite sides of the Rhine. The final treaty was delayed for over a year, while Charles and Louis sent their representatives to make a detailed inventory of the empire to make a fair division. Lothar protested the delay, but was forced to concede.

On 13 December 842 at the church in Quierzy, while the inventory of the Carolingian Empire was being complied, Charles II was married to

Ermentrude, daughter of Odo, Count of Orleans, in a political arrangement to strengthen his base of support among the heartland magnates and clerics of his new kingdom. During their marriage of twenty-seven years, they developed a close and loving relationship, the queen frequently travelling with Charles on his diplomatic missions and military campaigns. In 846, Ermentrude secured the continuance of the Carolingian dynasty with the birth of the future King Louis II. The marriage went on to produce ten additional children. Ermentrude was considered a strong-willed woman by her contemporaries, and devoted to the Christian Church. The queen was associated with several convents, actively supporting them with financial contributions. As queen, she directed the education of her children and was responsible for the management of the royal household. In 866, Ermentrude was consecrated queen in recognition of her wise and loyal reign and being wife to Charles II. When she died in 869, Charles II remarried the following year to Richildis of Provence to augment his recent seizure of lands in Lotharingia. Richildis, daughter of the Count of Ardennes, was authoritative and self-assured as queen, governing the kingdom during the absences of the king.

King Charles II spent the remainder of the harsh winter and spring of 843 with Ermentrude in Aquitaine, continuing his fight against Pippin II and his allies. In August of that year, the three brothers met near Verdun to finalize the terms of their treaty for the partition of the Carolingian Empire. The signed agreement was the first stage in the dissolution of the empire and foreshadowed the formation of the modern countries of Western Europe. Under the agreement, Louis the German was ceded the region east of the Rhine and north of the Alps, while Lothar acquired the central kingdom, including parts of modern Belgium, the Netherlands, western Germany, eastern France, Switzerland and much of Italy, along with the title of emperor. Charles was given the western area from the Scheldt to the Rhone River, current-day western France. The West Frankish king's realm largely comprised the lands previously designated for him by Emperor Louis I.

In the aftermath of the signing of the Treaty of Verdun, a period of relative peace prevailed among the Carolingian brothers, Charles II being involved with securing his rule in his West Frankish Kingdom. Over the following months, he had to respond to the relentless threats of revolt in Aquitaine led by Pippin II, Moslem armed incursions into his southern borders, the renewal of pillaging raids by the Vikings into the plains of the Loire and Seine rivers and the continued attempts by Lothar to gain support from his youngest brother's vassals. To secure his inheritance, Charles first moved against the persistent attacks of Pippin II. In 845, Charles travelled into

Aquitaine, meeting personally with Pippin II to resolve his rebellion. An agreement was hammered out, with Charles pledging to give direct control of Aquitaine to Pippin in exchange for his homage and acknowledgement as overlord.

With peace finally restored to Aquitaine after several years of bloody rebellion, the king made plans to march against the Duchy of Brittany, where Duke Nominoe had been expanding his domain into Frankish lands with impunity. Charles' spies had told him that a large faction of disgruntled Bretons would defect to him if he hurried to their aid. The West Frankish king assembled an army of nearly 3,000 soldiers in November and marched against Nominoe's forces. Using his knowledge of the Breton terrain, Nominoe lured Charles into the marshlands near Ballon Abbey, where on 22 November he unleashed an assault against the Franks. The Bretons, with a large force of light cavalrymen, outmanoeuvred Charles and forced him to retreat.

In 845, the Vikings renewed their raids along the Seine and Loire rivers, pillaging many farms and towns, leading Charles to issue orders for his vassals to assemble their troops for a campaign against the raiders. A fleet of over 100 Norse ships had recently sailed up the Seine and threatened Paris, compelling the Frankish king to advance his army to protect his subjects and lands. Confronting the pagans, Charles separated his forces into two divisions to defend both sides of the Seine. The Vikings took advantage of the king splitting his army, defeating each one in detail. With the Frankish defences weakened in strength and size, the Vikings were free to advance against the city of Paris. To save the city and other towns along the Seine, Charles was compelled to pay a tribute of 7,000 pounds in silver. When the Northmen returned the following year, they raided Aquitaine and Brittany. To clear his kingdom of the Vikings, the Frankish king marched his soldiers south into Aquitaine, destroying the new Norse settlement at Bordeaux. After the Northmen were driven out of Aquitaine, many of the local warlords and churchmen abandoned Pippin II and swore allegiance to Charles.

As King Charles II secured his power over his lands, in February 847, the three brothers signed an agreement pledging to cooperate in the mutual defence of their kingdoms against internal revolts and attacks from the Vikings and eastern pagan tribes. Lothar had continued his interventions into the West Frankish king's territory, attempting to expand his kingdom, but now honoured the provisions of the new accord, giving Charles a period of relief from his incursions. The three brothers promised to meet periodically to reaffirm their oaths of friendship and peace. Nevertheless, the scheming Lothar soon broke his vow and resumed his support of the rebellious nobles and high clerics in Aquitaine. Charles and King Louis met in 849 to quell the dangerous conspiracies of their older brother, strengthening their opposition against him.

In 845, the Franks had been defeated by Duke Nominoe of Brittany at the Battle of Ballon to re-establish the borders of the duchy to the east into Charles II's lands. Four years later, the Bretons renewed their campaign of expansion against the West Frankish king, advancing to seize Nantes and Le Mans. When Nominoe moved against Chartres, he suddenly died and was succeeded by his son, Erispoe, who continued the advance into Frankish territories. With the Bretons raiding unchecked into his realm, Charles the Bald mustered his army, and with German reinforcements from Louis marched west against Erispoe. On 23 August 851, the two armies clashed at Jengland, where Charles deployed his forces with the Germans in the front line and his men in the second. The battle began with the Bretons unleashing volleys of javelins into the lightly armoured Germans, causing heavy losses. Erispoe's foot-soldiers then charged into the enemy, but were beaten back with many casualties by a counter assault of Charles' troops. The fighting raged throughout the day and into the next, the Bretons continued to attack the Franks with fierce charges, feints and sudden withdrawals, forcing King Charles to abandon the field after sustaining heavy casualties. In September, the adversaries signed the Treaty of Angers, under which Erispoe pledged to acknowledge Charles II as his overlord and the Frankish crown honouring the Bretons' possession of the areas around Rennes and Nantes, establishing the boundaries of Brittany.

The continued defiance of Pippin II to Charles' rule over Aquitaine remained a source of opposition to the king. When the rebel leader again broke his pledge of fealty in 852, the Moslem allies of Charles launched an attack against him in support of their overlord. They quickly defeated Pippin and handed him over to the West Frankish king. After consulting with Emperor Lothar and gaining his approval, Charles had Pippin tonsured at the monastery of St Medard and sent to a priory, removing him from any future involvement in court intrigues. Lothar had relentlessly upheld Pippin II's rights to Aquitaine, but his abandonment of him and acknowledgement of Charles as ruler in the realm was recognition of his brother's rise to power in the West Frankish Kingdom.

Following the removal of Pippin II from Aquitaine, Emperor Lothar acknowledged Charles' overlordship, the two half-brothers developing a bond of trust and collaboration. The move to closer cooperation came at the expense of straining Charles' association with Louis of Germany. Later in the year, when Charles and the emperor campaigned together against the

Vikings, their relationship with Louis was weakened further, pushing them closer to war.

In 853, the health of Lothar began to rapidly decline, the two younger brothers starting to plot to gain the advantage in his Middle Kingdom and northern Italy. Charles manoeuvred to be acknowledged as the protector for the inheritance rights of Lothar's two sons to extend his kingdom to the east. Despite his intrigues to secure the appointment, when the assembly of magnates and bishops met, Louis of Germany was appointed to safeguard the Middle Kingdom's transfer to Lothar's eldest son, Louis II the Younger. The alliance between Charles and the German king was weakened further when Louis was approached by a faction of discontented Aquitanian churchmen and magnates, who pressed him to overthrow Charles II. The plot against the western Carolingian king was soon abandoned when the son of the German king, Louis II the Younger, travelled to Aquitaine to rally support but was forced to withdraw after the local warlords and churchmen refused to join him.

The equilibrium and political landscape in the Carolingian Empire was dramatically altered in September 855 at Prum in Germany, when Lothar I died after a long illness. The emperor's death eliminated a strong centralized force and a common unifying source in the empire for Charles II and Louis the German. Without their older brother to rally against, the two brothers' already precarious coalition threatened to break apart. New tensions and conflicts quickly developed between them, as each plotted to gain control and influence over their three young nephews. Under the instructions for the division of his lands, Lothar I named his eldest son, Louis II, his successor to the monarchy of Italy with the title of emperor, and the second son, Lothar II, was recognized as sovereign for the northern Kingdom of Lotharingia, while the youngest son, Charles, was awarded Provence. With his agreement with Louis the German now breached, the West Frankish king soon forged an alliance with Lothar II, forcing his older brother to negotiate an understanding with Louis II to maintain the balance of power.

As Charles II manoeuvred to secure his dominance over the empire, the Vikings resumed their plundering attacks against his lands. They sailed down the Seine and Loire with a large army and again threatened Paris. Meanwhile, to the south, new dangers emerged when factions of local magnates and bishops rallied to Pippin II's inheritance rights to the Aquitaine monarchy. The foremost Aquitainian warlord, the charismatic Count Robert the Strong, became closely associated with Pippin II's claim to the throne, rallying the nobles and clerics from Aquitaine, Neustria and Brittany to his cause. As the son of the influential count, he was assigned the lay Abbey of

Marmoutier in north-eastern France and was later appointed royal lord for Maine, Anjou and Touraine by Charles the Bald, as he steadily grew in power and dominance among the Frankish churchmen and warlords.

Along with the threats posed by the Vikings and Robert the Strong, Louis the German remained ready to seize upon any weakness or failure by Charles II and turn it to his advantage. To safeguard his Western Carolingian monarchy, the king launched a series of diplomatic and military initiatives to push back the German king and his allies. Charles' treaty of cooperation with Lothar II was renegotiated to strengthen his defences on his eastern frontier against an attack by his older brother. To protect his homeland against an internal revolt, he reinforced his support with the local Frankish warlords and churchmen. Meanwhile, in Aquitaine, Pippin II had ignored his vows to the Church and agreed to aid Charles against the threats of Robert the Strong for the pledge of lands and other bribes. Through a combination of military campaigns, bribes and alliances, he weakened the impact of the Northmen's pillaging raids on his Frankish kingdom. Charles II's successful measures had thus reduced the dangers to his kingdom and enhanced his powerbase.

By late 856, the political stability of Charles II's West Frankish kingdom began to break down. The Northmen returned in large numbers, sailing up the Seine towards the rich city of Paris. They constructed a fortified town at Jeufosse, 37 miles from Paris, to serve as the site for their pillaging raids. From their base of operations, the Vikings unleashed plundering forays into the Vexin and Perche regions of north-western France, sacking towns, burning farmlands and slaughtering inhabitants. As the Norse raiders intensified their destruction across Charles' lands, he assembled his vassals and soldiers and advanced to protect his heartland. His brief campaign inflicted large losses on the Northmen, compelling them to return to Jeufosse and spend the winter at peace.

During his campaign against the Vikings, Charles II was joined by Aethelwulf of Wessex, who was returning to his homeland after making a pilgrimage to the Holy See with his young son, Alfred (the later King Alfred the Great). The Wessex king had visited the Frankish court the previous year on his way to Rome and was royally entertained by Charles II. After meeting with Pope Benedict III and receiving his blessings, he travelled with his son through Italy into France and was reunited with Charles at his palace of Verberie-sur-Oise outside Paris. The Frankish king escorted Aethelwulf and his son through his expansive royal house, with its magnificent rooms and vast gardens. During his earlier stay at the Frankish court, the two kings had discussed the marriage of Charles II's daughter, Judith, to the Wessex king.

Both regimes were eager to expand and coordinate their defences against the escalating Viking raiders, and the union between the two families was pursued. Negotiations were now resumed and a final treaty signed. On 1 October 856, amid the majesty and splendour of Charles' court, Aethelwulf and Judith were married by the Archbishop of Rheims, binding the two realms to mutual support.

In 856, Charles' heir-designate, the 10-year-old Louis the Stammerer, was invested with the sub-kingdom of Neustria, with its principal cities of Paris, Tours and Orleans. Louis was the first son of Charles and Queen Ermentrude. From the city of Le Mans in Neustria, Louis the Stammerer ruled his realm through a chancery led by the Duke of Brittany, Erispoe. The appointment of Erispoe had disrupted the balance of power in the Lower Loire region, with the local warlords and churchmen threatening to rise up against the Carolingian regime. Count Robert the Strong felt endangered by the presence of Erispoe, joining with other local disaffected magnates and a faction of rebellious Aquitainians to invite Louis the German's intervention on their behalf. The attempt to form a united front against Charles II fell apart when Louis refused to respond. Despite the failure to bring Louis the German into their alliance, Count Robert continued to resist Charles' presence in his region and remained a rallying point for other potential rebel warlords.

The prospects for war generated by Robert the Strong's intrigues convinced Charles II to modify his relationships with his vassals to ensure their continued alliance. He sent several envoys to meet with the noblemen and clerics to confirm their loyalty. The Frankish king's representatives assured his liege subjects that he would always seek their counsel in the future before taking action, and that all loyal vassals would be protected. The nobles were told they should not fear his wrath as they would seek to peacefully resolve their disputes. Safe conduct would be issued to those magnates who wished to discuss their issues with the overlord. In spite of Charles' initiatives to regain the loyalty of his vassals, many continued to look to Robert the Strong as their leader.

In 857, the Northmen renewed their raids into the West Frankish kingdom in force. The Vikings at Jeufosse had not been driven away by Charles, and they continued their attacks on towns, raiding Paris in December. Paris was pillaged again during the following summer, the Jeufosse raiders and newly arrived Vikings from the north striking out across Charles II's heartland, killing, looting and burning.

As the Northmen ravaged the West Frankish kingdom, Robert the Strong rallied the still-disaffected Franks in a new challenge to the Carolingian king.

The Frankish leaders persuaded a faction of prominent Aquitaine warlords to revive the cause of Pippin II's kingship against Charles' rule. The rebels also forged an alliance with the Vikings and sacked the city of Poitiers. The attacks of the Northmen and Pippin II's supporters left Charles II's peace policy in Neustria in disarray. Robert the Strong seized the opportunity to negotiate an alliance with the rebellious Breton faction and unleashed an assault against Louis the Stammerer. Louis' troops were quickly overrun and his followers driven out of Neustria. Meanwhile, a large Viking force sailed up-river from Jeufosse, raiding the Abbey of St Denis and carrying off the abbot as their captive, as Charles II's control of his West Frankish lands continued to weaken under the attacks.

With his kingdom assailed by both Frankish rebels and Vikings, Charles countered the threat by arranging to meet with Lothar II in March 858 at Quierzy in central France to reaffirm their alliance and shore-up his eastern border defences. At Quierzy, he held meetings with his Frankish vassals and received their oaths of fealty, while pledging his protection to them. During the assembly of his liege lords, Charles II raised the funds necessary to secure the release of Abbot Louis of St Denis from captivity by the Northmen. To further reduce the plundering raids of the Scandinavians, he induced them to abandon the Seine area and vacate their fortress at Jeufosse by a combination of alliances, bribes and military campaigns. The withdrawal of the Northmen freed the Paris region from their forays and reinforced the allegiance of the warlords and clerics to the king. Charles continued to strengthen his kingdom's defences, and in early 858 persuaded the Viking warlord, Bjorn, and his men to join his army. In July he convinced Pippin II to abandon his alliance with Count Robert the Strong, weakening the ability of the Aquitainians to withstand his assaults.

While Charles II was shoring up his resistance to internal uprisings, he confronted a new threat from the Count of Troyes, Odo, and Abbot Adalard of St Bertin, who abandoned their allegiance to him and joined Count Robert. They were soon sent by Robert as envoys to Louis the German to convince him to overthrow his half-brother and take his throne. Odo and Adalard conferred with the East Frankish king, telling him that Charles had allowed the Northmen to plunder their lands with impunity and had continually broken his oaths to them. Sensing an opportunity to expand his domain to the west, Louis the German agreed to intervene against his brother, entering West Frankish territory in 858 and travelling south to Orleans. He met with warlords and churchmen from Neustria, Brittany and Aquitaine, who agreed to pledge their fealty to him. As the rebels gathered against the West Frankish king, he sent envoys to them with a liberal offer of peace, which was swiftly rejected. After the repudiation of his peace overtures, Charles II gathered an army and advanced to Brienne to quell the gathering storm. When the battle lines were drawn up on 12 November 858, the West Frankish king quickly realized his forces were inadequate to defeat Louis the German and his allies, and retreated into the safety of Burgundy.

After King Charles abandoned the battle, Louis the German advanced northward to Rheims and pressed the local churchmen to consecrate him as king in place of Charles. The Archbishop of Rheims, Hincmar, refused to perform the ceremony, giving evasive excuses to deflect Louis' demands. Meanwhile, in Burgundy, Charles rallied his supporters and prepared to move against the rebels. The bishops of Auxerre and Autum, along with Count Conrad of Auxerre, pledged their allegiance to Charles, while in Francia former dissidents now left Louis the German to join their forces with the West Frankish king. When Charles advanced his newly mustered army back into his kingdom, the military power of the two rivals was reversed and Louis the German was compelled to retreat.

The abandonment of Louis the German's attempt to seize the West Frankish kingdom signalled a reversal in Charles' political and military outlook. In February 859, Lothar II hastened to meet his uncle south-east of Paris at the town of Arcis-sur-Aube to personally assure the king of his loyalty. The Frankish king received assurances from his vassals in Francia, Burgundy Aquitaine and Septimania of their continued loyalty, while the lords and clerics of Neustria withheld their oaths. Charles now advanced against his remaining disloyal vassals, depriving them of their privileges and properties, while richly rewarding his loyal followers with grants of lands and titles.

Throughout 859, the Frankish king's political situation continued to strengthen, but he was then confronted with a new wave of Viking warbands operating in the valley of the Seine. The valley served as the agricultural centre of the king's realm and he could ill-afford to suffer the loss of its resources. When a new band of warriors led by Weland appeared in the Somme region, Charles the Bald was able to recruit its services against the raiders in the Seine valley and inflict heavy losses on them. The Frankish king's successful attacks against the Northmen encouraged the local warlords and their men to move against the raiders independently of aid from the throne, inflicting further large numbers of casualties on them.

As the West Frankish regime fought against the incursions of the Scandinavians, Charles II was confronted with the renewed revolt of a faction of his vassals. Salomon, Duke of Brittany, was at the forefront of the rebelling warlords. After pledging his fealty to the Frankish throne, Count Salomon had been granted the counties of Rennes and Nantes and parts of Brittany. In 857, he was acknowledged by the Bretons as their overlord after arranging the assassination of Erispoe, Duke of Brittany. As Salomon then reigned over Brittany, he formed an alliance with Robert the Strong and rebelled against King Charles II. He had earlier participated in Robert the Strong's overthrow of Louis the Stammerer in Neustria, forming an alliance with him. After securing the Duchy of Brittany, Salomon rose up against Charles with Robert's support and defied his king. Attempts were made by the Archbishop of Tours to encourage the Breton duke to recognize the sovereignty of Charles II, but he remained in defiance of his overlord.

In 860, Louis the Stammerer was granted the lay Abbey of St Martin's in Tours by his father after reaching the age of 15. The city was located in Neustria, and the transfer of the lay abbacy to Louis heralded the rebirth of the former sub-kingdom under the rule of Charles II's family. Many of the Neustrian warlords recognized Louis the Stammerer's overlordship of the fiefdom. Without the support of the local magnates and clerics, Robert the Strong was forced to make peace with Charles II. During the previous year, King Charles had successfully established his second son, Charles the Younger, in Aquitaine as sub-king, signifying his acceptance by the local warlords and church officials, while denying Count Robert a source of supporters for his continued defiance of the Frankish regime. The West Frankish king's political campaign expanded his acceptance as overlord and eliminated sources of resistance to his crown.

On 1 November 861, Louis the Stammerer reached the age of majority, and soon revolted against the Frankish king by marrying without his father's consent. In early January, Louis moved his court to the Breton Marches and with the support of Duke Salomon attacked his long-time enemy, Robert the Strong, ravaging his countship of Anjou. The uprising soon fell apart, however, Robert outmanoeuvring Louis and forcing him to surrender. Louis' independent actions resulted in the loss of Neustria from West Frankish control.

Charles II's successful political and military interventions against his rebellious vassals and clerics created a loyal powerbase in his kingdom. While maintaining a watchful eye on the Vikings and his liege warlords, he began intriguing to gain control of neighbouring Lotharingia on his eastern border. The King of Lotharingia, Lothar II, had no recognized successor and was actively seeking to dissolve his childless marriage. Once the divorce was sanctioned by the Church, Lothar planned to marry Waldrada, with whom he had fathered a son and potential heir. The acceptance of his new marriage would make their son, Hugh, the legitimate successor and ensure the continuation of the Middle Kingdom. Lothar secured the support of his bishops, but when they were sent to Rome to secure Pope Nicholas I's approval, the pontiff refused to sanction the second marriage and excommunicated Waldrada. Pope Nicholas I's decision now made it highly unlikely that Lothar would have a direct heir, opening the door for Charles II to intercede on his own behalf.

Lothar II's continued plotting to gain the Holy See's approval of the second marriage failed to alter the pope's decision. Pope Nicholas I died in 867 and Hadrian II was elected to the papacy. Lothar II was still without a direct heir, and in 869 he made the long and dangerous journey to Rome to personally petition Hadrian II. Before any decision was made by the Holy See, Lothar II became seriously ill with malaria and died. The unexpected death of Lothar created the opportunity for Charles II's seizure of the Kingdom of Lotharingia. Upon learning of his nephew's death, he assembled his army and marched quickly into the Middle Kingdom to enforce his rule. As he travelled through the realm, the lords and clerics rendered their allegiance. Charles the Bald was able to gain sufficient endorsements to be anointed king on 9 September at the church of St Stephen in Metz. As the sovereign of two kingdoms, Charles issued edits to his vassals and high churchmen proclaiming his assumption of the title of emperor. He had earlier made an arrangement with Louis the German to divide Lotharingia equally should their nephew die without an heir, but ignored the agreement to expand his kingdom to the east by seizing control of Lothar II's entire realm. With Queen Ermentrude having died the previous year, to secure a strong hold over his new lands, Charles married Richildis, who had strong Lotharingian family ties.

At the end of 869, Charles II was acknowledged as King of Lotharingia and appeared to have established his rule. While the king was enforcing his sovereignty over the Middle Kingdom, Louis the German became severely ill and was not expected to survive. When the East Frankish king made an unexpected recovery, he posed a threat to his brother's assumption of the Lotharingian crown. To challenge his half-brother's right to the Middle Kingdom, Louis mustered his army and advanced west to Frankfurt to impose his rights to the Lotharingian regime. He was recognized as overlord by the gathered Lotharingian magnates and high churchmen in the city. Louis sent an envoy to his half-brother telling him if he did not abandon the Middle Kingdom he would be brutally driven out by his army. Louis commanded a larger military force than the West Frankish king, compelling him to negotiate a settlement. Charles II sent representatives to Attigny to meet with Louis' emissaries. After several months of talks, Charles and Louis met at Meersen on 8 August to finalize their agreement. Under the terms of the Treaty of Meersen, Charles was forced to divide Lotharingia, with his brother receiving the eastern portion while he gained possession of the western region. The King of West Frankland was unable to obtain all the territory he had prized, but did add significant holdings in the Frankish heartland. The agreement of 870 replaced the earlier Treaty of Verdun.

By the beginning of 870, the western region of Lotharingia was securely under the control of Charles II. The uprising of his first son, Louis the Stammerer, had been suppressed, but now his second surviving child, Carloman, also defied his father and moved to gain possession of an independent realm. Carloman was born in 848, the fourth son of Charles II and Ermentrude. He was tonsured in 854 to further his father's policy of limiting the partitions of his kingdom. In 860, he was ordained a deacon and acquired Saint-Medard de Soissons Abbey, with several other abbacies later being ceded to him. After the deaths of Charles' second and third sons, Carloman became second in the line of succession. Sensing an opportunity to acquire his autonomous monarchy in the Middle Kingdom, he moved to confront his father's sovereignty. Carloman gathered a force of disgruntled warlords and churchmen from Flanders and Lotharingia and prepared to advance against the king. Upon learning of his son's revolt, Charles II ordered his arrest and confined him to a monastery prison at Senlis, while seizing his abbacies.

Carloman had gained a strong following from the nobles and clerics of Lotharingia, who rallied to his intervention against his father, while Pope Hadrian II and Louis the German also interceded in his favour and lobbied for his release. The potential encroachment of Louis the German was a serious threat to Charles, but occurred while his half-brothers' two sons were also in revolt against their father. To resolve the potential crisis, a meeting of reconciliation between the two brothers and their sons was arranged for August 871. Under the provisions of the settlement, Carloman returned to his father's favour, but he remained a potential danger to the Lotharingian throne with a growing political base of support. When a plot to place Carloman on the Middle Kingdom's throne was discovered, Charles II ordered his son put on trial and blinded to secure his sovereignty over the western region of Lotharingia. Before his imprisonment, Carloman escaped to the court of Louis the German, where he was given sanctuary.

The papacies of Hadrian II and his successor, John VIII, were beset with repeated forays by the armies of the Byzantines on the east coast of the papal lands and the Muslims to the west, while in northern Italy, the local warlords threatened to advance against the recognized territories of the Holy See. With the pope's domain under attack, Emperor Louis II had provided military and financial support to the papacy, but when he died on 12 August 875 without a direct heir, the political status quo was thrown into turmoil.

Shortly after securing his Frankish regime following his absence in the Middle Kingdom, Charles II quickly advanced south-east across the Alps into northern Italy to claim the imperial lands and title of emperor, while providing protection to the Holy See against rogue warlords and marauding Muslims along his south-western coastline. Before Louis II died, he had named his cousin, Carloman of Bavaria, as his successor. Carloman now assembled an army and prepared to cross the Alps to claim the imperial crown, while his uncle, Charles II the Bald, asserted his rights to the regime. To avert war with his nephew, the West Frankish king sent envoys to his court in Bavaria to forge a peaceful settlement. An agreement was finalized with Carloman, who pledged to forfeit his rights to Italy and the imperial title. Charles now moved quickly south to Rome, gaining the homage and support of the Italian nobles and clerics to solidify his rights to the imperial throne. Pope John VIII had earlier looked to the emperors as a base of defence and patronage, agreeing to perform the coronation ritual of Charles II to secure his favour. At St Peter's Basilica on Christmas Day 875, Charles was anointed by Pope John VIII with the imperial crown in a re-enactment of his grandfather Charlemagne's inauguration as Emperor of the Romans in 800. While in Italy, the King of the West Franks gathered enough local backing from the magnates to provide the pontiff with a protective coalition. Charles II completed his Italian triumph in January 876 at Pavia, where at a great assembly of the nobles and churchmen, he was elected King of Italy.

While in Italy, Charles II received reports of Louis the German's incursion into his eastern lands and was forced to hurriedly return to his kingdom. He hastened north over the Alps, reaching his homeland in time for the Easter celebrations at St Denis in Paris. At his Easter court, he reasserted his kingship over the Western Frankish kingdom, while putting his newly acquired empire under the protection of his heavenly Father. There was considerable resentment among the West Frankish magnates over Charles II's involvements in Italy, but they gave their consent to the decisions made in Rome and Pavia at the assembly of Ponthion. At the gathering of nobles, representatives from Louis the German, who had earlier withdrawn from his half-brother's kingdom, sent envoys to acknowledge Charles' title as emperor.

On 28 August 876, Louis the German died at Frankfurt, setting in motion the struggle for his East Frankish throne between his son, Louis the Younger, and Charles II. The death of the king gave his half-brother the opportunity to recreate the empire of his father and grandfather, Charlemagne. He sent envoys to the German warlords seeking their allegiance, while ordering his army to assemble for a campaign to the east. The West Frankish king led his troops to confront his brother's successor, Louis the Younger, who rallied his forces in defence of his claims to the throne. The two armies faced off in September across the Rhine near the town of Deutz, located on the right bank of the river opposite Cologne, while Charles sent emissaries to recruit new nobles on the west side of the river. In early October, Louis the Younger moved his troops upriver to Andernach and crossed the Rhine to challenge Charles. The West Frankish king followed his adversary and decided to unleash a surprise attack at dawn on 8 October. As Charles prepared to attack, the Archbishop of Cologne was informed of the planned battle and warned Louis the Younger. Forewarned, Louis was prepared for the assault and beat back Charles' men at Andernach with large losses, including many prominent counts.

Following the disaster at Andernach, the King of the West Franks was forced to retreat to his kingdom and for the next several months reasserted his sovereignty over his western vassals, ensuring their continued allegiance. In late November, an assembly of nobles and clerics was held at Samoussy, where Charles II reasserted his rule, as attempts were made to reinforce the loyalty of the nobles and clerics who had joined his campaign in Germany against Louis the Younger.

After the death of Emperor Louis II, Pope John VIII petitioned Charles II to intercede to protect the Holy See, which was threatened by the advance of the Muslims into southern Italy. Despite the risks of Viking raids, growing discontent among his magnates, escalating danger of attacks by his German nephews and his own failing health, the West Frankish king made preparations to travel to Rome. Before departing, the king summoned his vassals to meet at Quierzy on 14 June 877 to reinforce his rule. At the assembly, he named his son, Louis the Stammerer, as regent and arranged for him to govern under the advice of an appointed council of bishops and counts.

By the summer of 877, Charles II the Bald had received pledges of loyalty from his warlords and high church officials, meaning his throne was secure enough to respond to Pope John VIII's request for military intervention. He had earlier in the year paid the Viking raiders a large tribute in silver and gold for their pledge not to plunder his kingdom, and with his vassals' recent oaths of fealty was now ready to advance his army to defend the Holy See. In June, the West Frankish king, with Richildis and a large war chest, set out for Rome. He met Pope John VIII in September at Vercelli, where he learned that the oldest son of Louis the German, Karlmann, was at the head of a large army moving into Italy to assert his rights to the imperial crown. While travelling through Burgundy, Charles had gained the oaths from his wife's brother, Boso of Provence, to bring his troops into Italy to reinforce the king's army. With Karlmann fast approaching, the West Frankish king was anxious for the arrival of the much-needed reinforcements, but they never came. After Charles had deployed for Italy, a large faction of his vassals, including Louis the Stammerer, banded together and refused to aid their overlord. The Emperor of the Romans was forced to abandon his expedition to support the papacy and return north to his homeland to defend it against the fresh rebellion. He sent Richildis back north with the gold and silver cache, soon following her out of Italy and across the Alps. The king stopped near Maurienne on the present-day border of south-eastern France and sent messages to Richildis to join him, as his health rapidly declined. Now near death, he entrusted the royal regalia and his sacred sword to his wife with instructions to give them to Louis the Stammerer as his only direct heir. Before the West Frankish king died on 6 October 877 at the age of 54 after a reign of thirty-seven years, he requested to be buried at St Denis Abbey in Paris. Despite his wishes, he was interred at the Abbey of Nantua in Burgundy, but several years later his remains were transferred to St Denis, where his tomb remains today.

During his rule, King Charles II the Bald was an enthusiastic patron of education and the arts. He attracted many scholars and artisans to his court, while actively supporting their work. The king made numerous grants of exceptions and privileges to the Church, actively protecting its wealth and properties against pillaging invaders and rogue Frankish magnates. He was a consistent supporter of the Church and made many appointments to its offices. The Frankish crown's policies served to strengthen the union between the monarchy and Church, while providing a source of rewards for the king's loyal vassals. He frequently called upon the Church for capable court officials and advisors. Charles II ruled his vast kingdom through the Carolingian practice of sending his personal representatives throughout the realm to enforce his laws and wishes. The king retained the periodic assemblies of his bishops and counts to resolve outstanding disputes and problems, while acting as a means to impose his overlordship. Charles II was a forceful and dedicated ruler, who defended his inheritance from Louis I the Pious and protected it from attacks by his rival brothers, magnates, high church officials and pillaging Vikings and Muslims. The West Frankish king was the last great Carolingian overlord to maintain his family's sovereignty over the western portion of Charlemagne's empire that would in time become the nation of France. During the reign of Charles, many of the splendours of the Carolingian Renaissance were resumed, and his close association with the Church enhanced his recognized authority and prestige. Carolingian art embraced classical Mediterranean forms, setting the stage for the rise of Gothic art. At the king's court, attempts were made to attract scholars to increase the education of his priests and nobles. During his kingship, there was an expansion in literature, the arts, writing, poetry and biblical studies.

In the wake of Charles II's death, Louis II the Stammerer was acknowledged as successor to the West Frankish kingdom. Despite his appointment as king by his father, Louis' rule was not universally accepted, forcing him to make extensive grants of titles, lands and court offices to secure his regime. The concessions weakened his power and compelled him to confront the rebellion of his southern warlords. He reacted quickly, mustering an army of loyal nobles and marching into Aquitaine to overwhelm the rebels and re-establish his authority. The successful military campaign consolidated his hold over the realm and ended the spirit of independence among the lords and churchmen to secure his monarchy. However, the heir of Charles II only held the reins of power for sixteen months before dying in April 879 of unknown causes, to be succeeded by his young son, Louis III.

Selected Sources

Castries, Duc de, *The Lives of the Kings and Queens of France*
Dunbabin, Jean, *France in the Making*
James, Edward, *The Origins of France*
Maurois, Andre, *A History of France*
McKitterick, Rosamond, *The Frankish Kingdoms Under the Carolingians*
Nelson, Janet L., *Charles the Bald*
Potter, Philip J., *Kings of the Seine*
Riche, Pierre, *The Carolingians*
Tilley, Arthur, *Medieval France*

Philip II Augustus

In late October 1187, Pope Gregory VIII issued a call for the kings and knights of Europe to unite and launch the Third Crusade to restore Christian control over the Holy Lands and Jerusalem. The King of France, Philip II, took the cross of a Crusader in January 1188 and prepared his army to advance against the Saracens led by Saladin. The French Crusader fleet landed in the Levant on 20 April 1191 at Tyre, the only remaining fortified town occupied by the Christians. Philip II united his troops with the small army of the Latin Kingdom and travelled south to the ongoing siege against the port of Acre. Under the command of the French king, preparations were begun for an assault against the Muslim-held citadel, while the Crusaders awaited the arrival of the English king, Richard I, and his army. The French began constructing siege engines, breaching towers and trebuchets to storm Acre. Shortly after Richard I joined the Crusaders, relations between him and Philip II grew increasingly strained. With the cooperation between the two kings continuing to deteriorate, Philip pounded the Moslem fortifications with his artillery pieces and sent his men against the enemy without English support, but his forces were thrown back. As the siege engines continued to fire projectiles against the defences, two frontal attacks with English reinforcements were made, only to be repelled. Meanwhile, under the steady bombardment by the French and English siege engines, the defensive works slowly began to collapse. With the battlements breaking down, the garrison surrendered to the Crusaders on 12 July, Philip II entering Acre in triumph.

After twenty-eight years of marriage, King Louis VII was still without a direct successor to his French throne, but on 21 August 1165, his third wife, Adele of Champagne, had given birth in Paris to a healthy son. The infant was baptized the following day and given the name of Philip. He spent his first years under the care of nurses in the royal household before beginning his education at a young age under the tutelage of learned scholars appointed from the Church. Philip possessed an inquisitive and energetic intelligence, excelling in his studies of reading, writing, Latin and some mathematics. His training in the administration of the royal government began early, attending council meetings and watching his father hold discussions with foreign envoys and Church officials. Around the age of 7, he was taught the fighting skills of a feudal warlord and spent long hours practicing with the sword and spear of an infantryman, while learning to ride a warhorse and charge into the enemy's ranks. The future king was an enthusiastic hunter and enjoyed participating in field sports and games. Under the influence of his father, Philip exhibited a strong pious nature and devotion to the Church, while gaining a widespread reputation for his many acts of charity.

Unlike most previous kings, Philip's succession to the French throne was not threatened by a rival magnate or relative and no formal anointment ceremony for his accession had been performed. During the spring of 1179, Louis VII suffered a near fatal attack of paralysis, and following his recovery agreed to secure his son's inheritance by having him crowned king. Despite the continued urgings of the pope and the nobles, Louis VII refused to share power with his son. When he summoned his vassals to gather in Paris at the bishop's palace to hear his will in late April, the prelates and lords unanimously pressed him to enthrone his heir and a date was set for the ritual.

While waiting for the coronation ceremony, Philip went hunting on horseback with a group of friends in the forest near Compiegne. The party soon found a wild boar and gave chase, with the king's 14-year-old son leading the pack. He became separated from his friends and was lost in the great dense forest. Surrounded by the darkness, he became afraid and asked the defender of French kings, St Denis, for his intervention. Shortly after his prayer, he saw a man burning charcoal in the distance, who returned him to the town. Philip, greatly fatigued by the encounter, soon became dangerously ill. When the king learned of his son's illness, he was in great despair and prayed for his recovery. During the night, he had a vision of St Thomas of Canterbury, who told him to make a pilgrimage to his tomb in Canterbury, England.

With England being the enemy of the French regime at this time, Louis hesitated to make the journey, but after the vision reappeared three times, a decision to visit Canterbury was reached. The king and his advisors crossed the English Channel to Dover on 22 August, where they were warmly welcomed by King Henry II. The French party was escorted to Canterbury, where Louis remained for two days praying at the tomb of St Thomas. Before returning to his kingdom, he made rich offerings to the Church. When the French king arrived home, he discovered his son had recovered from his serious illness, which was attributed to the intervention of St Thomas. The king's cordial reception by Henry II facilitated the beginning of friendly relations between the two realms.

Soon after returning to Paris, King Louis VII made his way to St Denis to offer thanks for his son's recovery. During the journey, he was struck by a new attack of paralysis and was paralyzed on his right side. Despite the declining health of the king, the coronation ceremony was held at Rheims Cathedral in November 1179 as scheduled, with the archbishop placing the crown on Philip's head. The ceremony was attended by three of Henry II's sons, who acknowledged Philip's overlordship for their cross-Channel lands. Due to his illness, the French king was unable to attend the service.

Shortly after his succession to the Capetian throne, the 15-year-old Philip II was married to Isabella of Flanders. The marriage had been arranged by Louis VII as a political agreement binding the Capetian dynasty to the powerful and ambitious Count of Flanders, Philip. Isabella was described by contemporaries as possessing great beauty and charm, while being a most holy woman. She brought the County of Artois as her dowry to the French domain. A month after the marriage, Isabella was crowned Queen of France at St Denis. The union between Philip and the queen remained childless until September 1187, when she gave birth to a son, Louis, who would inherit his father's throne.

After Philip was anointed king, he possessed sovereign powers alongside his father. As Louis VII's health continued to deteriorate, Philip assumed greater control of the regime under the tutelage of Count Philip of Flanders. The young king quickly found the Flemish count a useful ally in his developing dispute with his mother's family, who soon mounted a diplomatic and martial campaign to usurp him. Adele of Champagne and her four brothers were a rival family to control of Flanders and resented the influence Count Philip would now have over the king. To eliminate the threat of the Champagne faction to his independent reign, Philip II gained the support of the Flemish count and Henry II of England.

At the time of his assumption to the Capetian crown, Philip II was described by contemporaries as tall, with a powerful arm in the use of weapons, and well-proportioned in stature with a ruddy completion. He was noted for his piety and introduced a fine of 20 sous for swearing at his court. During his time in power, the king had little interest in supporting music, arts or literature. He was fond of wine, and even when ill continued to drink it, against the advice of his physicians.

In the early years of his rule, the king remained on friendly terms with his father's English rival, using him on several occasions to mediate disputes.

In 1180, he signed a treaty of friendship with Henry II, reconfirming the peace accord previously negotiated by his father. Philip II was able to exploit the ensuing period of peace with his greatest adversary to consolidate his powerbase over his magnates, high churchmen and towns to rule over the French kingdom unchallenged.

The reign of Louis VII had been tolerant and protective of the French Jewish population, but in 1180 his son issued a proclamation against the Jews. The royal order resulted in the seizure of properties and arrests of many Jews, who were held for ramson. Only those who converted to the Christian faith were exempt, while debts owed by Christians to Jews were cancelled. The declaration produced a short-term windfall for the French regime's treasury. In 1182, Philip expanded his decree by expelling all Jews from his domain. The king's policy brought about only a brief period of financial gain, and was later reversed with the expelled Jews encouraged to return to the French kingdom.

After enforcing his rule over the rebellious family of his mother, in 1181 Philip Augustus and the Flemish count argued over the Vermandois area in north-western France, which the king claimed as part of his wife's dowry. As the conflict intensified, Philip of Flanders invaded the region north of Paris, ravaging the area as far south as Dammartin. With his lands under attack, Philip II mustered an army of 2,000 knights and over 100,000 men to advance against the invaders. At the approach of the royal troops, the Flemish count retreated to his great castle at Boves. The king besieged the stronghold, surrounding the defensive works while building siege engines to pound the fortifications and sending his miners to dig tunnels under the walls. When French soldiers broke through the gate, they surged forward into the castle, overwhelming the defenders. Philip of Flanders was compelled to go before the Capetian king and humbly ask for a pardon. He was forced to accept the Treaty of Boves in July 1185, which ceded to the French crown his counties of Amiens and Montdidier and the castles of Roye and Thourotte, plus the rights to Artois after the death of the count. With the submission of the Flemish count, Philip II had defeated the challengers to his inheritance and enforced his rule over France against internal uprisings.

During the early years of his reign, Philip II was challenged for the monarchy by numerous French warlords, who sought to expand their territorial holdings at the expense of the Capetian regime. The king countered the dangers by negotiating advantageous alliances to strengthen his military might, while turning his enemies against each other. The success of his manoeuvres secured his realm and allowed him to renew his father's struggle against Henry II to add newly English-occupied French lands to his kingdom should the opportunity arise.

In 1180, Philip II met the English king at Gisors to renew their treaty of friendship. Henry acknowledged the Capetian monarch as his overlord for his French lands, which comprised much of modern-day western France. Both kings made pledges of peace and continued cooperation. Following the meeting at Gisors, Henry II found it to his advantage to maintain the agreement with the French when he was forced to intercede against his rebellious sons over the allocation of their inheritances. With the English king distracted by the revolts of his three sons – Henry the Younger, Richard and Geoffrey – Philip II offered his support to them to weaken the ability of the Plantagenet monarchy to defend its western French lands.

While Philip II was fending off the aggression of the Count of Flanders, Henry the Younger and Geoffrey rose up together against their father in 1183, seeking more lands and involvement in the ruling of the Angevin Empire, while Richard rallied to the support of the king. As tension between the brothers grew, Henry the Younger formed an alliance with the disgruntled warlords of Aquitaine and threatened to attack Richard. When Geoffrey moved against Richard with his mercenary army, Henry the Younger mustered his troops and advanced against his father and his ally, Richard. During the march into Aquitaine, the eldest son became ill with dysentery, dying on 11 June. With the death of Henry the Younger, the English king was compelled to rearrange the inheritance of his realm. Under the terms of the reorganization, Richard was named heir to England and Normandy and Geoffrey retained Brittany, while the youngest son, John, was given Aquitaine. Richard was deeply attached to Aquitaine, which had been under the rule of his mother, Eleanor, refusing to accept its loss. Philip II had pursued a policy of promoting the rebellion of the English sons to weaken the Angevin Empire of Henry II, and now with the death of Henry the Younger threw his support behind Geoffrey. When Geoffrey was later killed during a martial tournament in Paris, the French king befriended John in opposition to Richard.

In the aftermath of the deaths of Henry the Younger and Geoffrey, the Capetian monarch demanded the return of the strategically important Vexin and Gisors regions of Normandy from Henry II, which had been the dowry of his sister, Margaret, wife of the English king's first son. The English king claimed the lands were part of Normandy and refused to transfer them to the French regime. While Philip II continued to pursue his quest for the Vexin and Gisors, he also made demands for the regency of Geoffrey's Duchy of Brittany. To further press the English realm, he led armed incursions into

Angevin territory, sacking towns and destroying crops. To maintain the fragile peace, numerous meetings were held by the two kings to prevent a declaration of war, but Philip remained determined to renew the armed struggle to expand his territorial holdings in English-occupied western France.

After attending several unsuccessful conferences with Henry II to resolve their dispute over the recovery of the Vexin, Gisors and Brittany, the French king launched an attack into English-occupied Berry, capturing two towns and occupying the lordships. The French offensive resumed with the king's troops advancing into Normandy. As Philip expanded his campaign of conquests, Henry II sent Richard against the French in Berry, while he hastened with his army to drive the Capetians out of Normandy. Pressed on two fronts, Philip II was compelled to seek terms, agreeing to a two-year truce.

Shortly after the peace conference, Richard returned to Paris with the Capetian king, who attempted to gain his loyalty but had only limited success. Exasperated by the failure to gain the allegiance of the English heir, Philip II made a second foray into Angevin territory, advancing into the Loire River region before withdrawing at the approach of Richard with his army. When Philip and Henry held another conference near Gisors, it only resulted in further hostilities between the two kings. In frustration, Henry II ordered his army to sack Mantes, 30 miles west of Paris. When the French king saw the flames from the burning houses, he hastened to Mantes with his troops, driving off the English king's forces and saving the town. In the wake of the Angevin attack, the French king and Henry II held another conference in November 1188 to resolve their differences. During the meeting, Philip II offered to return his recent conquests if Henry would recognize Richard as his successor and authorize his marriage to the French king's sister, Alice. When the Angevin king refused to give an answer, Richard dropped to his knees in front of Philip II, offering his homage and allegiance. All attempts at reconciliation failed, and the French monarch and Richard renewed the war against Henry, taking Le Mans and Tours and compelling the battered English soldiers to retreat. As his empire crumbled around him, the gravely ill Henry withdrew to Chinon. When the adversaries again met 13 miles north of Le Mans at Ballon, the ruler of the Angevin Empire was forced to accept the humiliating treaty dictated by the allies, agreeing to the marriage between Richard and Alice, recognizing his eldest son as heir, while the French monarch retained his conquests and the English barons pledged to join forces with the French if their king failed to honour the agreement.

Following the conference at Ballon, the French king acknowledged Richard I as the rightful and legal successor to England and the French

Angevin lordships, while Henry returned to Chinon broken in body and spirit, dying on 6 July 1189. Philip II's political and military campaign had overwhelmed the powerhouse of Europe and succeeded in expanding the lands under his rule and securing the allegiance of the ruler of western France.

While the French and English were fighting for sovereignty over France, in the Holy Land, the leader of the Islamic war against the occupying Crusader forces, Saladin, led his army to victory at the Battle of the Horns of Hattin on 11 July 1187, igniting the campaign against the Christians. After the Crusader defeat, the Moslems continued their offensive, taking the cities of Sidon and Acre, then on 3 October Jerusalem surrendered to Saladin, leaving only the fortified town of Tyre on the Mediterranean coast under the control of the Crusader troops.

With the continued Christian presence in the Holy Lands in peril, the papacy issued a decree calling for a crusade to restore the Church's order. Soon after the summons was issued, Philip, Richard and Henry II took the cross of a Crusader in early 1188. Still at war with the English regime, Philip ignored his pledge and continued his attacks against Henry II. Following the death of Henry II and the succession of Richard I to the throne, Philip and the new English king agreed to settle their differences and participate in the Third Crusade. Both kingdoms issued what was known as the Saladin tax to raise money for the arms, equipment and supplies necessary to field an army, while arrangements were made for a fleet to transport the Crusaders to the Levant. To govern his kingdom during his absence, the French monarch appointed his mother and her brother, Guillaume de Blois, the Archbishop of Rheims, as co-regents, imposing strict limitations on their rule. In the late spring of 1190, the Capetian army was assembled and on 4 July marched out of Paris to begin the journey to the Holy Land. The French Crusaders headed over the Alps to Genoa in north-western Italy, where they boarded ships for the voyage south to Sicily and a reunion with Richard's army. Philip reached the island on 16 September, and Richard I and his ships arrived six days later. Soon after landing in Sicily, the English king became involved in a dispute with the island's ruler. The King of Sicily had recently died, and Richard, whose sister had been married to him, demanded the return of her dowry. As the dispute intensified, Richard ordered his soldiers to pillage several Sicilian towns to enforce his demands. With the journey to the Holy Land delayed, Philip personally intervened to work out a settlement. The disagreement and the resulting interruption of the crusade caused a breach of trust and friendship between the two Crusader kings that would only expand in the coming months. At the end of March 1191, the

French Crusaders sailed from the Sicilian port of Messina to Acre, and the English following two weeks later.

While Philip proceeded to the ongoing siege at Acre, Richard I made an unscheduled stop at the island of Cyprus, where a storm battered his fleet and forced some of his vessels ashore. The English king's sister, Joanna, and his future wife, Berengaria, were aboard one of the ships and were taken prisoners by the island's king, Isaac Comnenus. Richard demanded the immediate release of the captives, but Comnenus refused. As he prepared to attack the Cypriot king, the defeated ruler of Jerusalem, Guy of Lusignan, landed on the island with several Latin princes and their soldiers, joining forces with the Englishmen. Guy had left the siege of Acre to encourage Richard to hasten to the Crusader kingdom. The Cypriot monarch now withdrew to the fortress town of Famagusta to defend his realm. The Crusaders followed him to the stronghold but found it deserted by the Cypriots, who had withdrawn to Nicosia. At the approach of the Crusaders, Isaac Comnenus also abandoned Nicosia and attempted to escape to the castle at Kantara. While Richard and his troops were pursing the Cypriot king, Guy and his followers captured the young daughter of Comnenus. When her father learned of her imprisonment, he surrendered, begging for her release. The daughter was placed in the household of Joanna and her father put into chains. In less than a month, Richard had seized the island and enthroned himself as king. After leaving men to maintain his authority over the island, he set sail on 5 June, crossing the eastern Mediterranean for Acre, located in current-day northern Israel, reaching the siege lines three days later.

Acre was first besieged by King Guy of Lusignan and his army of 7,400 men in 1189, but his forces were too weak to seize the stronghold. When Philip II landed at Acre, he took command of the siege operations, ordering his men to construct siege engines, towers, battering rams and trebuchets to pound the city walls with large heavy stones and fire pots. The city was surrounded by trenches and mobile towers built by the French which reached the top of the fortification's walls. The French tunnelled under one of Saladin's defensive towers, setting the supporting timbers on fire, while the siege engines continued to batter the walls. One of the king's large catapults was named 'God's Own Sling' by the soldiers as Philip continued battering the walls while waiting for the arrival of Richard and his army.

The English fleet finally anchored at Acre on 8 June, and Richard's men joined the siege. Relations between the two kings, which had already deteriorated in Sicily, soon became further strained after Richard offered to pay four gold coins a month for the services of any knight who would join his army, against the three currently paid by Philip II. When the English king sent a message to Saladin asking for a peace conference without conferring with the French, Philip was enraged. Their relationship had degenerated to a dangerous level, and was worsened by the illness of both monarchs. The French king became impatient with Richard's lack of cooperation and continued delays, ordering an assault against the fortification with his army, but his troops were repelled. By early July, the defensive works had been breached in several locations through the work of the French sappers and siege engines. Philip decided to attack the walls without the support of the English soldiers, but his men were again repulsed. He launched a second foray three days later, but was beaten back once more. Several additional attacks were made, but the Saracens continued to hold the city. Finally, after Richard recovered from his illness, the English troops joined the attack and forced the Muslims to surrender on 12 July. Under the terms of the resulting treaty, the Saracens agreed to pay a large indemnity, release their Christian prisoners and return the True Cross, which had been taken at Hattin four years previously.

After the capture of Acre, dissension between the Crusader monarchs continued, Richard pressing for the election of Guy of Lusignan to the vacant throne of the Jerusalem kingdom, while Philip threw his support behind Conrad of Montferrat. The French king was forced to accept a compromise, agreeing to acknowledge Guy as King of the Latin Kingdom, but upon the latter's death the crown would pass to Conrad. As part of the settlement, Conrad was promised the immediate possession of the northern part of the Christian kingdom in the Holy Land.

With the dispute of the succession to the Latin Kingdom resolved, Philip now demanded half of Richard's spoils from Cyprus under the terms of their earlier treaty to share all conquests equally. Richard refused and made additional ultimatums on the Capetian king. As Philip's relationship with Richard continued to deteriorate and the lingering effects of his recent illness left his body swollen and weak, he was persuaded to return to his kingdom.

At the end of July, Philip II sailed from Acre for home, first stopping in Italy to confer with Pope Celestine III and report on the conquest of Acre and plans to take Jerusalem. After the papal conference at the Vatican, Philip travelled overland through Italy into France, reaching Paris in late December. As the French king journeyed to France, Richard remained in the Holy Land, marching his army down the coast and expanding the lands under Christian control by seizing several fortified towns. He next moved his troops inland toward Jerusalem, attacking Saladin's forces, but soon realized his army was too small to defeat the Saracens. Unable to take Jerusalem, he negotiated a settlement with Saladin that gained access to the Holy City for Christian pilgrims and acknowledgment of the Latin Kingdom's control over the coastal towns and countryside. While the Third Crusade had failed to recapture Jerusalem, it reenergized the Crusader spirit across Europe and saved the Christian kingdom from destruction by the Muslims. Philip's leadership and participation in the crusade enhanced his stature and standing among the lords and high clergymen of Europe, and he was thereafter regarded as a devoted son of the Church.

Richard I's continued presence in the Latin Kingdom gave the Capetian regime the opportunity to attack the French Angevin lands. The pope had earlier issued an edict barring any warlord from attacking the properties and rights of the Crusaders while they were in the Holy Land. To press his expansion into Richard's lordships and avoid the intervention of the papacy, the French king began a series of indirect assaults against the English realm. To the warlords and high churchmen who were in dispute with Richard, he provided the support and protection of his French throne to enforce their feudal rights to gain their allegiance. He issued grants of privileges and exceptions to numerous towns in English-occupied territories, winning favour for his expansionist campaign. As part of an earlier agreement between the two regimes, Richard had pledged to marry Philip's sister, Alice, but later decided against the marriage. The French king claimed the Vexin lordship, which had been part of the dowry. Philip now possessed the legitimate right to seize the Vexin by arms but delayed his attack, fearing a violation of the Papal guarantee. In late 1192, Richard lost the protection of the papacy when he departed from the Holy Land and was captured and held for ransom by Leopold of Austria. Philip was then free to actively pursue his claims against all of the English king's properties in France.

While Richard remained a prisoner in Austria as the large ransom was collected, Philip negotiated an alliance with his brother, John, in 1193. During their meeting in Paris, the French king recognized John as heir designate to the Angevin Empire, while receiving his homage as overlord. They agreed to a dual campaign against Richard's lands, with John rebelling in England and the French advancing against English-occupied Normandy. Capetian troops began their offensive by marching into the Vexin on 12 April, quickly taking the lordship and moving west to attack the Norman forces of Richard. The French army swiftly overran much of north-eastern Normandy, but a siege of Rouen was repelled. Uncertain whether their English overlord would ever return from captivity, many Norman warlords gave homage to Philip, thereby expanding the territory under his monarchy.

After fighting for most of the year, Philip II Augustus met with Richard's representatives at Mantes and agreed to halt the invasion, but the French monarch was allowed to retain the conquered towns and countryside. Hostilities were resumed the following year, with the French occupying all of Normandy east of the Seine, along with all key fortifications.

By early 1194, Richard's vast ransom had been paid and he was released. During his slow journey back to England, he made his way through Germany, stopping at strategic towns to forge alliances against Philip to threaten the eastern French borderlands. On 16 March he was in London, easily regaining his throne from his rebellious brother. After securing his monarchy, he made preparations to renew the war against France to regain his lands lost during his absence in the Latin Kingdom. On 10 May, the king crossed the Channel and landed at Barfleur in Normandy, where he prepared to advance against the French monarch with his army. He supplemented his forces with mercenary troops to begin the reconquest of his lost lands. On 3 July 1194, the two rivals clashed at Freteval Woods, where Philip's large baggage train was plundered and his rearguard routed. Among the captured French luggage was the royal seal for the regime, archival accounts, financial records, a large treasury and charters utilized to administer the kingdom. As Philip withdrew, the English and their mercenary allies continued to harass his rearguard. With the French retreating, the English king renewed his offensive, first taking Verneuil before recapturing Beaumont-le-Roger. The English next turned south, moving into Aquitaine and recapturing several fortifications. Richard continued his campaign by taking control of Anjou and driving the Capetians out of Aquitaine, while in the north the French overran the forces of Prince John, who had by now been reconciled with his older brother. With both armies exhausted by the relentless fighting, a truce was arranged, with both kings retaining their recent conquests.

During 1195, the French army made substantial gains against two vulnerable Angevin regions, Philip sending his troops into the Norman borderlands and the lordship of Berry. He next advanced into north-eastern Normandy, sacking Dieppe. While Richard was in Aquitaine reconquering his lost lands, Philip continued to take fortified towns in Normandy. Neither regime possessed the military might to risk a decisive encounter, and the war quickly deteriorated into a series of inconclusive clashes followed by intermittent truces. When the Angevin king started forming alliances with his neighbouring barons, his campaign against the French began to drive Philip out of his recent Norman gains. English coalitions with Raymond of Toulouse and Baldwin of Flanders allowed the allies to assault the Capetians on three fronts, forcing Philip's men to withdraw and abandon their conquered lands.

In 1198, Richard led his army into the strategic lordship of Vexin, compelling the French to retreat. As the Angevin forces continued to expand the territory under their control, by the end of the year they had regained most of the area captured by Philip II. The Capetian monarch was then compelled to seek peace terms with the English throne. As negotiations for peace continued along the Epte River in Normandy, with Philip prepared to accept the loss of Normandy, events unexpectedly turned to his advantage. In March 1199, as Richard was preparing to besiege the castle of a rebellious baron, he was struck in the upper chest by the bolt from a crossbow while making a reconnaissance. The stricken king was taken to his encampment, where he steadily grew weaker after his surgeons failed to extract the projectile. On 6 April 1199, King Richard I died from his wound. When Philip learned of his great rival's death, he rode to the Angevin-occupied town of Evreux with his men-at-arms and infantry, forcing the garrison to surrender in a display of his determination to continue his war of conquest.

Richard's only surviving brother, John, succeeded to his English crown and the Angevin continental lands. The new English king lacked the military skills and governing experience of his brother, rendering continued allegiance by his subjects questionable. While he had been involved in ruling England and Normandy and was acknowledged as king by the local lords, churchmen and commoners, in the other French lordships he was unknown. His succession to the Angevin Empire was further weakened when his nephew, Arthur of Brittany, challenged his rights to the crown. Arthur was born in 1187 and was the son of Geoffrey of England and Constance of Brittany. At birth, he was second in the line of succession to the English throne behind his uncle, Richard. In 1196, his mother proclaimed Arthur co-ruler of Brittany, and six years later he was allied with Philip II against John in Normandy and later Poitou, fighting for recognition as successor to the English-held lands.

Philip II acknowledged Arthur as king, receiving his homage for the English-occupied French territories. Richard's wars against the French had created a large tax burden on the English nobles and churchmen, who vigorously opposed any further intervention against the Capetian crown. Confronted with the strong opposition of the warlords and the Church, John agreed to talk with the French king and negotiate a peace treaty. The two monarchs met on 15 January 1200 on the island of Le Goulet on the Seine, near the town of Vernon in Normandy. Under the resulting agreement, Philip was ceded eastern Normandy, the Vexin and parts of Berry. To bind the two kingdoms closer together, the Capetian heir, Louis, was betrothed to John's niece, Blanche of Castile. The French regime recognized John as the English king and pledged to return the occupied lordships of Limoges and

Angouleme to him. While negotiating with John, the Capetian king came to terms with numerous rebellious French magnates, ending their allegiance to the English regime as their overlord. The strategy further isolated and reduced the English crown's strength and presence in France. Philip then remained in his newly occupied lands, consolidating and strengthening his authority and establishing his government.

In 1200, the French king came to terms with Baldwin of Flanders, receiving his pledge of fealty, and the following year he was acknowledged as overlord by Renaud of Boulogne to further isolate John's power in France. In 1202, Philip II knighted Arthur of Brittany, while encouraging him to oppose John's presence in Aquitaine. The Count of Boulogne's daughter was married to the French king's illegitimate son, Philip Hurepel, to further bind the two realms. Following the marriage, Hurepel was legitimized by Pope Innocent III. While Philip claimed dominion over his vassals, John refused to appear at the French court to offer his pledge of allegiance. After failing to receive the English king's oath, the Capetian regime claimed hegemony over Aquitaine and in 1202 invaded Normandy, seizing many fortified towns in the north, while steadily moving westward toward the capital at Rouen. While Philip II Augustus was attacking John's followers in Normandy, his ally, Arthur of Brittany, was active in Poitou, capturing towns under the jurisdiction of the English king's mother, Eleanor of Aquitaine. When Arthur besieged the Aquitaine fortress of Mirebeau, Eleanor became trapped in the keep. Learning of his mother's endangerment, John set out to rescue her, catching the attackers by surprise and freeing Eleanor. During the fighting, Arthur was captured and taken to the stronghold at Falaise. While under guard, Arthur disappeared, most likely killed on the orders of John. Following the disappearance of their overlord, many Breton warlords abandoned the English king and pledged their oaths of homage to Philip.

In 1203, Philip renewed his war of conquest in Normandy, moving against the great castle at Gaillard, which was key to the capture of Rouen. He first ordered his troops to eliminate the outer defences of the fortification. By August, the network of bastions protecting the approaches to Gaillard was under Capetian control and the king's army moved against the main fortification, which had been designed and constructed by King Richard I to withstand the attacks of a mighty army. The castle was besieged and French siege guns began pounding the defensive works, while archers fired volleys of arrows at John's men on the walls. The garrison was commanded by Roger de Lacy, who showed unwavering resistance to hold Gaillard for King John. As the fighting for the stronghold continued unabated, de Lacy sent several hundred men, women and children out of the castle to save food supplies for his garrison soldiers, leaving them to survive in the wilderness no-man's land between both armies. When Philip learned of their plight, he issued instructions to feed them and allowed their passage through his lines. The battle for the citadel continued into the winter months as the French slowly advanced, seizing the outer bailey in February 1204 and the inner defensive works in early March, finally compelling the surrender of the fortification by de Lacy. With the fall of Gaillard, John's hold on Normandy quickly collapsed, his remaining castles and towns submitting. In May 1204, Philip led his army to Rouen and initiated siege operations. On 1 June, the garrison commander agreed to submit if no relief aid arrived within the next thirty days. John made no attempt to relieve the city and the garrison capitulated on 24 June, ending all resistance against the French in Normandy.

Shortly after the fall of Normandy, King Philip II continued his war of conquest against the English monarchy of John, sending his army into the Loire region. In quick succession he captured Chatellerault, Poitiers and Loudun, before taking Chinon and Loches by siege. By late September, a large part of the area south of the Loire, including Tours and Amboise, was under the control of the French king. While Philip marched through the south and established his sovereignty in Normandy, his son, Louis, led an expeditionary force into Brittany in 1205. During the following year, Philip joined the soldiers in Brittany, gaining control over Nantes and Rennes to complete his conquest of the duchy. When John finally sent troops to recapture his captured towns, the French crown lost control of Poitou and Philip halted his expeditions of conquests to concentrate on enforcing his rule over his recent acquisitions.

John crossed the English Channel in June 1206 to initiate a campaign to regain his lost French territories, landing at the coastal city of La Rochelle in the Bay of Biscay. He sent his army against the Capetians and soon retook numerous towns in Gascony, and the northern region of Poitou County was again placed under his authority. As the Angevins marched toward Anjou, Philip II moved his troops against the English king in a lightning offensive of relentless attacks, forcing him to withdraw to La Rochelle and later back to England. The adversaries then opened negotiations for a peace treaty and a two-year truce was quickly arranged, with the Angevins retaining Gascony and parts of Poitou but the remainder of their continental lordships were lost to the French. The defeat and break-up of the Angevin Empire was the foremost accomplishment of Philip II's reign, bringing him great wealth and increased military might, while tripling the territorial size of his kingdom. By following a strategy of first destroying the Angevins' lands and then besieging their castles, the French regime was transformed into a major European power.

When Philip II took the crown in September 1180, the French realm had no naval force to protect its coastline. After the recent conquests of the western lordships, the French monarchy gained new outlets to the sea and a larger coast to defend. Under the direction of the king, the French began a construction programme for a fleet of warships along its western coastline, and by 1208 a sizable number of vessels had been built. The galley, the primary warship used by the French navy, was propelled by rows of oarsmen and sails and carried a crew of over 150 sailors and soldiers. The galley was first used by the Greeks and had remained the dominant warship through the centuries. It was highly manoeuvrable and could pass through shallow waters, making the vessel highly effective for raiding harbours and during ship-to-ship fighting. The French augmented their fleet with requisitioned merchant ships known as cogs, which were used as transports but could easily be converted into a warship by fitting raised fighting platforms at the bow and stern. The emplacements were manned with archers, who could fire their projectiles down on the crews of enemy ships. Cogs were generally about 60ft long and carried a crew of six sailors and fifteen archers and men-at-arms. They were propelled by a fitted mast and large square sail.

At the conclusion of his campaigns against the English, Philip began initiatives to integrate the conquered territories into his kingdom. He placed loyal magnates in the principal towns and castles to enforce his rule and keep the peace. The lands of the lords and high churchmen who had remained loyal to John were forfeited to the French crown and now governed by supporters of Philip. To secure the loyalty of the seized towns, the Capetian monarch granted them liberal privileges and exceptions. Philip remained vigorously involved in the administration of his newly acquired towns and fortresses, forming a strong bond with his new vassals.

As the French king strengthened his relationship with his new subjects, he was also intent on imposing his royal suzerainty over neighbouring lordships. In return for his protection, he received pledges of allegiance from numerous lords that expanded his powerbase. Through his mother, the French king was related to the House of Champagne, and he intervened in the county to receive the homage of the ruling count, Theobald III. Similarly, he received the oath of allegiance from Burgundy after the reigning duke died and Philip II agreed to support his young son, Hugh IV, as the new ruler. When the Count of Flanders, Baldwin IX, took part in the Fourth Crusade and was later elected Emperor of Byzantium, Philip was instrumental in the choice of Ferdinand of Portugal as his successor. The French king's involvement in the appointment of the new duke enhanced his already substantial standing in the duchy, while increasing his royal authority. By way of his repeated interventions, Philip influenced political and military affairs in Western Europe while in the process expanding the sovereignty and esteem of his kingdom.

The future succession of the House of Capet remained in question, with only one son to inherit the throne, and was thrown into further disarray when Queen Isabella died in 1190 during childbirth. Soon after Philip's return to his Paris court from his participation in the Third Crusade, the search for a second wife was begun around the other European regimes. After giving consideration to many princesses, and their military and political advantages, a marriage contract was signed with Ingeborg of Denmark, sister of the Danish king, Canute VI. It was felt that a marital union with the powerful Baltic kingdom would serve as a deterrent against an invasion from the Holy Roman Empire and ally France with a strong naval realm. The wedding ceremony was held on 15 August 1193, but soon after Philip renounced his new queen and attempted to send her back to Denmark. He quickly petitioned the papacy for a divorce on grounds of non-consummation due to sorcery. Outraged, the queen fled to the convent in Soissons and sought the intervention of Pope Celestine III. The pontiff refused to grant the divorce, but the king continued to press his petition. Three months after the wedding, Philip called an ecclesiastical council to Compiegne, claiming a too-close family relationship existed with Ingeborg. The council agreed and voted to declare the marriage void. With his matrimonial union with Ingeborg now annulled by the French Church, the king married Agnes of Merania. When Queen Ingeborg protested to Celestine III, he declared the annulment cancelled. Philip was pressured by the Holy See to renounce his third marriage, but he refused, relations with the papacy consequently deteriorating further. Despite the threat of a papal interdiction against his kingdom, the Capetian king would not agree to an invalidation and the dispute was only settled in 1201 after the death of Agnes. Following further negotiations, a reconciliation with Rome was finally arranged. Under the agreement, Philip pledged to reinstate Ingeborg as his wife and queen, while the new pontiff, Innocent III, recognized the two children resulting from the third marriage to Agnes – Marie, born in 1198, and Philip, born in 1200 – as legal issue.

Meanwhile, King John had not lost hope of recovering his lost French lands. When his nephew, Otto, was elected Holy Roman Emperor, he formed an alliance with him against France. While he was preparing to invade France, John was excommunicated by Pope Innocent III for refusing to accept his newly appointed candidate for the vacant post of Archbishop of Canterbury. In Germany, Otto IV was engaged in a power struggle with his rebelling German nobles. The distractions in England and Germany gave Philip the opportunity to expand his sovereignty into northern Europe. He sent financial and martial aid to support the German uprising, and made plans to invade England. The French king summoned his vassals to meet at Soissous to secure their oaths of loyalty and participation in the coming English invasion. The warlords and allies of the Capetian regime answered the call, but the Count of Flanders, Ferdinand, refused to reply to the muster called by his overlord.

While Philip continued his preparations for the expedition against the English kingdom, John negotiated a settlement with Innocent III, who agreed to lift his interdiction against England in exchange for the king's recognition of him as his overlord. John would now rule England for the pope as his papal fief. With John accepted as a vassal of the Holy See, Philip was compelled to abandon his attack on England, not being willing to incur the wrath of the papacy. With The English eliminated as a threat, Philip quickly decided to deal with the disloyal Ferdinand of Flanders, massing his warlords and new naval forces.

The Capetian fleet of approximately 500 vessels was assembled at Boulogne and loaded with supplies for the army. The naval force sailed north to Gravelines and then on to the Flemish port of Damme, which served as the harbour for the city of Bruges in current-day north-western Belgium. While the fleet navigated up the coast, King Philip was leading his army overland to Ghent. After reaching the fortified city, the French opened siege operations. Meanwhile, in England, John had mustered his forces and fleet in May 1213, sending them to support his Flemish ally, Ferdinand. The expeditionary force of 500 ships, 7,000 English and Flemish men-at-arms, infantrymen and a large contingent of mercenary troops, under the command of the Earl of Salisbury, William Longespee, set sail across the English Channel on 28 May, and two days later reached Damme. The earl soon located the anchored French flotilla, heavily laden with equipment and supplies. At this time, the Capetian army was besieging Ghent and its fleet was only lightly guarded. On 30 May, Salisbury ordered his warships to attack the anchored French fleet, seizing 300 ships and killing their crews, while burning over 100 more vessels. The following day, they attacked the remaining ships, and the English earl then sent his infantry against Damme, assaulting the French garrison troops. As the English fought for the town, Philip arrived from his siege of Ghent on 2 June, forcing John's men to flee to their fleet. The French monarch ordered his soldiers to destroy his surviving warships to prevent them from falling into English hands and had the town of Damme burned. When the Capetians then began their retreat to the south, Philip ordered his men to burn every Flemish town the army passed through. The disaster at Damme had destroyed French aspirations of launching an invasion of England in 1213.

In the wake of his defeat of the French at Damme, John renewed his preparations for an expedition to recover his seized lands in France by first attacking the Poitou region in Aquitaine. Ferdinand agreed to join the English king's campaign during a visit to John's court in December 1213. The Angevin monarch expanded his alliance against Philip, bringing numerous rebellious French magnates and their retainers into his army. Late in the year, Otto IV threw his support behind John, agreeing to lead his forces southwards against the Capetians. John now had a broad-based alliance for his bid to recreate the Angevin Empire by force of arms. The members of the coalition pledged to assail the Capetians in a giant pincer movement; the dissident French warlords, a contingent of English soldiers and archers, the Flemish troops of Ferdinand and the Holy Roman Emperor would advance from Flanders, while John marched his army north from La Rochelle through the Loire Valley toward Paris.

In early February 1214, King John assembled his soldiers in England and crossed the Channel, landing in Gascony. In early spring, he advanced north with his army and was joined by many rebellious French lords, who had been compelled to give their oaths of fealty to Philip during the Capetian occupation of their lordships. As the English king pressed his troops forward, towns and castles surrendered without resistance and magnates readily paid homage to him. The English army advanced unopposed, occupying numerous towns and fortifications before reaching Angers on 17 June. Meanwhile, to the north, King Philip and his son, Louis, were marching their army to oppose the invaders, but when reports reached them that the Germans and Flemish were now moving toward the French border, they were compelled to divide their forces. The heir continued south to engage the English and their allies, while Philip II headed north to attack Otto IV and Ferdinand.

King John resumed his campaign of conquest from Angers, advancing against the citadel at La Roche-au-Moine. After the English reached the fortress unopposed, the garrison refused to capitulate, compelling John's men to deploy their siege engines and begin battering the defensive walls. As the garrison resisted his attacks, the English monarch constructed a gallows, threatening to hang every defender if they did not immediately surrender, but the French defiantly refused to submit. While the siege wore on, Prince Louis left Chinon with a contingent of soldiers to hasten to the relief of La Roche. When the French reached the stronghold on 2 July, King John ordered his troops to abandon the castle and retreat, leaving his siege engines and baggage behind. During John's withdrawal, his rearguard was attacked by Louis and defeated. After the abandonment of La Roche, the

English king returned to La Rochelle, sailing back to England in October after agreeing to terms with Philip II.

While Prince Louis was securing the south for the Capetian throne, Philip II proceeded north into Flanders to meet the approaching forces of Emperor Otto IV and Count Ferdinand at Bouvines. The French army of nearly 7,000 soldiers was composed of 1,300 knights, 300 mounted sergeants, over 3,200 foot soldiers from the lordships and towns and 2,000 mercenary troops. The right flank was led by the Duke of Burgundy, Odo III, and Robert II of Dreux held the left wing, while Philip was positioned in the centre of the battle line with his household cavalry and 2,000 infantry from the lordships of Normandy and Ile-de-France. The allied forces, estimated at 9,000 men, were under the command of Otto IV. Count Ferdinand of Flanders led the left wing of the allied formation, the right comprising the soldiers of Count Renaud of Dammartin and Boulogne. The contingent of English knights sent by John was led by William Longespee, Earl of Salisbury. Otto IV held the centre with infantry from the Duchy of Brabant and Germany. On the far right of the allied line, support was provided by a force of English archers.

The Battle of Bouvines, fought on a mile-wide plateau on 27 July 1214, began with the attack of the allies against the French rearguard. When Philip was informed of the clash, he entered a nearby church to offer a prayer for victory, then prepared for battle. During the afternoon, as the two armies faced each, the Capetian king told his gathered soldiers 'In God is all Hope', while clerics behind him chanted prayers and hymns. The fighting began soon after, with a charge by the French light cavalry on the left flank slamming into the Flemish horse soldiers. The Count of Flanders counter-attacked, beating back the French. Odo's knights re-formed, and with reinforcements surged into the Flemish; following several fierce and bloody charges, they smashed through the enemy's line and wheeled back into the fray. The battle continued on the left wing for three hours before Count Ferdinand was unhorsed and taken prisoner, his surviving horsemen then withdrawing from the melee.

Meanwhile, in the centre, the 2,000 French infantrymen deployed in front of Philip Augustus were assaulted by the allied knights and foot soldiers led by Emperor Otto IV and beaten back in a bloody and fierce clash. When Otto's men regrouped and attacked again, they broke through the French line, reaching the king and knocking him off his horse with their pikes, Philip's armour deflecting the blows from an enemy lance. Philip mounted a fresh horse and led his cavalry and foot soldiers in a counter-charge. During the French attack, Emperor Otto was unhorsed and rescued by his

German knights in the vicious and bloody melee. The battle in the centre became a savage fray between the two armies, personally led by Philip and the emperor, the soldiers fighting with sword, spear and battle axe. As the French continued to throw more troops into the fray, Otto fled the battle and the fighting in the centre ended with the French holding the field. During the struggle, the emperor's standard was captured and taken to the French king.

While Philip II's forces were gaining the upper hand in the centre and on the right wing, on the left, Robert II of Dreux's horsemen and infantrymen were initially hard pressed, but rallied and drove the German and Flemish soldiers from the field to complete the French victory. With the Germans and their allies retreating, Philip ordered his men to pursue, but only for a couple of miles, not willing to disperse his forces too widely. He spent the night on the battlefield, and the following day the dead were buried in the grounds of the local abbey. Both the French and allied armies sustained heavy casualties, but the unrelenting charges of Philip's cavalry had broken the resistance of Otto's men and secured victory. The morning after the battle, Philip gave thanks to God for his victory at a nearby church.

During the fighting at Bouvines, French troops captured numerous allied warlords, including William Longespee, Count Ferdinand of Flanders and Count Renaud of Boulogne. After the battle, Renaud refused to submit to Philip and was forced to remain in prison for the remainder of his life, dying by suicide in 1227, while Earl William of Salisbury was soon ransomed and returned to England. Ferdinand of Flanders remained a prisoner for the next twelve years before his release in 1226 by Blanche of Castile, who was serving as regent for King Louis IX.

The triumph at Bouvines ended all hope for the rebirth of the Angevin Empire and left the English with greatly reduced territories on the continent. The defeat so weakened King John's power over the English barons and bishops that he was soon compelled to submit to them and agree to accept the Magna Carta. Meanwhile, in Germany, Emperor Otto IV was overthrown and replaced by Frederick II Hohenstaufen. In the aftermath of his victory at Bouvines, Philip returned to Paris in triumph, marching his prisoners behind him in a long procession as his subjects crowded the streets to greet their victorious king with great shouts of joy.

During the reign of Philip II, Catharism spread widely through the lordships of southern France, centred on Toulouse. The Cathars began as an anti-materialist reform coalition within the Christian Church, advocating a return to poverty and a message of perfection. The movement was in reaction to the perceived excesses of the clergy, especially in southern France. The dissidents believed Jesus was a normal human being, who had been adopted by God as his son. To purge Christendom of the sect, Pope Innocent III sent his clerics into southern France to eradicate the heretical faction from the Church. When a papal legate was killed, the pope declared the Albigensian Crusade to eliminate the Cathars. King Philip II took up the Holy See's banner, supporting Innocent III's campaign to destroy the Cathars, while taking the opportunity to expand and strengthen his rule over southern France. Under the sponsorship of the Capetian king, hundreds of his knights travelled south into the County of Toulouse, killing more than 20,000 Cathar heretics. While Philip did not personally take part in the Albigensian Crusade, he sent Prince Louis to Toulouse to fight the Cathars in 1209. The prince joined his army with the English knight Simon de Montfort and they campaigned together against the leader of the Cathars, Count Raymond VI of Toulouse. The French prince and de Montfort advanced against the town of Marmande, overrunning the defensive works and massacring most of the 5,000 garrison troops and residents. Louis continued his attacks against the Cathars, besieging Toulouse on 14 June, but after six weeks was forced to abandon his offensive and return to the royal court. Without the Valois prince and his troops, de Montfort was unable to hold his recently reoccupied lands. In June 1222, King Philip II sent an army of 200 knights and over 10,000 foot soldiers into the Toulouse province to renew the war against the heretics, but the campaign accomplished little. While the French king's interventions had failed to defeat the Cathars, it led to new areas acknowledging his overlordship, producing an expansion of the monarchy's influence and power into southern France.

With the exception of the conflict developing in the aftermath of Philip's second marriage to Ingeborg of Denmark, the Capetian king maintained a mutually beneficial relationship with the French Church and Holy See. Following his occupation of the King of England's continental lands in western France and subjugation of his warlords, Philip Augustus had become too powerful and useful an ally in European affairs for the papacy to alienate. The size of the royal demesne was now four times larger under the rule of Philip, and the power and influence of his warlords had been greatly weakened. During his reign, he was a devout ruler, supporting and protecting the Church and the poor. He had taken the cross of a pious Crusader and took part in the Third Crusade, while later sponsoring the crusading spirit in Europe. When the papacy issued the summons for the Fourth Crusade to the Latin Kingdom, the Capetian king encouraged his vassals to participate, while financially backing their campaign. The monarch's association with the Holy See was further enhanced with his financial and military sponsorship of Innocent's call for the Albigensian Crusade. The continuation of a wide-ranging bond with the pope and French Church remained a vital part of Philip Augustus' reign, but he actively defended his sovereign rights against any papal interference in Capetian activities.

By late 1222, Philip's health had begun to decline from the stresses of his many military campaigns and the governing of his expanded kingdom. He wrote his will at St Germain, leaving money for crusades in the Holy Land and gifts for St Denis, the poor, orphans and widows. In July 1223, his physical condition rapidly deteriorated and the king summoned Louis and his council to his bedside. He told his son to fear God and protect the poor. On 14 July, at the town of Montes 30 miles west of Paris, Philip II Augustus died at the age of 58, following a reign of forty-three years. His remains were taken to Paris, and in a grand procession transferred for burial at St Denis. The rule of Philip established the political and geographic foundation that led to the creation of the France of today.

In the aftermath of the death of King Philip II, his heir succeeded to the throne of France unchallenged. On 6 August 1223, he was crowned King Louis VIII at the Rheims Cathedral. The year after Louis' ascension to the throne, relations with the English regime once again deteriorated into dissension. With the English King Henry III's refusal to give homage for his French county of Gascony and parts of Poitou, a just cause was created for Louis to enforce his royal rights to the lands. Through a combination of threats, bribes and the gifts of privileges, he won his acceptance by the magnates, high churchmen and towns in Poitou, while Henry III's sovereignty in Gascony was destabilized. Louis VIII's reign over France was short-lived, lasting only slightly over three years before his death on 8 November 1226.

Selected Sources

Castries, Duc de, *The Lives of the Kings and Queens of France*
Bradbury, Jim, *Philip Augustus – King of France 1180–1223*
Bradbury, Jim, *The Capetians – Kings of France 987–1318*
Dunbabin, Jean, *France in the Making 843–1180*
Fawtier, Robert, *The Capetian Kings of France*
Hallam, Elizabeth M., *Capetian France – 987–1328*
Hutton, William Holden, *Philip Augustus*
Masson, Gustave, *Medieval France*
Potter, David, *A History of France, 1460–1560*
Sumption, Jonathan, *The Albigensian Crusade*
Tilley, Arthur, *Medieval France*

Louis XI

The French and English kings fought for over 100 years for the rights to reign over the Kingdom of France. Five generations of sovereigns from two rival dynasties – the houses of Valois and Plantagenet – struggled for possession of Europe's largest realm between 1337 and 1453. Following the defeat of the English at the Battle of Castillon during the rule of Louis XI's father, Charles VII, there was a period of peace between the two nations. In 1474, war threatened to resume when Charles, Duke of Burgundy, formed an alliance with King Edward IV of England for a combined military campaign against the reigning French monarch, Louis XI. In June 1474, English troops landed on the French coastline and began marching toward Rheims to renew the conflict against the Valois regime, while Louis stood ready to defend his lands with his army of knights, men-at-arms and foot soldiers assembled from his loyal vassals. As Edward advanced deeper into the interior, the Valois king sent envoys offering to begin peace talks to break his alliance with the Burgundians. Edward refused to meet with the French, but when Charles of Burgundy failed to support the invading English forces with his army, he agreed to peace negotiations with Louis XI. The two kings met on a wooden bridge at Picquigny near Amiens and hammered out a settlement to the war. Under the terms of the treaty, Edward agreed to withdraw and not renew the war in defence of his claims to the French crown, while Louis was to pay him a yearly pension of 50,000 crowns and a large upfront payment in gold. The Treaty of Picquigny ended the danger of an English offensive against France and finally concluded the Hundred Years' War.

Louis XI, the first son of the French king, Charles VII, and Queen Mary of Anjou, was born at the castle of Bourges on 3 July 1423 during the Hundred Years' War. In 1425, as the English army threatened to attack Bourges, the young Valois prince and heir to the crown was taken to Loches Castle for protection. The dauphin – the name given to the eldest son of the King of France – remained at the castle for the next eight years while the war against the English and forces from Burgundy continued to rage. He was raised at Loches by throne-appointed guardians while the king was involved with the defence of his kingdom. When the dauphin reached the age of 6, Charles appointed tutors for his education and he quickly demonstrated an inquisitive intelligence and broad interest. Under the instruction of his teachers, Louis learned to read and write, studying Latin, religion, history, mathematics and music. As the Valois prince remained separated from the royal court, he received martial training in the art of war from experienced warrior lords, becoming skilled fighting with the weapons of a knight. He mastered the handling of the sword, spear and battle axe, while learning to attack the enemy from a charging warhorse.

Shortly before the birth of Louis, the Valois monarchy had reached its lowest point in May 1421 when the Treaty of Troyes was signed between England and France, naming the English King Henry V regent for France and his successors rulers of the realm, while Charles VII was disinherited. After the English occupied the northern part of France, including Paris, Charles VII was recognized as monarch only in the region of central France centred on the city of Bourges. He continued the war against the English and their Burgundian allies, but in 1423 his poorly led army was again decisively defeated at the Battle of Crevant, weakening his hold on the Loire Valley. The following year, the Valois throne's army was reinforced with Scottish troops and 2,000 Italian mercenaries. The king then sent his army to attack the enemy at Verneuil, where the 15,000-strong French and allied force was decisively routed, with over half of the men killed or captured. The military position of Charles now appeared hopeless, the English and their Burgundian allies moving deeper into the Loire and seizing towns against little resistance. The king's plight was made worse by the numerous unscrupulous and incapable advisors and ministers in his government, who openly stole from the royal treasury, weakening the French war effort. By the beginning of 1429, it appeared the southern region of France would soon be occupied by the English and Burgundian troops. Despite the hopelessness of his position, Charles' seemingly certain defeat was turned into victory in February with the arrival at his court of the Maid of Orleans, Joan of Arc.

Joan was a young peasant girl from the small village of Domremy, and around the age of 14 she claimed to have been visited by angels and later saints with a message from God to break the siege of the city of Orleans. Driven by the word of God, she made her way to the royal court at Chinon, and after some hesitation was granted an audience with the king. At their first meeting, Joan was unable to convince Charles of her mission from God, but her persistence eventually resulted in her being given command of the royal troops. At the end of April 1429, she began to advance towards

Orleans with the Valois army. Joan rode ahead of the slow-moving soldiers, and with a small cavalry escort evaded the English forces to enter the city. She assumed command of the garrison troops and held Orleans until the rest of the army finally arrived. As the English king's forces approached, Joan led the garrison soldiers from the citadel, catching the enemy between the two French forces and compelling them to withdraw. She continued the campaign by pushing the English back to the west. When Rheims was freed of occupation forces, Charles entered the town on 17 July and was finally anointed King of France in the city's cathedral. Joan resumed her attacks on the enemy, beating them back toward Paris, but when John of Lancaster, the Duke of Bedford, took personal command of the English army, the French advance was halted and they withdrew into winter quarters.

During the pause in the war, Joan visited Loches and was introduced to Louis. The meeting with the Maid of Orleans had a lasting influence on the young dauphin, who developed a passionate worship of the Virgin Mary and belief in the destiny of his family's rule over France through the intervention of God. While at Loches, Joan is said to have told Louis: 'You will be a great king but not until you are nearly 30.' Louis later accompanied Joan on a pilgrimage to Clery, east of Lyons, to worship at the sacred shrine of a wooden image of the Virgin Mary.Remaining at Loches, Louis grew up in an environment void of stability or loyalty away from the royal household. He received little support or love from the king or his mother, his years of continued separation creating a rebellious spirit.

As the dauphin remained isolated from the royal court, Joan continued her campaign of conquest, advancing west to besiege Paris, but was beaten back by the English under the command of John of Bedford and compelled to retreat. In the spring of 1430, the Valois offensive resumed, but soon lost momentum as the English and their allies regained lost towns and territory. The French army's failure to take Paris and the ensuing victories of the enemy caused Charles VII to lose faith in Joan, but she continued to fight the English and Burgundians. While attacking the Burgundians at Compiegne on 23 May 1430, Joan was captured and later ransomed to the English. Under the control of the English, Joan was taken to Rouen in secure western France and put on trial for heresy and witchcraft. She was declared guilty of being a witch and was burned at the stake on 30 May 1431. In the aftermath of Joan's death, in 1456 she was declared innocent of the charges by an inquisitional court ordered by Pope Callixtus III. Joan of Arc was beatified and canonized in 1920, and today she is recognized as a patron saint of France.

The death of Joan of Arc at Rouen ignited the flame of a new nationalist spirit in the French warlords, who met with Charles and forced him to summon the Estates General. When the legislative body of clergymen, nobles and commoners met, they imposed their will on the king, compelling him to replace his ministers and advisors with better-qualified men. Under the new government, Louis was moved from Loches to the household of his mother at Amboise. At the queen's court, the young Louis was treated as the dauphin of France, receiving the homage of the town's nobles, clergymen and merchants in a ceremony of veneration. At Amboise, Louis' education was resumed and he began preparations for his reign over France by first receiving training in the governing of the kingdom. In 1434, he was sent to Tours to gain experience in the administration of the town by attending council meetings and resolving issues affecting the residents, while gaining support for the king's war effort from the warlords. The prince's academic education was continued in Tours, where he had access to more qualified scholars and better libraries.

While the dauphin remained in the south of France, Charles VII was reconciled with his former constable, Arthur de Richemont. De Richemont, the younger son of Duke John IV of Brittany and Joanne of Navarre, was born on 24 August 1398 at the castle of Suscinio in Brittany. In 1410, Arthur joined the Armagnacs in their fight against the Burgundians, later entering the service of the Duke of Guyenne. He fought against the English at the Battle of Agincourt, where he was wounded and taken prisoner. After his release, Arthur returned to France to serve with the dauphin, and was later appointed to the office of constable. As Constable of France, he served with Joan of Arc at the Battle of Patay. After the death of Duke Peter II of Brittany in 1457, Arthur ascended the ducal throne as Arthur III, reigning until his death on 26 December 1458.

With Arthur de Richemont's appointment as Constable of France, many corrupt court officials were removed and improvements made to the French army. Under the reform measures brought in by de Richemont, the Valois forces regained their fighting spirit, and with the English suffering from the lack of support from the government of King Henry VI – who displayed little interest in pursuing the war – Charles VII's soldiers battled the enemy to a standstill. With the war at an impasse, Duke Philip III the Good of Burgundy agreed to negotiate a settlement with the French. Following several meetings at Nevers between envoys of the Valois regime and Burgundian representatives, a preliminary agreement was signed, to be finalized at a conference of the belligerents.

Charles VII resumed the war against the forces of Henry VI, with de Richemont sending the French troops to make sorties against the English-held fortifications of Paris. After the loss of their Burgundian ally and with the Valois army attacking the defences of the capital, the English agreed to open talks for the resolution of the conflict. In May 1435, the Congress of Arras began with emissaries from France, England, Burgundy, the German Empire and Holy See. When the congress opened, Charles VII demanded the English terminate their claims to his throne and withdraw from occupied France. Following the king's ultimatums, the English envoys withdrew from the conference with no resolution to the war. Philip III of Burgundy remained at the congress and continued to negotiate a settlement, offering to abandon the English and sign a separate peace if he was permitted to retain his conquered lands. The terms were accepted by Charles VII's representatives.

Following the Arras agreement, the fighting spirit of the French was energized and their forces attacked the English in Normandy and the Ile-de-France, expanding the territory under Charles' control. As the Valois monarchy continued the war against the occupation forces of Henry VI, the terms for the marriage between Louis and Margaret Stewart, daughter of the Scottish king, James I, were finalized in 1436 after prolonged negotiations. The political agreement included a pledge by the Scots to provide troops and supplies for the war against England. The dauphin had little interest in the marriage, but reluctantly agreed to the treaty. In the aftermath of the wedding ceremony, he was given his own household with experienced and capable ministers. Now under the influence of his advisors, he viewed his father as a weak and easily influenced king at a time when the French regime needed a strong and energetic leader, which he was determined to become.

The dauphin had received a broad military training under experienced warlords, and in 1437 he had his first encounters against English forces, participating in the campaign against the enemy troops defending Paris. He commanded a division of soldiers during the siege operations, leading several attacks against the defensive works. When the Valois army forced the troops of Henry VI to surrender Paris in November 1437, Louis rode alongside his father in triumph into the city as the newly freed inhabitants welcomed their king and dauphin. Following the procession through the streets of Paris to Notre Dame, the king and his son attended a service of thanksgiving.

While Louis remained at the royal court, becoming closely associated with his father's rule, the war against the English continued. In 1439, the dauphin was given his first independent command when Charles VII named him lieutenant general for the district of Languedoc in the south-east of the kingdom. During the fighting against the English, the area had been ravaged and was now prey to roving bands of brigands, who raided the towns and farmsteads. Widespread unrest spread among the people and the local economy was in ruin. On 25 May, Prince Louis made his state entrance into Toulouse. To restore order, the dauphin established his government in the city and carefully chose capable and loyal ministers. He introduced new measures to end the plundering attacks, re-establish order and revive the economy. Louis travelled throughout the region establishing his rule, while receiving homage from the local nobles, clergy and merchants. Lacking troops and money, he raised funds from the region's lords and towns to buy off the brigands. During his journeys through the district, he listened to appeals from the inhabitants, attempted to rectify abuses and curbed the excesses of the warlords. After six months under the prince's administration, the reform programmes began to produce results, with the economy showing signs of recovery and the throne's laws now enforced. After remaining in the Languedoc area until November, the prince was recalled to the royal court at Tours by Charles VII to take part in the suppression of the Praguerie Revolt. In the coming years, the residents of the Languedoc area would remember the benefits derived from Louis' energetic and competent command.

During the war against the English and their Burgundian ally, the regime of Charles VII had instituted numerous military reforms to restructure the army, which had the effect of reducing the power and autonomy of the warlords, prohibiting their private armies. As the king continued to suppress the independence of his vassals, a faction of magnates bonded together to regain their self-rule, led by Charles of Bourbon and John of Armagne. In February 1440, the rebel lords revolted, intending to replace the king with the dauphin and remove Constable de Richemont from the government. Their insurgence was known as the Praguerie Revolt due to its similarity to another uprising in Bohemia. The warlords advanced against the king, taking the towns of Niort, Melle and Saint Maixent. As the uprising spread, Charles VII sent troops to subdue the rebellion and appointed Louis as lieutenant general for the Poitou region, the centre of the revolt. Taking control of the county, he received homage from the noblemen and clerics to establish his rule. The dauphin introduced new measures similar to those employed in Languedoc to ensure the loyalty of the local lords, churchmen and people, while securing the region for the Valois regime.

After bringing peace to Poitou, Prince Louis was placed in command of the French army and sent to relieve the English siege of Dieppe in the summer of 1443. The port city had been surrounded by English forces, who had constructed a fort on the heights of a nearby hill to bombard the

French fortifications. Louis mustered a relief force of 1,600 men and set out for Dieppe, arriving on 11 August. After making a reconnaissance of the English position, on the morning of 14 August, to the sound of trumpets, Louis led his men in an attack against the English encampment. As the prince's troops advanced, reinforcements from Dieppe joined the fight and the combined French army overran the enemy, compelling them to flee, leaving their dead and wounded on the battlefield. In the aftermath of his victory, Louis returned to the royal court, where he was warmly greeted by his father. While the dauphin had won the favour of the king with his success at Dieppe, he continued secret negotiations with numerous mutinous warlords to seize the Valois crown.

After his victory at Dieppe, Prince Louis remained on friendly terms with his father, and in 1444 was appointed to lead an expeditionary force to the Swiss cantons in support of the German emperor, Frederick III. The emperor had formed an alliance with the French and appealed to Charles VII for reinforcements in his ongoing conflict against the Swiss. With the French monarchy having long-standing claims to the cantons, the king agreed to take part in the war against the Swiss to reclaim his lost lands. The conflict against the English was at this time at a stalemate, and the unemployed mercenary soldiers were pillaging and raiding French towns and the surrounding countryside. To reduce the size of the marauding mercenaries and provide a military force for Frederick, Louis was placed in command of the Valois army with orders to hire the vagrant soldiers for the campaign against the Swiss. The dauphin recruited an army of over 10,000 men and advanced east, attacking the city of Basel in current-day north-western Switzerland.

The dauphin's infantry and cavalry moved into the Swiss Confederation, meeting only scattered resistance. When Louis' troops approached Basel, the Swiss commander sent an advance force of 1,300 pikemen to assault them. In the early morning of 26 August, they mounted a surprise attack against Louis' vanguard at Saint Jacob. The Swiss soldiers deployed into squares as they clashed with the French forces. The bloody fighting lasted for several hours before Louis ordered his cavalry to charge into the enemy formation. As the French horsemen repeatedly crashed into the pikemen, the Swiss ranks were decimated by heavy losses and the survivors withdrew. Following the defeat of the Swiss, the French besieged Basel and Louis soon began negotiations with the city leaders, who agreed to abandon their alliance with the cantons and accept his protection for the region.

In the wake of his victory against the Swiss, Louis continued to loyally serve the king while maintaining his alliance with the rebel lords until he felt strong enough to revolt against his father. Louis' natural rebellious temperament and lack of confidence in the government of his father prompted him to negotiate an agreement with the rebel warlords for his self-rule. When the king learned of his son's negotiations with the magnates, he sent his army, led by Constable de Richemont, to suppress the insurgent alliance. Moving his army against the rebels, the constable quickly overwhelmed Louis' forces, compelling him to negotiate a reconciliation with the king. Following protracted talks, and with his support from the warlords beginning to weaken, the dauphin was forced to accept the king's demands. In exchange for his oath of loyalty, Prince Louis received a full pardon and was appointed to govern the rebellious Dauphine Province in the south-east of the realm. The rebel lords were compelled to disband their armies and agree not to recall their forces without the approval of the king.

In January 1447, Louis took the reins of power for the Dauphine and began to enforce his authority over the rebellious warlords and high churchmen. He issued laws prohibiting private wars between the nobles and compelled them to acknowledge him as ruler. Louis required the nobles to perform military service for him at their expense and respect the government of the province. The Valois prince also moved against the defiant clerics, forcing them to obey his laws. In 1453, he transformed the local governing Dauphine Council, which dealt with judicial and military issues for the region, into the Parliament of the Dauphine. Under the dauphin's reign, the province was fully integrated into his father's kingdom. He expanded his authority by compelling the Archbishop of Vienna, Bishop of Grenoble and the Holy Roman Abbot to pledge their allegiance to him, while taking control over the town of Montelimar in south-eastern France. To revive the region's economy, the prince ordered the construction of roads and approved the creation of new marketplaces. He placed a tax on wheat imported from France to stimulate the growth of local agriculture, while offering financial incentives to his merchants. During Louis' reign over Dauphine, the size of the lordship was doubled and a well-organized and functioning government was created. In July 1452, the Valois prince established a university at Valence for the teaching of law, medicine and theology. Away from the royal regime, he ruled independently without consulting the king. The dauphin's years away from his father's court served as an apprenticeship for his future assumption of the French throne. As Louis continued to expand his opposition against Charles VII, he was forced to abandon his rule over Dauphine and the province was again placed under the authority of the Valois monarchy.

While Louis was in Dauphine, the English had broken their truce with the French in 1449, upon which Charles VII sent his army to attack their forces in Normandy. During the truce, Henry VI's regime had largely ignored its army in Normandy, leaving the region unprepared against an attack. Led by Arthur de Richemont, the well-trained and heavily armed Valois troops swept into Normandy, capturing Rouen, and by the end of the year the southern part of the region was again occupied by French royal soldiers. After the defeat of his occupation troops, Henry VI ordered a relief force to regain the lost territories. On 14 April, a force of 6,000 English soldiers led by Lord Thomas Kyriell reached the village of Formigny, while the French moved from the east to intercept them. As the Valois forces approached, the English formed into a long line behind a thicket of stakes and earthworks. The French launched an attack with their 3,000 infantrymen against the fortified English position, but were thrown back. The French then deployed several artillery pieces to open fire on their enemy. In danger of being decimated by the cannons' volleys, the English attacked and seized the guns. While the French were pulling back, Arthur de Richemont led 1,500 cavalrymen in a charge against the English left flank. As Arthur's mounted warriors swept into the English, the French footmen rushed across the battlefield, massacring Kyriell's troops. The remaining isolated Norman fortifications fell quickly to the French, and by August 1450 all of Normandy was in Charles VII's hands, leaving the Duchy of Gascony and Calais Pale as the only remaining provinces in France under Henry VI's control. As the regime of Henry VI was losing control of its French lands, factional differences erupted across England that led to the Wars of the Roses. This civil war, which was fought over the next thirty-two years, distracted the attention of the English away from the war in France.

In July 1445, the dauphin's wife, Margaret of Scotland, suddenly died at Chalons-en-Champagne. Louis had spent little time with Margaret and had never approved of the negotiated marriage. The Valois prince continued to reign over Dauphine, but began secret talks with the Duke of Savoy, Louis, for marriage to his daughter, Charlotte. The marital agreement would give the dauphin a loyal ally on his southern border, while providing a rich dowry. When the king learned of the talks, Charles refused to approve the nuptial treaty. The prince sent numerous envoys to the royal court to secure the king's endorsement, but his opposition remained. Despite his father's disapproval, Louis disregarded the king and he married Charlotte on 9 March 1451. The future queen was born in 1441, the daughter of Louis of Savoy and Anne of Cyprus. At the time of her marriage to the dauphin, Charlotte was just 9 years old but was recognized as Dauphine of France. On 22 July 1461, Charlotte became Queen of France. The then Louis XI saw little of his wife, sending her to reside at Amboise castle, where she maintained her household. She spent her days with her courtiers and sisters, supervising the education of her daughters and attending to religious duties. Only on rare occasions did the queen fulfil royal ceremonial duties, entertaining foreign guests. After the death of Louis XI, the queen served on the regency council, governing the realm for the minor King Charles VIII. Queen Charlotte was the mother of eight children, but only three survived to adulthood.

Charles VII responded to his son's marriage by cancelling his pension, with rumours spreading around the realm that he was to be disinherited. Relations between father and son continued to deteriorate, but when the English landed an expeditionary force in Guyenne, Louis quickly offered his sword to the crown. The king refused to allow his son to participate in the Guyenne campaign, but when his uncle, Rene – who was contesting the throne of Naples – sought help in gaining his kingdom, Louis volunteered his services. When Rene sailed to Naples to attack his rival, Louis crossed over the Alps with his small army and his uncle's French troops. When the Valois prince descended into Piedmont in north-western Italy, he met his uncle and proposed a joint attack against Genoa to place the city under his protection. As he manoeuvred to secure a new kingdom in Italy for himself, Rene was pressed by his northern Italian allies to protect them from Louis' seizure of their lands. The dauphin made appeals to several cities for their aid, but they refused to intervene. Without the support of his uncle and the denial of the Italian allies, Louis was compelled to return across the Alps to Dauphine.

In the wake of his failure to expand his independent rule into Piedmont, Prince Louis dispatched emissaries to the king asking for his pardon and reconciliation. He attached two conditions to his plea, demanding to remain in Dauphine and retain his advisors. Charles VII refused to forgive his son's disobedience and prepared to send troops to forcibly bring him to his court. Louis continued to dispatch representatives to the king, telling him he wanted to obey but that his orders were too harsh and threatening. Charles then sent a final message to his son, telling him to return without conditions or he would move against him with his military forces.

As the French regime's envoy was making his way to Dauphine with the king's message, the royal army was nearing the border of Louis' province. When the prince learned of the approaching soldiers, he fled to the court of his father's most feared enemy, his uncle the Duke of Burgundy, Philip III. Early on the morning of 30 August 1456, he mounted his horse and with a small escort galloped away from Dauphine, riding north towards Burgundy. At the beginning of October, the dauphin arrived at the court of his uncle in

Brussels, where he was received by the duchess and escorted into the castle. He was royally entertained at the ducal court, and on 15 October met the duke, who had been on campaign in Holland.

Duke Philip welcomed the prince to his duchy, and during their talks provided a pension to his nephew and his own household at the castle of Genappe. Louis quickly settled into the formalities and pomp of the ducal court in Brussels. He met frequently with his uncle, discussing his reign over Dauphine and his relationship with his father. In the spring of 1457, he toured the wealthy Burgundian cities with the duke, enquiring about trade and commerce. During the summer, Charlotte of Savoy joined her husband and they established their court at Genappe. They routinely entertained the Burgundian lords and high churchmen with banquets, hunting parties and festivals. From his castle in Brussels, the dauphin remained in contact with his many friends and secret agents in Dauphine, keeping informed of local activities, while maintaining a watchful eye on events at his father's court through a network of spies and allies.

While Louis remained in Burgundy, Duke Philip III sent his nephew with a large force of Burgundian soldiers to England in early March 1461 to reinforce his ally, Edward of York, in his war against the House of Lancaster. After sailing across the English Channel and travelling overland to London, the dauphin and his troops joined the Yorkist army. Advancing with Edward's forces on 29 March, Louis led his soldiers in the pivotal Battle of Towton. The two armies collided near the city of York during a snowstorm. The Yorkist soldiers opened the battle by advancing against the enemy, deployed on a fortified ridgeline. When Edward's archers fired devastating volleys of arrows, the Lancastrian troops abandoned their defences, charging across the snow-covered field into the ranks of Edward's and the French prince's men in a fierce and bloody hand-to-hand encounter. As the battle raged for hours, Yorkist reinforcements under the Duke of Norfolk finally arrived and the enemy was beaten back. During the battle, Louis fought alongside Edward under his Dauphine flag, helping lead the Yorkists to victory.

In mid-1461, while Louis was still in England, he began to receive reports that his father's health was worsening. As Charles VII's condition deteriorated further, his son began to make preparations for his return to France, diplomatic measures being undertaken with the powerful French warlords and leading clerics to ensure their loyalty against any attempt by his brother, Charles of Valois, to usurp the crown. On 22 July 1461, King Charles VII died, his acknowledged successor receiving the news of his death three days later. Having returned to Burgundy, he sent messages to his followers telling them to assemble their men and meet him at Avesnes near the city of Rheims to ensure his assumption of the Valois throne. In the aftermath of Charles VII's death, many French nobles, prelates, members of parliament and government officials converged on Avesnes to pay homage to the new king. Louis ordered a Requiem Mass for the dead king but forbade his household to attend. The next day, he rode with a large military escort to the border with France at Avesnes to meet Duke Philip III, his lords and churchmen.

Dressed in mourning clothes, Louis attended the Mass for his father on 3 August, and during the afternoon went hunting dressed in the red and white colours of the Valois family. The following morning, he made his way to Rheims, escorted by Philip III. The elaborate coronation was held in the cathedral on 15 August, with the realm's leading lords and clerics in attendance. Following the time-honoured rituals, the peers of the realm anointed Louis with holy oil over the upper body. During the ceremony, Louis swore an oath to the saints proclaiming to regain all of his lands, including those sold, divided or pledged by his predecessors. Philip of Burgundy then took the crown, raising it into the air for all to see before placing it upon the 38-year-old Louis' head, recognizing him as King of France. Philip then shouted, 'Long live the King'. The cry was taken up throughout the cathedral and into the streets of Rheims. The coronation service was followed by a grand banquet presided over by King Louis XI.

Shortly after the anointment ceremony, Philip of Burgundy organized the grand entry of Louis XI into Paris. On the afternoon of 31 August, with four trumpeters sounding his arrival, the king reached the city under a canopy of blue satin embellished with fleur de lys and carried by six local citizens. He proceeded through streets richly decorated with displays of chivalrous feats to Notre Dame, where his was greeted by the Bishop of Paris at the doors of the cathedral. A grand procession escorted the king up the brilliantly lit aisle to the high altar, as the Te Deum was sung. Soon after the singing ended, the organ played and the bells rang out, while the crowd cried out, 'Noel, Noel'. Following a short prayer by the bishop, the monarch made his way to the royal palace for the welcoming banquet. After the dinner, the king withdrew to the Hotel des Tournelles to establish his temporary residence, living as simply as he had done at Genappe castle. Louis remained in the city for a few days before announcing his departure for Tours to begin his rule.

With his authority now acknowledged by the nobles, prelates and towns of his realm, Louis XI quickly began to build his government. Most of his father's counsellors and officials were dismissed and replaced by the new king's loyal allies and friends. He introduced new programmes to lower his regime's expenditures, while seeking ways to raise additional revenue. The king travelled extensively throughout his realm, receiving homage from his subjects while establishing his rule. During his earlier journeys across France and with Philip III in Burgundy, Louis had acquired a special interest in the welfare of his towns and put in place measures to strengthen their economies and prosperity. The Valois court issued individualized grants of special trading privileges to the towns and sought ways to expand their local commercial activities. Under the reign of Louis XI, his heavy presence was felt in every aspect of government as he monitored the effects of his changes. In return for the Valois crown's economic initiatives, the towns became a base of solid support and loyalty for the king. To encourage the growth of commerce, Louis built new roads and waterways, while existing ones were enlarged and repaired.

While the king was expanding his authority across his kingdom, his court took measures to increase its influence over the appointment of the French clerics and enhance its ability to tax the Church's properties. Soon after his succession to the Valois throne, Louis XI had revoked the Pragmatic Sanctions, which had been enacted by his father to increase his crown's power over the Holy See and weaken the influence of the pope, while restricting its sources of income. When it became evident that the pontiff's recent actions intended to expand his sway over his kingdom, Louis reimposed the Pragmatic Sanctions and enacted new decrees to tax the papacy.

Following his assumption of the French monarchy, Louis XI also instigated a new policy to restrict the power of the nobles and prelates, while consolidating the sovereignty of the realm solely in his hands. As the king pressed his political campaign to act as an independent ruler, the two estates – the nobility and Church – became increasingly alarmed at their loss of influence and forced subjugation to the will of the king. The warlords and high clerics began to conspire against Louis XI, their plot beginning with the revolt of the Duke of Brittany, Francis II, who endeavoured to maintain his quasi-independence from France against the initiatives of the Valois king. Francis, the son of Richard of Brittany and Margaret of Orleans, was born on 23 June 1433 at the Chateau of Clisson on the west coast of France. At his birth, Francis was not in the direct line of succession to the Breton throne, but after the death of his two cousins he was acknowledged as heir designate. During the Wars of the Roses in England, he supported the Lancastrian claimant to the crown, providing money and troops to Henry Tudor's campaign for the

English throne. In 1465, Francis participated in the Public Weal's quest for self-government from the rule of Louis XI.

Soon after his assumption of the ducal throne, Francis II paid only marginal homage to Louis XI, which at first was accepted by the monarch. As the relationship between the king and Duke Francis continued to vacillate, the Breton duke began to rule as an independent lord, forming alliances with regional rulers without the approval of his overlord. The conflict between the king and Francis II erupted when the duke required Amauri d'Acigne, Bishop of Nantes, to offer homage to him instead of Louis. D'Acigne remained loyal to the French regime, whereupon the duke moved against the prelate, forcing him to flee from his bishopric and seek protection from the Valois monarchy. Louis agreed to intervene, ordering his warlords to muster in Tours for an incursion against Francis to compel his submission. Perceiving the opportunity to regain their lost independence, the French magnates formed an alliance in support of the duke. They assembled in Paris, and in opposition to the king formed the League of the Public Weal. The king's brother, Charles of Valois, was chosen to lead the league, with Duke John of Bourbon appointed commander of their forces. To defy their overlord, the rebel magnates began raising an army and money.

In March 1465, as the rebels prepared to confront their king, Louis XI offered peace terms and a pardon to all who abandoned the League of Public Weal. The peers of the kingdom refused to accept the crown's proposal, but many lesser lords and towns assured Louis of their continued loyalty. As the threat of revolt intensified, Count Charles of Charolais, the son of the Duke of Burgundy, was acknowledged as the leader of the Public Weal. Charles was born in November 1433 at Dijon, Burgundy, the son of Duke Philip III and Isabella of Portugal. He was raised at his father's court, which was at the centre of the renaissance of European arts and commerce. Renowned tutors were employed for Charles' academic and military education, and under their guidance he excelled in his studies. At the Burgundian court, he was exposed to his father's quest for the unification of his scattered duchy into a single kingdom, which the duke aggressively pursued during his rule. In April 1465, Philip III relinquished his regime to Charles, who commanded the duchy's troops in battle for the first time during the Public Weal. Under the command of the count, an army of over 5,000 cavalry, 14,000 infantry and a large contingent of artillery was mustered during 1465 and began to advance against Paris. The rebel forces reached Paris unopposed and laid siege to the city. Meanwhile, Louis had begun the defence of his crown by attacking the lands of the Duke of Bourbon. When the king learned of the threat against his capital, he halted his attack and moved north to defend Paris. As his regime's forces of 12,000 mounted soldiers and 3,000 footmen neared the capital after a hard march, they clashed with the rebels on 16 July 1465 near the castle of Montlhery. On a hot summer's day, the opposing armies deployed across an open field, each with two divisions at the front and a third in the rear. The fighting at Montlhery began with the charge of the rebel cavalry, led by Count Louis of Saint Pol. Shortly after the count's horsemen collided with the royalists, Charles of Charolais sent his horse soldiers into the fray. The fierce and bloody encounter lasted until nightfall, when Louis ordered his men to fall back. Following the encounter at Montlhery, the French king withdrew to the north and reorganized his battered army, while the forces of the Public Weal resumed their siege operations against Paris.

After resting and regrouping his army, Louis led his men toward Paris, occupying a fortified position along the Seine opposite the rebels. With his forces secure behind their defensive lines, the king rode to Normandy to rally additional troops to his banner. Returning to Paris with reinforcements, he offered to negotiate a settlement with the Public Weal to avoid risking his monarchy on the results of a single encounter. As the two armies prepared for battle, leaders of the league agreed to meet and discuss a peace treaty. After prolonged talks, Louis pledged to transfer Normandy to his brother, Charles of Valois, in exchange for the County of Berry, and cede the Picardy towns along the Somme River to Burgundy, along with several minor concessions, while the League vowed to acknowledge Louis' sovereignty. During negotiations for what became the Treaty of Conflans, the French king made a separate peace with the Duke of Brittany, separating him from the league.

Soon after the signing of the Treaty of Conflans, Charles of Valois travelled to his new duchy to receive the homage of his subjects. While the king's brother remained in the duchy, he was joined by Duke Francis II from the bordering Duchy of Brittany. With the Breton duke in Normandy with Charles, visiting the towns and meeting the local nobles and churchmen, the Norman warlords and prelates began to fear his seizure of their lands. To ensure their continued independence, the Normans seized Charles of Valois and held him prisoner. When Louis XI was informed of his brother's capture, he assembled his army and moved against the Normans to free his brother and reimpose his rule. As the royal troops marched into the duchy, the Norman lords surrendered without resistance and pledged their loyalty to the monarch. Louis then forced Charles to transfer the duchy to his crown. The king's swift advance into Normandy with his soldiers re-established his reign over the region, while overturning an unfavourable clause of the Treaty of Conflans.

During the French regime's conflict against the Public Weal, civil war had erupted in Spain between the King of Castile and John of Aragon. The Valois monarchy threw its support behind King Henry IV of Castile, intervening to negotiate a peaceful settlement between the two warring factions. In 1463, war again broke out between the two Spanish kingdoms, and with John of Aragon occupied with the defence of his lands, Louis XI sent his troops into the Aragonese counties of Roussillon and Cerdagne to establish his rule. With the Aragonese leader now fighting the Castilians, the French troops overwhelmed the enemy's resistance and annexed the two lordships into Louis' kingdom. This occupation of the northern Spanish region remained unchallenged until 1473, when the Aragonese launched an invasion into Roussillon. However, the local forces of the French regime drove out the enemy troops and Louis' sovereignty over the region remained secure.

In June 1467, Philip the Good of Burgundy died and his son, Charles, was recognized as his successor. Taking the reins of power, he was resolved to create a new European kingdom by joining his scattered lordships with his lands from France and Germany. To wage war against the Valois monarchy, Charles the Bold of Burgundy negotiated a military league with Duke Francis II of Brittany, Edward IV of England and numerous rogue French warlords. After receiving homage from his subjects, Charles assembled his well-trained and armed Burgundian army to attack Louis' realm. He supplemented his forces with units of heavily armoured cavalry and infantry, while also hiring Italian mercenary soldiers. With his powerful army prepared for battle, the Burgundian duke attempted to gain the fealty of the lords in southern Flanders by threatening to invade them. Despite the danger to their fiefdoms, the nobles remained loyal to the French throne, compelling Charles the Bold to march into Flanders with his troops and occupy the towns.

As Charles was spreading his rule over Flanders, Louis XI was occupied with Francis II of Brittany's invasion of Normandy, where his duchy had territorial claims. With his rights to the duchy challenged, Louis was compelled to delay his response to the Burgundian attacks against Flanders and sent his formidable army against Francis. The Breton soldiers in Normandy were quickly defeated by the French and forced to withdraw from the duchy and pledge their fealty to the Valois regime.

In the aftermath of his repulse of the Bretons' attack into Normandy, Louis XI sent envoys to the Burgundian court to resolve their recent incursions into Flanders. The French representatives met with the duke, who offered to negotiate with Louis under a safe conduct pass at the town of Perrone on the Somme. As Charles continued to enlarge the area under his ducal control, the town of Liege – in current-day eastern Belgium – threatened to revolt against the Burgundians, and Louis sent emissaries to the town's officials to encourage their resistance. When Louis reached Perrone for his conference with the Burgundians, he was escorted into the city by the duke. Soon after their meeting to settle border issues, the inhabitants of Liege rebelled against Duke Charles' harsh rule, declaring their fealty to the French throne as their protector. When the Burgundian duke was informed of the uprising, he flew into a violent frenzy, ordering the seizure of the French monarch. Louis was held prisoner for three days. The duke eventually offered to release him if he and his troops would participate in the suppression of the Liege rebellion and accept peace terms dictated by him. Fearing for his life, Louis agreed to the demands, and on 15 October 1468 advanced against Liege with the Duke of Burgundy. Liege was brutally attacked by the French and Burgundian soldiers, with many thousands slaughtered and the city burnt to the ground. By the time the Valois king departed from Liege, he was committed to the destruction of the power of Charles the Bold.

After leaving the Burgundians, Louis XI travelled to his court in Paris and began to plan his revenge against Duke Charles. To secure the allegiance and military support of his brother, Charles of Valois, the king pledged to transfer to him the Duchy of Gascony in south-western France. The duke agreed to the offer, and with the Valois duke now aligned with his crown, Louis manoeuvred to separate the remaining French warlords from their Burgundian allegiance, while raising new troops and money for his attack against Charles.

As Louis XI continued to increase the number of French magnates, clerics and towns under his regime's authority, he summoned Duke Charles of Burgundy to his court in 1471 to answer charges of treason. After the duke refused to appear to defend himself, the French king declared war and mustered his army of loyal vassals and their troops. He ordered part of his forces to assail the enemy from Dauphine, while a second army advanced into Picardy in northern France. The French marched into the Somme region and overran numerous Burgundian towns, the garrison at Amiens surrendering without offering resistance. With the French troops now seizing his towns and occupying his lands, Charles the Bold unleashed a counter-attack into Picardy, desolating the region in a savage campaign. The Burgundians continued their assaults, overwhelming the resistance of the Valois supporters and then moving against Amiens. The city was besieged and battered by the duke's large cannons. However, despite the bombardment and bloody attacks against its defensive works, the city's garrison troops repelled the Burgundians, compelling Charles to abandon his siege. Unable to take Amiens after three weeks, and with his men exhausted and supplies depleted, the duke agreed to negotiate a ceasefire with Louis. After holding talks, a truce treaty was signed.

In the aftermath of his campaign of 1471, Charles the Bold spent the duration of the truce rebuilding his battered army and recruiting additional troops. By June, he was ready to renew the war against Louis and sent his forces back to the Somme region to attack the Valois-supporting nobles. The duke laid siege to town after town, but when he attacked the castle at Beauvais, the garrison threw back his assaults. Rebuffed, Charles was compelled to abandon the siege and advance south into Normandy to pillage the Pays de Caux. The Burgundian duke left a trail of destruction across the area, but in late autumn his offensive began to stall and his treasury was nearly depleted. Charles was compelled to abandon Normandy and go into winter quarters. In November 1473, Louis agreed to a truce with Charles, which was extended into the next year.

While Louis XI was occupied with the war against the Burgundians, he moved to strengthen his support against potential rebellion by his vassal warlords. In May 1471, Louis' brother, Charles, died and his Duchy of Gascony was reoccupied by the Valois regime, then when Francis of Brittany threatened to break his oath of fealty to the French crown and unite with Charles of Burgundy against the French kingdom, the king sent troops into the duchy to force the duke's pledge of loyalty. While the monarchy was confronting Duke Francis, John V, the Count of Armagne, disregarded his oath of fealty to Louis and joined the Burgundians. To prevent other lords from abandoning their allegiance to the French, and to reassert his authority, Louis XI ordered his soldiers into Armagne to force John's fidelity. As the French marched into his lands, John submitted and again pledged his homage, whereupon the monarch pardoned the rebel count and withdrew his soldiers. However, shortly after receiving amnesty, John rejoined the Burgundians and their war against his overlord. Confronted by the count's treason, Louis XI ordered his army back into Armagne to unleash a fierce attack against the rebels. The countship was pillaged, with John killed during the attack against the castle at Lectoure. The count's rogue fiefdom was then annexed into the Valois kingdom. By 1474, through his campaign of bribery, negotiations and military intervention, the French king had regained his rule over his vassals and secured his hold on the throne.

To further reinforce his power over the nobles and clerics, and to isolate and weaken Charles the Bold, the French king pursued an international policy of dividing the duke's lands. When the Duke of Austria asked for French aid in his dispute with the Swiss Confederation, Louis refused the request to maintain his friendly relationship with the cantons. Rebuffed by the French, the Austrian duke, Sigismund, negotiated an alliance with Burgundy. As part of the agreement, Charles gained dominion over the Duchy of Alsace on the borders of present-day eastern France and northern Germany in exchange for a large cash payment. The acquisition of Alsace and the later seizure of the Duchy of Guelders solidified his northern lordships, and he now sought to acquire German lands to unite his duchy into a new kingdom.

Following his acquisition of Alsace, Charles the Bold met with the emperor of the Holy Roman Empire, Frederick III, at Trier in 1473 to discuss the marriage of his daughter, Mary, to the emperor's son, Maximilian, and the establishment of a new kingdom under his rule. The German emperor became alarmed by the creation of a potential enemy near his border and the talks ended quickly, with Frederick hastily departing. Undeterred by the rejection of the emperor, Charles marched his army into Cologne, occupying the Rhineland city to renew his quest to form a realm.

While Charles was expanding his lands by occupying additional Rhineland counties, the French king sent envoys to the Swiss Confederation, Duke Rene II of Lorraine and imperial free cities along the Rhine to form a counter-alliance to contend the mounting danger of the Burgundians. Under pressure from Louis XI's representatives, the Swiss and the Austrian Duke Sigismund agreed to a ten-year alliance against the Burgundians. As part of the treaty, Sigismund was granted enough money to repurchase the Alsace region, as per the terms of his earlier agreement with Charles the Bold. In return, the Austrians acknowledged the independence of the Swiss Cantons. In early April, the Austrian duke notified Charles that funds had been paid for the return of Alsace. In less than a month, the Alsace towns drove -away the Burgundian troops and welcomed Sigismund's forces. While Louis' campaign against Charles was reducing the lordships allied with his regime, Rene II shifted his allegiance to the French when Charles began to secretly establish garrisons in his duchy's castles.

As Louis XI continued to press his opposition to the Burgundians, Charles assembled a large army and advanced to recover his lost allies and lands. The duke began his campaign on 30 July by besieging the small town of Neuse, which served as an outpost for Cologne. With the city of Cologne threatened by the duke, Louis sent his envoys to the Swiss Confederation to secure its agreement to join the fight against Charles. On 26 October 1474, a treaty was signed, with the French agreeing pay a yearly pension to each canton that pledged to attack Charles. The Swiss cantons declared war against Burgundy and advanced their army over the Jura Mountains to attack Charles, crushing his forces at Hericourt near the Austrian border. As the cantons were attacking Hericourt, the Holy Roman Emperor, Frederick III, issued a call to arms and his forces prepared to move against the Burgundian duke.

While Louis was politically manoeuvring to isolate the Duke of Burgundy along the Rhine, Charles negotiated the Treaty of London on 25 July 1474 with King Edward IV of England, who agreed to cross the Channel and attack the French. As part of the treaty, England acknowledged Charles as the rightful King of France. Edward had recently reclaimed the English throne from the Lancastrian claimant, Henry VI, and was now eager to reacquire French lands lost during the Hundred Years' War. Under the terms of the settlement, Charles of Burgundy pledged to fully support the campaign and acclaim Edward as the French king, while the English agreed the Burgundians could recover their ducal territories along with new lands. In July 1475, the troops of Edward IV crossed the Channel, landing in the Pale of Calais to launch their invasion of France.

Edward IV expected to begin his advance into France soon after reaching Calais, but his campaign was delayed while Charles remained in the east fighting the Swiss and Germans. Finally, in the autumn, the Burgundians were ready and the English marched into Picardy to attack the town of Saint-Quentin with the support of the duke. The town was besieged by the allies, but Charles soon abandoned Edward to return to his deteriorating campaign along the Rhine. The English were attacked at Saint-Quentin by Count Louis of Saint-Pol, who had recently deserted his alliance with the Burgundians to rejoin the French. As the siege dragged on, the English king became disillusioned with Duke Charles, believing he had been deceived into attacking the Valois monarchy. When the opportunity came for negotiations with the French, Edward readily consented to a meeting. Following several days of talks, the two kingdoms came to terms. Under the resulting treaty, each side pledged to honour a seven-year truce, the Valois regime agreed to pay an annual fee to the English and Edward was to peacefully withdraw his invading army. The Treaty of Picquigny was signed on 29 August 1475 by Louis XI and Edward IV, ending the English involvement in the Burgundian war. The loss of his English ally in the west and the continued resistance of the Swiss and Germans in the east destroyed Charles' grand strategy for the conquest of France and creation of a new kingdom, compelling him to agree to a nine-year truce with Louis in September.

Shortly after the withdrawal of Edward's army, Duke Charles returned to the east to pursue his war against the Germans and Swiss, while King Louis continued to support his eastern allies as they fought against the Burgundians. To guard against the renewal of the war in his realm by Duke Charles, the Valois king strengthened his defences and army. Meanwhile, along the Rhine, the duke's troops were repeatedly overwhelmed by Swiss forces. Despite his defeats, Charles refused to abandon his quest for a separate kingdom, and in early January 1477 was before the walls of Nancy with his war-weary soldiers. On 5 January, the Burgundian army was again crushed by a joint force of Swiss and troops from Lorraine; during the fighting, Charles the Bold was killed. When Louis XI learned of his great adversary's death, he quickly began preparations to march into Burgundy with his army.

In the aftermath of the death of Duke Charles, Louis XI ordered his army into northern Burgundy in March 1477 to seize the towns in the Picardy region north of Paris. As the powerful French forces marched into the area along the Somme, the towns swiftly paid homage to the Valois throne without putting up a fight. When the soldiers of King Louis advanced further north into Flanders, however, the local towns refused to submit, declaring their allegiance to the daughter of Charles the Bold, Mary of Burgundy. In August, the Burgundian duchess married Archduke Maximilian of the Habsburgs, who pledged to defend his wife's lands against the French invasion. Maximilian took command of the Burgundian soldiers and began a campaign to recover the lost territories of Mary recently occupied by Louis' army.

While the French pursued the occupation of the northern Burgundian region, Louis XI sent emissaries to negotiate his overlordship with the southern lordships of Duchess Mary. To gain their peaceful submission, they were offered large pensions and positions in the Valois court. The towns were promised sizable tax exemptions and special privileges for their allegiance, while gifts were granted to the churches. With the pledge of liberal royal patronage, the Duchy of Burgundy now declared its fealty to Louis. The French regime's representatives in the duchy formed a council of state in the Burgundian capital, Dijon, to rule in the name of the Valois king.

Soon after the French crown's envoys attempted to bring the County of Franche-Comté under the king's rule, the region rebelled, pledging allegiance to Mary of Burgundy. The king appointed a new commander for the local militiamen, ordering him to enforce his rule against the followers of Mary. When a general loyal to Mary advanced his troops to capture a castle in Franche-Comté, Louis ordered his men to retake it.

The castle was soon reoccupied by French supporters and the campaign continued, Louis expanding the lands under his kingship. The region was soon fully under royal control, and on 31 July 1477 Louis XI made a triumphant entry into Dijon, to the cheers of the inhabitants. He rode into the city mounted on a warhorse, beneath a large golden canopy held by the city's notables. He was presented with a ring to symbolize his new alliance with Dijon. During Louis' visit, the privileges and exemptions to the city previously granted by the Burgundian duke were reconfirmed. When Louis departed the Duchy of Burgundy, the area was firmly under the Valois regime's authority.

Soon after receiving the fealty of the southern Burgundian nobles and churchmen, the French monarch returned to the war against the Flemish. As the conflict wore on without resolution in 1477, both belligerents became exhausted and agreed to a one-year ceasefire. The war was resumed the following year, but a stalemate soon developed. In 1478, Mary of Burgundy was killed while riding her horse, her death becoming the stimulus for the renewal of talks to end the fighting. When Archduke Maximilian learned of the new negotiations, he made contact with Edward IV, seeking his intervention, but the English king was involved with preparations for an invasion of Scotland and was unable to offer any support.

As the conflict with the French continued, the Habsburg archduke moved against Cambrai with his army, forcing the French to evacuate the town. With Maximilian's men advancing against his occupied lands, Louis XI sent a force of 11,000 cavalry and infantry to enforce his rights to the region. On 7 August 1479, the two armies clashed near the village of Guinegate in the county of Artois. The Valois army was deployed with its cavalry on the flanks and the archers and infantrymen in the centre, while the archduke aligned his Burgundian and imperial footmen into two large squares, with his horsemen on the wings. The commander of the French forces, Philip of Crevecoeur, was located with the cavalry, while Maximilian was positioned with his infantry. The battle began with the attack of Louis' infantry, who drove back the enemy on the right, while the archduke's left flank was battered by the hard-rushing Valois foot soldiers. When the French knights broke ranks and chased after the fleeing Burgundians, the archduke's soldiers on the left held their line in a melee of savage fighting. Maximilian's men slowly gained the advantage on the left, and as the horsemen from the right rode back into the battle, the French forces were overwhelmed and fled the battlefield. In the wake of his defeat at Guinegate, Louis XI agreed to a truce under the auspices of Pope Sixtus IV, which was to remain in force for the following year.

Louis sent his envoys to negotiate in the city of Ghent, and the Treaty of Arras was signed in December 1482. Under the terms of the agreement, Mary's infant daughter, Margaret of Austria, was betrothed to Louis' heir, Charles, with the counties of Franche-Comte and Artois as her dowry. Meanwhile, France retained the regions surrounding the Somme and most of its Burgundian lordships, except Flanders, which was ceded to Maximilian of Austria. Louis sent the news of the treaty to the towns of his kingdom, ordering the singing of Te Deums in the churches and joyous processions in the streets. Six months later, at the city of Amboise, the 3-year-old Margaret of Austria was married to Dauphin Charles in the castle's church before a large crowd of magnates and prelates, sealing the Treaty of Arras. The partition of the Burgundian duchy was now complete. As a result of the Burgundian wars, Louis of France eliminated the threat of Charles the Bold and occupied most of his lands. Later, in 1491, the then Charles VIII renounced his marriage to Margaret and was wed to Anne of Brittany to secure his dominance over the strategic duchy.

The Treaty of Arras secured the borders of the Kingdom of France and brought peace to the king's subjects. To strengthen his monarchy against internal revolt, Louis continued his political and military campaign against his nobles to prevent their armed revolt by maintaining a formidable army and ruling with a firm hand. When Charles of Anjou died without a direct successor, his counties of Anjou, Maine and Provence were absorbed into the Valois monarchy. The French crown also expanded its territory into the County of Bar after Rene I died.

King Louis XI now reigned over his kingdom unchallenged and had laid the foundation for a united and powerful France. However, in 1480 he began to experience periodic strokes, which left him temporarily unable to talk or walk, and increasingly the crown's ministers governed in the name of the king. In the aftermath of his seizures, Louis withdrew from public appearances and was visited by only a few close officials. After a period of rest, the effects of the attacks lessened and he was able to resume partial control of the monarchy.

Louis now made large offerings to shrines and churches to gain God's favour for the extension of his life. He wrote to the patriarch of Florence, Lorenzo de' Medici, asking to borrow the precious ring of the patron saint of the city, which was said to have special powers of healing. The king also sought to obtain the holy oil used in the French coronation ceremony. After securing a dispensation from the pope, the sacred oil was brought to the royal chambers along with several other relics, which remained in Louis' room until his death.

To prolong his life, Louis also sought the intercession of holy men, in particular Francis Paole from the Kingdom of Naples, who was renowned for his years of piety. The monk was summoned to the French court, and following the personal intervention of Pope Sixtus, he agreed to travel to France and pray with the king. He made the journey to Rome for an audience with the pontiff before sailing to Marseille, and then up the Rhone River by small craft to Lyons. Following a brief stopover in the city, he continued to Plessis south of Paris for his meeting with Louis XI. When the hermit appeared before him, the monarch fell to his knees, imploring Francis 'to pray to God for him that the Lord might be willing to prolong his days'. The presence of Paola greatly consoled the slowly dying Louis.

As Louis XI continued to comfort himself with religious relics and visits from holy men, he suffered another cerebral attack on 25 August. With his life now close to its end, he acknowledged his approaching demise by sending his close counsellors and royal guardsmen to his heir, Charles, at Amboise. On the morning of 31 August, he called his priests and made his last confession, repeating the words of the Psalmist. From his death bed, he spoke his final words: 'In thee, O Lord, do I set my trust. Let me never be put to confusion. I shall praise the mercy of my Lord for evermore.' In the early evening, King Louis XI died at the age of 60, and two days later his body was taken to St Martin Church in Tours for his funeral. The Valois king was buried on 6 September at Our Lady of Clery, south-east of Lyons.

France was ruled by Louis XI for twenty-two years, and the Valois realm was assumed by his only surviving son, Charles VIII. The new monarch was born on 30 June 1470 at the castle of Amboise, and was 13 years old, when he ascended the throne. During the king's minority, a regency government was created, led by his sister, Anne, who served as regent with her husband, Peter of Bourbon. However, the French magnates revolted against the centralization policies of the regime, igniting what became known as the Mad War. Following four years of fighting, the war ended with the young king's victory and a pledge of fealty from the warlords to the Valois crown. In 1491, Charles negotiated his marriage to Anne of Brittany, expanding his sovereignty over her duchy. When Pope Innocent VIII offered the throne of Naples to the Valois regime, Charles moved south with his army in September 1492 to gain possession of the Italian kingdom. The French forces overran Pisa and Florence before reaching Naples, which quickly surrendered. Fearing the domination of the French over Italy, the new pope, Alexander VI, formed an anti-French league, forcing Charles VIII to abandon his conquests and return to France. The king attempted to rebuild his shattered army to renew the Italian war, but died on 7 April 1498 at Amboise without a direct heir, ending the reign of the House of Valois. His death was followed by the assumption of the Valois-Orleans line to the throne of France, led by King Louis XII.

Selected Sources

Castries, Duke de, *The Lives of the Kings and Queens of France*
Champion, Pierre, *Louis XI*
Cleugh, James, *Chant Royal*
Gisserot, Jean-Paul, *The Family Trees of the Kings of France*
Kendall, Paul Murray, *Louis XI*
Knecht, Robert J., *The Valois – Kings of France 1328–1589*
Law, Joy, *Fleur de Lys – The Kings & Queens of France*
Masson, Gustave, *Medieval France*
Maurois, Andre, *A History of France*
Potter, David, *A History of France, 1460–1560*
Potter, Philip J., *Kings of the Seine*

Louis XII

In the spring of 1509, King Louis XII of France led his army over the Alps into northern Italy to renew his quest for the expansion of his domains into Lombardy. Having earlier compelled the surrender of the Duchy of Milan, the objective of his new campaign was to end the Republic of Venice's occupation of Lombardy. After marching his troops to the city of Milan in mid-April, Louis XII moved his forces east to invade Venetian-occupied territory. To oppose the advancing soldiers of the king, the Venetian Republic mustered a mercenary army commanded by Bartolomeo d'Alviano and Niccolo di Pitigliano. Acting under orders from Doge Leonardo Loredan, the Venetian commanders avoided battle against the French troops, engaging them only in minor skirmishes. On 9 May, Louis crossed the Adda River, threatening the doge's men and compelling the Venetians to move south toward the Po River in search of a strong defensive position. On 14 May, the Republic's rearguard of 8,000 soldiers was attacked by the French near the village of Agnadello. Louis sent his men up a hillside to clash with the Venetians along a ridge line, but they were driven back. The French king brought up his reserves and surrounded the enemy troops on three sides before launching a fierce assault of the Venetians' defensive front. With his army hard pressed, d'Alviano ordered his cavalry to charge the centre of the French line, but their assault was thrown back with heavy losses. D'Alviano was taken prisoner during the fighting and his forces were shattered, with over 4,000 killed. Following the defeat of the Republic of Venice at Agnadello, Louis XII proceeded to occupy the remainder of Lombardy and consolidated his power over the Milanese.

Louis had been born at the chateau of Blois on 27 June 1462, the son of Duke Charles of Orleans and Mary of Cleves. As the only son of the 68-year-old duke, Louis' birth ensured the house of Orleans-Valois would remain uppermost in the line of succession to the French crown. When Duke Charles died in early 1465, Louis was acknowledged as his father's successor and placed under the protection of his mother, along with his two sisters. Despite possessing many estates, Mary of Cleves had only a small income and was compelled to maintain a frugal household. Under the influence of King Louis XI, Mary appointed the Count of Saint-Pol, Guyot Pot, as her son's governor, and the young duke was sent to reside at Blois chateau in the Loire Valley. Pot was responsible for Louis' academic and military training, and named experienced tutors and soldiers to instruct him. The young Duke of Orleans' education entailed learning to read and write, along with studying the basics of Latin, mathematics and history. Under his instructors, Louis became well-versed in French literature and history, while learning to read and write in Latin. He had a keen interest in the study of ancient history, art and especially music. At Blois, he had access to his father's extensive library but had little interest in reading, preferring to hunt deer and wild boar in the dense woodlands and practice his martial skills. During his adolescent years, he received military training from renowned masters of arms and was taught the techniques of jousting, fencing and horsemanship. He spent long hours drilling with the weapons of a warrior, learning to fight with the sword, dagger, mace and lance. As part of his military education, he was exposed to castle warfare, learning the strategies of laying siege to and storming a fortress. As the duke grew older, he frequently took part in many jousting tournaments, exhibiting exceptional martial skills.

On 23 April 1464, the wife of Louis XI, Charlotte of Savoy, had given birth at th castle of Nogent-le-Roi to a daughter, who was named Joan of France, but as the princess grew older it had become apparent she was physically deformed and incapable of bearing children. She was described by contemporaries as very short, with one leg longer than the other and hunchbacked. To eliminate the Orleans duchy and annex it to his kingdom, the French king had forced Charles of Orleans to agree to the marriage of his son, Louis, to his daughter. Reluctantly, the duke signed the nuptial treaty. During the following ten years, the disfigurements of Joan became increasingly noticeable and Louis XI demanded Mary of Cleves renew the marriage contract following the death of her husband to ensure its compliance. The duchess refused to sign the contract, but after the king threatened to place Duke Louis in a bag and throw him into a river, she begrudgingly agreed.

Louis and Joan were second cousins, and under Church canon law their marriage would violate the permitted degree of consanguinity. A papal dispensation was required for the wedding to be performed, and in February 1476 Cardinal Giuliano della Rovere arrived from Rome with a papal bull from Pope Sixtus IV permitting the ceremony. On 8 September 1476, at Montrichard castle near Tours, Louis of Orleans was married to Princess

Joan by the Bishop of Orleans. When the nuptial service was performed, neither Louis XI nor Mary of Cleves were in attendance. In the wake of his marriage, the Duke of Orleans abandoned his wife, returning alone to his chateau at Blois. Despite his protests, he was compelled to return to Joan and spent the next seven years with her at Linieras chateau. At the chateau, Louis had little contact or interaction with his wife, spending his days in the pursuit of jousting tournaments and hunting, while having numerous adulterous love affairs with the women of the French court. When Louis became seriously ill with smallpox, Joan attended to his care, nursing him back to health, but she received no sign of gratitude or affection from him.

Joan of France had been raised by Baron Francis de Linieres and his wife, being lavished with love and affection. The baron took charge of her education and she was taught reading and writing, while studying poetry, mathematics and art. Raised in the household of devout Catholics, Joan became a devoted follower of the Christian faith, spending long periods in meditation and prayer. In the aftermath of the annulment of her marriage to King Louis XII by the papacy, Joan had made plans to establish a new religious sect named the Order of the Annunciation of the Blessed Virgin Mary. After receiving approval from Pope Alexander VI in early 1502, construction of the first monastery was begun the following year. Joan spent the remainder of her life dedicated to her Christian Order, following the ways of the Virgin Mary. She died on 4 February 1505 and was buried at Annonociade Monastery. During the revolt of the Huguenots in 1562, Joan's gravesite was desecrated and her body burned by the French Protestants. Soon after this, miracles and healings attributed to her were reported, giving cause to her beatification in 1631 and recognition as a saint by Pope Pius XII in 1950.

In 1483, the minor Charles VIII succeeded to the French throne following the death of Louis XI. The new king was the only remaining male in the direct Valois line of succession, and as his nearest male relative Louis of Orleans was recognized as dauphin. As the next in line to the crown, Louis pressed his right to the regency against the counter-claims of the king's older sister, Anne. Before his death, Louis XI had named his daughter, Anne, and her husband, Peter of Burgundy, as co-guardians for his 13-year-old heir. With the power to rule over France, the Valois princess outmanoeuvred the Duke of Orleans and seized the regency, using her new authority to consolidate her reign and compel Louis to publicly acknowledge her as regent.

In an attempt to pacify Louis, Anne appointed him to her ruling regency council as royal governor for the Ile-de-France region. The duke, not satisfied with this position in the government, held secret talks with Duke Francis II of Brittany and numerous other French warlords to gain their support for his assumption of the guardianship of Charles VIII. As the danger of rebellion grew, the Estates General was assembled to resolve the growing rift in the regime. The assembly of the nobles, churchmen and commoners met at Tours in early January 1484. After the representatives heard presentations from the rivals, they voted to continue with Anne's administration.

Following his failure to be appointed as regent, Louis began to seek allies to seize the government. When Anne learned of the duke's planned rebellion, she moved against him, forcing Louis to flee to avoid imprisonment. He made his way from Paris to Brittany, rallying supporters to his cause against Anne's regime. As the threat of civil war escalated, Anne's regency council assembled the royal army and sent the powerful force into Brittany to quell the festering uprising, igniting the Mad War. At the approach of the royal troops, Louis and his allies were outnumbered and compelled to submit. Nevertheless, Anne imposed lenient terms on Louis for his rebellion, only denying him his continued governorship of the Ile-de-France but allowing him to retain his freedom, estates and offices in the government after his pledge of loyalty.

Despite the Duke of Orleans' first attempt to seize the monarchy having been thwarted by the quick response of Anne, Louis soon renewed his quest to overthrow the regency. In 1486, he again held negotiations with Duke Francis II of Brittany and other discontent French nobles to seize control of the ruling council. He appealed to the 15-year-old Charles VIII to dismiss his older sister from the government and take personal control of the kingdom. Supported by his sister, the king rejected the duke's demands and sent the royal army to enforce his rule. At the approach of the troops, Louis again submitted and withdrew from the regency council. The Duke of Orleans still refused to abandon his pursuit of the regency and began to muster a formidable military force to confront the regent. Learning of the duke's preparations, Anne assembled the Valois army and ordered the commander to seize Louis' castles in the Loire region, compelling him to surrender to the crown. Louis was forced to accept the terms of the Peace of Bourges, agreeing to the garrisoning of royal troops in his strongholds and pledging his homage to end the Second Mad War.

Louis of Orleans remained determined to overthrow the regency government of Anne, despite his previously failed uprisings. When the French regime became involved with Maximilian of Austria's punitive campaign in Flanders, Louis seized the advantage created by the distraction to re-establish his plot against the Valois monarchy. He resumed his friendship with Francis II of Brittany and attempted to regain the support of his earlier French and Breton allies. However, the duke's appeals were rejected and many of the warlords united with the king against him. With his army now reinforced with the former rebel warlords, Charles VIII ordered his troops into Brittany, where they captured the southern lordships before the start of the winter season. In 1488, the Third Mad War was resumed, Louis mustering his French forces and those of Francis II before clashing with the royalists at Saint-Aubin, near the Breton capital of Rennes, on 28 July. At the beginning of the battle, the Breton forces and the other rebel soldiers were aligned along a ridge. At the approach of the loyalists, Francis II's vanguard launched an assault, pushing through the centre of their enemy's front. When the centre of the line moved forward to attack the withdrawing troops of Charles VIII, a large opening was created in their position and the French unleashed a devastating cavalry charge, breaking through their position. Charles VIII's commander poured more troops into the gap, forcing the Bretons and French insurgents to withdraw in panic, sealing the victory for the royalist army. Duke Louis of Orleans was captured during the fighting and held captive for the following three years.

As the prisoner of the Valois monarchy, Louis was held at the town of Sable in western France before his transfer to Lusignan in the district of Poitou, where he was guarded by 200 knights. When an attempt to free the duke was made by his loyal allies, he was transferred to Bourges in central France and held in the great fortified tower. While in the tower there. While in the tower, he was maltreated by his jailer, being fed only bread and water and denied visitors. When Louis complained about the lack of food, he was told to eat the rats in his cell. The duke's treatment improved slightly after a guard was convinced to travel to the royal court and petition the regime for better conditions.

When a new chief jailer was appointed, Louis was provided with better food and allowed visitors. Despite his continued harsh treatment and abandonment of his wife Joan, she went to see her husband frequently, bringing him fresh food and new clothing. She wrote to her older sister, Anne, and the many friends of the duke, appealing to them to intervene on behalf of her husband. At the request of Joan, numerous friends of Louis petitioned the king to pardon him. As conditions in the prison slowly improved, Joan was permitted to stay in the cell with Louis. While he remained in confinement, his wife managed his finances and properties. Despite his wife's frequent visits and care, Louis continued to treat her harshly, showing no love or appreciation.

While Louis remained in captivity, his friends at court continually petitioned King Charles, telling him the duke would now be a loyal servant and useful ally for his regime, while being grateful for his freedom. In late June 1491, the king rode to Bourges and issued orders for the release of Louis. When the Duke of Orleans was brought before the king, he fell on his knees in a show of obedience and gratitude. He pledged to loyally serve Charles, for which he was returned his estates and appointed royal viceroy for Normandy. Louis became a devoted supporter and friend of Charles VIII. The strong bond between the two former rivals was further confirmed when the duke was named godfather for the royal couple's first son and heir, Charles Orlando.

During Duke Louis' three years in captivity, the French army of Charles VIII had destroyed the resistance in Brittany, forcing Francis II to agree to peace terms on 20 August 1488. Shortly after the signing of the treaty, the Breton duke died, leaving the survival of an independent Brittany in question. The duke was survived by two young daughters, and the uncertainty of their guardianship rendered control of the duchy in further doubt. Following his defeat of the Bretons, Charles VIII claimed the right of custody, although several rival factions challenged this entitlement. To enforce its sovereignty over Brittany, the French regime invaded the region, and by December 1488 had seized most of the duchy. Although the French had occupied Brittany with little opposition, it was in the vital interest of neighbouring realms to preserve the independence of Brittany to protect their borders. The monarchies of Spain and England formed a coalition with a faction of rebellious Bretons and attacked southern Brittany, compelling the French to withdraw. As winter approached, the government of King Charles agreed to a six-month truce with members of the coalition in October 1490. During the ensuing pause in the fighting, England and Spain were distracted away from Brittany and withdrew their soldiers, leaving only the rebel Bretons to resume the war against France. Without the support of their allies, the remaining warlords of Brittany were soon defeated and the region was retaken. Peace negotiations were initiated with Francis II's successor, Anne of Brittany, and following prolonged talks a treaty was signed. Under the terms of the agreement, Anne pledged to marry Charles and acknowledge the end of Brittany's quasi-independence. The wedding took place at the chateau of Langeais in early December 1491, Louis attending the ceremony and holding the crown over her head.

While Charles VIII was subduing the rebellion in Brittany, Maximilian of Austria formed an alliance with England and Spain against the French occupation of Brittany. To fashion a lasting peace on his frontier and counter the plans of the hostile league, the Valois king began a series of diplomatic initiatives. When the English king, Henry VII, landed a large army at Calais, threatening to invade northern France, the French monarch sent emissaries to him to pursue peace terms and the withdrawal of his troops. The English, having little enthusiasm for the war against France, soon agreed to abandon their invasion for the payment of an annual indemnity. Following his treaty with Henry VII, Charles VIII also came to terms with the Spanish, pledging to return the counties of Roussillon and Cerdagne to Castile in return for a vow to honour the border between the two kingdoms.

The new treaties resulted in the withdrawal of two potential allies for Archduke Maximilian in his quest to expand his empire to the west. To advance his claims to lands in south-eastern France, the archduke sent his army into the Franche-Comte region in December 1492. The French put up little resistance, and the imperial troops quickly occupied the county. The archduke soon agreed to negotiate a settlement, and in May 1493 a treaty was signed. Under the terms of the agreement, the Valois regime pledged to cede the counties of Franche-Comte and Artois to the Austrians, while Maximilian promised to honour the new French borderlands. The three treaties negotiated by Charles secured his borders against foreign invasion and established a period of peace for France.

After abandoning his quest for the throne of France, Louis of Orleans remained a loyal servant of the king and was occupied serving on the royal governing council, managing his personal estates and serving as governor in Normandy. Charles' foreign initiatives had left his realm at peace and his monarchy's hold on power unchallenged, allowing him to begin planning to conquer the Kingdom of Naples in southern Italy to enforce his hereditary rights to the realm through his blood claim from his great uncle, Rene of Anjou. The decision to launch the campaign was solidified by the visit of Cardinal Giuliano della Rovere, who had fled Rome fearing arrest by his rival, Pope Alexander VI.

Alexander was born near Valencia in Spain on 1 January 1431 and given the name Rodrigo Borgia. Rodrigo's uncle, Alfonse Borgia, was the local bishop and financially supported the impoverished family of his sister. When Alfonse was elected Pope Callixtus III in 1455, Rodrigo's life changed dramatically, and he was sent to live in Rome. He was soon named a cardinal by Callixtus and given numerous well-paid offices and sees. Several years later, he was appointed vice-chancellor of the Holy See, a lucrative and powerful position. Rodrigo Borgia used his many appointments to amass great wealth and a large following among the cardinals. He openly maintained illicit relationships with several women and had five illegitimate children. When Pope Innocent VIII died in 1492, Rodrigo used his many offices and wealth to bribe the cardinals into electing him the new pontiff, and he took the name of Alexander VI.

Cardinal della Rovere encouraged Charles to invade Naples and free the kingdom from its tyrannical ruling family. In November 1493, the king ordered his generals to prepare for the Italian campaign. To finance this, taxes were raised against the throne's subjects and churchmen, while money was borrowed from Genoese bankers. When the French army was mustered at Tours, there were over 20,000 infantrymen, 6,000 Swiss mercenary pikemen, 9,000 cavalry and seventy artillery guns ready for the Italian war.

In mid-1494, Charles VIII led his army south over the Alps into northern Italy. A month before the French departed from Tours, Louis had travelled into Italy with a force of cavalry, riding to the County of Asti, where he had inherited claims to the lordship through his grandmother, Valentina Visconti. He also possessed similar rights to the Duchy of Milan and his presence in Italy threatened the ruling duke, Ludovico Sforza, also known as 'il Moro' ('the Moor') due to his dark complexion. Ludovico was born in July 1452 in Lombardy and was the fourth son of the Duke of Milan, Francesco I. Under the direction of his mother, Bianca Visconti, he obtained an education in the classical languages, arts and letters, while receiving instruction in warfare. When Francesco died in 1466, the family's lands and titles were taken by the older brother, Galeazzo Maria, who ruled until his assassination ten years later. The duchy then passed to his young son, Gian Galeazzo, and a bitter struggle ensued between the heir's supporters and Ludovico; in 1481, Ludovico seized control of the Milanese government and ruled as regent. In October 1494, he was recognized as duke after his nephew died under suspicious circumstances. During il Moro's reign, the Duchy of Milan became a centre for the Renaissance movement and his court was recognized as one of the most splendid in northern Italy. He was a patron of many well-known artists, including Leonardo da Vinci, who painted 'The Last Supper' for him.

Ludovico Sforza offered to transfer his city of Genoa to the French if Charles agreed to appoint Louis as its governor. To retain cordial relations and appease the duke's concerns, the Valois king ordered Louis to take charge of the city of Genoa. In August 1494, Duke Louis of Orleans arrived at the seaport of Genoa with his vessels, uniting his fleet with the Genoese ships. Shortly after reaching Genoa, the Neapolitan navy under Don Federigo anchored off the coast of Genoa and disembarked 4,000 troops at the village of Rapello to prevent the French from using Genoa for naval operations against Naples. Learning of the enemy's landing at Rapello, Louis assembled a force of Swiss mercenaries and Genoese, sending them overland against the Neapolitans, while he took a fleet of galleys and galleases (warships combining sails and oars) to attack their navy. Rather than risk a battle with the French, Federigo sailed away, leaving his soldiers on the coast. Louis then led his troops ashore and joined them with the Genoese and Swiss. He unleashed an attack against the Neapolitan force, and with support from his cannons on the ships drove the enemy from Rapello.

In the wake of his victory at Rapello, Louis rode to the city of Asti to meet with the French king, who was preparing his troops for the advance against Naples. It was in the personal interest of Louis to remain in Asti to take any opportunity to seize the Duchy of Milan, and he petitioned the king to leave him in the north. When the French moved south, Charles VIII ordered the duke to stay in Asti and guard his lines of communication with France, while serving as governor for the Lombardy region. As Charles led his soldiers south towards Naples, Louis took over the ruling council for the Providence of Asti and kept reinforcements and supplies flowing to the royal army.

The French army's advance on Naples met with little resistance, towns along its path submitting without opposition. While Charles was in Pisa, a delegation from Florence arrived, offering the homage of the city. The king travelled to Florence and met outside the city with its new governor, Piero de Gino Capponi, who had recently taken control of the government after the overthrow of the de Medici family. After the French king was compelled to reduce his demands, Capponi agreed to give fealty for the city. Charles remained in Florence for eight days, inspecting the city's Renaissance art and buildings. When the French troops resumed their trek and headed for Rome, they were greeted with open gates and offers of homage from the many towns, the campaign becoming a grand triumphant procession. On 31 December, the Valois army reached Rome and the king made his residence at the palace of a French cardinal. Negotiations were soon begun with the Holy See for a meeting between Pope Alexander VI and the king to gain the support of the Church for the invasion of Naples. The pontiff feared the creation of a strong foreign power independent of his authority to his south, and after two weeks of talks finally agreed to meet with Charles. As the discussions lingered on without agreement, the French departed from the city on 28 January 1495 without receiving the pope's blessings for the Naples campaign.

By 4 February, the French army was in the Kingdom of Naples before the fortified walls of the castle of Monte San Giovanni, midway between Rome and Naples. When the garrison commander refused to surrender, Charles besieged the fortification and pounded the walls with his powerful siege guns. When a large breach was blown in the walls, the French stormed forward, overpowering the defenders and compelling their submission. After occupying the castle, Charles resumed his advance south, encountering little opposition, and by March had conquered Naples. On 12 May, he was crowned sovereign of the Kingdom of Naples.

While the royal troops were occupying the kingdom in the north, Louis was protecting the flow of men, arms and supplies to his king and governing the occupied lands in Lombardy. The seizure of Naples had altered the balance of power in Italy, and the Italian states feared the presence of the powerful enemy's army in the south. To protect their interests, Pope Alexander, the Doge of Venice, Ludovico of Milan, the Kingdom of Aragon in Spain and Maximilian of Austria agreed to join a Holy League to drive Charles and his French soldiers out of Italy. The members of the league chose Viscount Francesco II Gonzaga of Mantua to lead the campaign to recover Italy from the invaders. In May, Gonzaga began attacking the French troops protecting the lines of communications, threatening to disrupt the king's flow of reinforcements and supplies. In danger of being isolated in Naples, Charles was forced to return to France. After leaving half of his army to guard his Italian conquests, the king departed from Naples on 20 May, heading towards Rome. The retreating soldiers bypassed Rome and advanced into central Italy, avoiding contact with the forces of the Holy League. As the 10,000 Valois troops moved north, the members of the Holy League assembled a formidable army of over 20,000 men; when Charles reached the town of Fornovo, southwest of Parma, the two armies clashed on the morning of 6 July 1495. The French opened the bloody and fierce encounter with an artillery bombardment of the Italian front before sending their heavy cavalry charging across the battlefield into the enemy's line, pushing them back in disarray. Meanwhile, Gonzaga's horsemen broke away from the battle to plunder the lightly guarded French baggage train. With the enemy thus distracted, Charles was able to push ahead with his army's move north, making his way safely to Asti.

In the meantime, the desertion of Duke Ludovico Sforza to the Holy League threatened Louis' presence in Asti, forcing him to reinforce his defences in preparation for an attack by the Milanese. The Duke of Orleans sent an urgent appeal to Paris for additional troops to defend his lands. Shortly after the arrival of the reinforcements, the opportunity to attack il Moro came when the inhabitants of the fortified town of Novara revolted against the Milanese duke's harsh rule and gave their fealty to Charles VIII. Louis quickly occupied the town with his troops to protect France's new ally. After the loss of the town, Ludovico marched his army to besiege Novara. As Novara's garrison and French troops continued to resist the Milanese attacks, their food and supplies neared exhaustion.

When the withdrawing King Charles reached Asti, he sent his troops to relieve the siege of Novara . As the French troops neared the town, Ludovico offered to negotiate a settlement. Under the terms of the resulting agreement, Louis was compelled to abandon Novara and the Valois king pledged not to support him in the quest for Milan, while Duke Ludovico Sforza acknowledged the Duke of Orleans' possession of the County of Asti.

In the wake of the signing of the treaty with il Moro, Louis of Orleans rejoined his men with the withdrawing forces of King Charles. By the end of October, the French soldiers had crossed the Alps into their homeland. During the retreat, Louis renewed his friendship with the king and served as a close advisor on the ruling council, later taking the governorship of the important region of Normandy. In December 1495, the Duke of Orleans was again recognized as dauphin upon the death of the 3-year-old Prince Charles Orland from measles. Two years later, the king's wife, Anne of Brittany, gave birth to a fourth son, Francis, who replaced Louis as heir designate. However, Francis lived for only a month, dying in July 1497, making Louis once again dauphin.

After returning from the Italian war, Louis rejoined the royal council and supported the policies of the king. The duke's personal relationship with Joan of France remained strained, despite his wife's continued acts of concern and affection. Louis did occasionally write to Joan from Italy, asking her to pray for him. Following his return from Italy, Charles pressed his friend to visit his sister, and Louis felt pressured to comply. When she was at court, Louis escorted her to dinners and parties, out of fear of alienating the king. He likely left court in late 1497 to pursue his duties in Normandy and avoid contact with Joan.

Soon after his withdrawal from Italy, Charles VIII began to plan a new expedition to Naples, with Louis named to lead the army into Italy. Despite his orders to depart, the duke delayed leaving court, believing the king was in poor health. While Louis was in Blois, a royal courier rushed into the castle with the news that Charles VIII was dead and that the duke was now Louis XII, King of France. Charles had died on 7 April 1498 at Amboise castle after striking his head on a low doorway. In late May, Louis travelled to Rheims for his coronation at the cathedral. On 27 May, he was escorted from the bishop's palace to the main altar of the cathedral for the service. The Archbishop of Rheims anointed the new king with sacred oil and placed the crown on his head. A solemn Mass followed, officiated by the archbishop, and Louis received Holy Communion. After the ceremony, the king was escorted back to the palace for a grand banquet. The next day, as was tradition, Louis XII rode to Corbeny in the shire of Saint Marcoul, where he offered prayers to the saint.

Taking up the reins of power, Louis moved to consolidate his new regime by first reconfirming the appointments of his predecessor, while travelling throughout the kingdom receiving the fealty of the nobles, churchmen and towns as their rightful sovereign. Many of the king's friends and supporters were appointed to high government offices, and an advisory council of magnates and high churchmen was created. During the first year of his reign, he introduced sweeping reforms to the judicial and financial systems to revive the stalled economy and end costly corruption. The tax burden on his subjects was reduced and additional regional parliaments introduced. He reimposed the Pragmatic Sanctions, which established the Catholic Church as a Gallic Church, with the power of appointments confirmed as the right of the king. The new measures produced an expansion of the economy and growing prosperity.

A condition in the provisions of the marital agreement between Charles VIII and Duchess Anne of Brittany stated that if the king died without producing a male successor, his wife was legally bound to marry the successor to ensure the Duchy of Brittany remained under French sovereignty. In August, Anne agreed to honour the pact and negotiations for the marriage were begun. A treaty was quickly arranged between Louis and the dowager queen. To end his matrimonial union with Joan of France, the king sent emissaries to Rome seeking a papal invalidation. Pope Alexander VI was desirous of establishing friendly relations with the new French regime and formed a papal commission to rule on the petition. The papal court met at Tours in October, and Louis XII's representatives presented his appeal. In his petition to the commission members, the king stated as justification for the annulment his too-close blood relationship with Joan, that the marriage had never been consummated and that he had not entered into their marital union voluntarily. The hearing ended in December with the judges voting in Louis' favour. When Joan learned of the decision, she consented to the ruling without objection and withdrew from court life.

In the aftermath of the papal judges' vote of annulment, Louis XII and Anne of Brittany were married in February 1499 at the Cathedral of Nantes. Following the nuptial ceremony, Louis abandoned his decadent practices and became devoted to Queen Anne. During their life together, the queen became an influential and trusted advisor to the king. She continued to defend Brittany and frequently intervened against Louis' decisions in support of her duchy. The union with Anne resulted in the birth of two daughters, Claude and Renee, but no surviving male created a succession crisis in 1515 upon the king's death.

During the first two years of his reign, Louis firmly established his authority and put in place vigorous reform measures that brought peace and prosperity to his kingdom, with France now recognized as the wealthiest and most powerful nation in Europe. With the realm at peace and his rule secure, the king began planning his return to Italy to gain possession of the Duchy of Milan as the legitimate duke. He sent envoys to the regimes on his borders to negotiate non-aggression pacts to safeguard France. Philip of Burgundy signed a treaty to ensure peace along the northern French frontier, while the Treaty of Etaples with England, earlier orchestrated by King Charles VIII, was reconfirmed to protect the western lordships. Meanwhile, an agreement of friendship was signed by Ferdinand II and Isabella of Spain to guarantee the southern region of the kingdom against invasion, and cooperation in the east was pledged by Emperor Maximilian of Austria.

While the Valois regime's envoys were securing the French borders, Louis XII's diplomatic manoeuvres secured allies in Italy to isolate the Milanese against his campaign of conquest. Following prolonged negotiations, an alliance was formed between Louis and the Republic of Venice, which pledged to provide an army of infantrymen and cavalry for the attack against il Moro. In March 1499, the French king negotiated an agreement with the Swiss Confederation, allowing him to enlist soldiers from the league for the payment of an annual fee, and a treaty was signed with the Duchy of Savoy, giving Valois troops the freedom to march across the duchy and to recruit militias and purchase supplies. Furthermore, in return for French support of the Holy See's planned interventions in the Papal States, Pope Alexander VI agreed to commit papal troops to Louis XII's expedition.

While France's political initiatives were detaching Milan from potential Italian allies, Louis XII was accumulating a large war chest to finance his campaign. A general tax increase was imposed, while money was also obtained from the nobles and the Church. The French army had been allowed to deteriorate during the latter years of Charles VIII's reign, and now Louis was involved with its rebuilding. Large quantities of war supplies were acquired and the armed forces mobilized. In early 1499, the Valois army began the invasion of Milan by utilizing the County of Asti as an assembly point. Before launching his attack against Milan, Louis XII made a final attempt to convince Ludovico Sforza to acknowledge his sovereignty, offering to allow him to remain ruling duke in return for an annual levy. In early August, after il Moro refused his offer, the French king ordered his army to begin the expedition to the Duchy of Milan. As his troops marched to war, Louis relocated his court to Lyons to be closer to the battlefront.

Under the command of Marshal Giacomo Trivulzio, the 27,000 soldiers, including 10,000 cavalry, advanced out of Asti into Milanese territory.

The French and their Swiss mercenaries soon reached the fortified town of Rocca di Arazzo in the western region of Milan. The town was besieged and the French artillery unleashed a fierce bombardment of the walls. Following five hours of battering by the guns, the walls were breached and the infantry rushed through the gaps into the town. To limit the resistance of other enemy fortifications during his offensive, the Valois king had ordered Trivulzio to slaughter the garrison and many of the inhabitants. After carrying out Louis' commands, the troops resumed their campaign by attacking and seizing Annone. When the garrison refused to surrender, the marshal ordered his men to kill those who had been captured. As the French resumed their march, the next three fortified towns opened their gates and submitted without a fight, fearing a massacre.

In late August, Trivulzio and his army reached the city of Alessandro, and when the governor refused to surrender, the French began to batter the defences with their cannons. The garrison put up a vigorous fight until the governor abandoned the town before dawn, and the Milanese troops soon yielded. While the French and their mercenary allies were seizing control of the western lands of Milan, their Venetian ally entered the duchy from the east, pushing back Sforza's men. The Milanese duke quickly realized further resistance was useless, and on 2 September, escorted by a force of cavalry, fled from Milan, making his way towards Austria and the court of Emperor Maximilian I.

Abandoned by Duke Ludovico, the Milanese ruling council opened talks for the peaceful submission of their city. Following several meetings, terms were finalized on 17 September. As the French steadily gained possession of the Duchy of Milan, Louis XII returned to Italy and on 6 October entered the city in triumph, riding through streets decorated with a large sculpture of the patron saint of Milan, St Ambrose, tapestries and family coats of arms, receiving the homage of the people. The king was congratulated by numerous Italian princes and high churchmen, including an envoy from Pope Alexander VI. He remained for six weeks while establishing his ducal government and securing his overlordship, appointing his friends and allies to high positions in the regime. Eminent Milanese families who had been persecuted by il Moro now pledged their loyalty to Louis, recovering their stolen properties and privileges from the French. To protect his conquest against rebellion, the king garrisoned the duchy's strategic fortifications with his troops. With his government in place and the duchy firmly under his control, Louis returned to France in late November.

Louis XII had left Milan with the duchy at peace and his ruling regime held in high regard by the people. However, shortly after the king's departure, his appointed council members began a reign of suppression and brutality against the Milanese. The Frenchmen freely abused and stole from the residents, while Trivulzio was unable to keep the peace. As dissension spread across the duchy, the cause for rebellion began to awaken. The presence of marauding Venetian troops in eastern parts of the duchy further escalated the threat of revolt. A rebel party was organized against the French presence, which supported the return of Ludovico Sforza as duke. Encouraged by the escalating spirit of rebellion, il Moro recruited troops from the Holy Roman Empire and employed Swiss mercenaries to reacquire his lost duchy.

In mid-January 1500, Ludovico Sforza led his army into the Duchy of Milan to reclaim his ducal throne. Trivulzio collected his scattered forces to defend Milan, while recalling the French soldiers who had been temporarily sent to reinforce the army of the pope's son, Cesare Borgia, who was preparing to launch an attack to recover papal lands lost in the Romagna. After Sforza's troops captured the great fortress of Como, the population of Milan rose up in rebellion against French occupation, compelling the marshal to withdraw his troops to nearby castles. Il Moro then entered Milan on 5 February to the welcome of large cheering crowds.

When the news of Milan's loss reached Paris, Louis XII was furious, initiating preparations to overthrow il Moro. To supplement the strength of his Italian army, he raised a force of French cavalry and hired 10,000 Swiss mercenary pikemen. The king appointed a new commander, Louis La Tremoille, who led the 27,000-strong force against Sforza. As the reinforced army invaded Italy, the Milanese duke moved his soldiers to the citadel at Novara to await their arrival. On 8 April, La Tremoille reached Novara and set up siege lines, positioning his cannons around the defensive works of the town. Both armies had large contingents of Swiss mercenaries, who refused to fight against each other. With a large segment of his forces now unavailable, il Moro was compelled to abandon Novara; dressed as a pikeman, he joined the Swiss as they mixed with their fellow countrymen. Nevertheless, he was soon identified and seized by the French. Sforza was placed under heavy guard and taken to Lyons under the escort of archers sent by Louis XII. When he reached Lyons, the king was among the large crowd which watched him taken to prison in the dungeon of the citadel. After an attempted escape bid, il Moro was transferred to Loches, where he died in 1508 while still under heavy guard.

With Milan once again occupied by the French, Louis sent a new and more capable viceroy to govern the duchy, who quickly re-established the royal ruling council while managing to curb the abuses of the soldiers to keep the peace. To enforce law and order, a large French army was permanently stationed in the duchy, which prevented the outbreak of revolt. Agriculture and commercial pursuits were now encouraged by the ruling regime, and the region once again became prosperous. A new government was put in place made up of a civil and military viceroy, while a Milanese parliament was established to aid in the administration of the duchy.

With his reign firmly established over the Duchy of Milan, Louis XII began planning for the further expansion of his Italian lands by the conquest of Naples, to which he possessed a claim through being successor to Charles VIII. Similar to his preparations for the campaign against Milan, he manoeuvred to secure allies and gain pledges of neutrality from potential enemies. The French regime renewed the alliance with Pope Alexander VI and the Doge of Venice to gain additional soldiers and supplies for the expeditionary force.

While he was building his army to invade Naples, Louis XII began talks with King Ferdinand II of Aragon for a joint attack against the kingdom. In the ensuing Treaty of Granada, signed on 11 November 1500, the two kings agreed to collectively invade Naples, with the French occupying the northern half of the duchy and Ferdinand retaining the south. Louis was to be acknowledged as King of Naples, while the title of King of Sicily was assigned to Ferdinand II. In May 1501, Louis mustered his army of 15,000 French and Swiss soldiers and marched south towards Naples, while the Spanish army moved to Cordoba in southern Spain in preparation for sailing to Italy. The French unleashed their attack in August, overrunning towns and slaughtering the garrison troops and inhabitants. As the invading army moved farther into the Duchy of Naples, the Neapolitan king, Federigo III, surrendered, begging for mercy, while the fighting continued in the southern lordships. When the Spanish landed an army south of Naples, the remaining Neapolitan forces were forced to seek peace terms. King Federigo was sent to France and spent his remaining years in exile in the Loire Valley, dying at Tours in 1504.

Immediately after the French victory in northern Naples, the regime's appointed viceroy organized a new government and ruthlessly enforced the king's laws. The administration soon alienated the Neapolitans, dissension rapidly spreading across the occupied lands. As the population's unrest grew, relations between the Valois viceroy and his Spanish counterpart became increasingly strained over the division of two provinces of Naples that had been omitted in the Treaty of Granada. The Spanish military commander, Gonzalo de Cordoba, expelled the French occupation troops from the two areas, as sporadic warfare developed. With the threat of war escalating,

Louis XII returned to Naples with reinforcements in the summer of 1502, leading his army in the capture of the two Spanish-occupied provinces. After reimposing his sovereignty, the king appointed Louis d'Armagnac of Nemours as his viceroy for Naples and returned to France.

Following the defeat of his army, King Ferdinand II sent additional troops and supplies for Cordoba with orders to attack the French. In April, Cordoba unleashed his counter-offensive, defeating a French force of 4,500 infantry and nearly 1,000 horsemen at the Battle of Seminara on 21 April 1503. A week later, the two armies collided again at Cerignola, where Cordoba's Spanish occupied the high ground and reinforced their position with trenches, while deploying the infantry – armed with pikes, swords and arquebuses – along the first line. The Spanish light cavalry was placed in front, with the artillery located on the top of the hill with a full view of the approaching enemy. Louis' army was composed of Swiss pikemen and French infantrymen and mounted troops. The French viceroy opened the fighting by sending his heavy cavalry charging into the enemy's centre but they were repulsed by the volleys of the arquebusiers and artillery pieces. During this encounter, d'Armagnac of Nemours was killed. The Swiss pikemen then entered the fray, as Cordoba sent his German landsknechts (mercenary pikmen) forward into the melee, while ordering his arquebusiers and light cavalry to attack the enemy's flanks. The French foot soldiers now joined the pikemen but were unable to break through Cordoba's line, and were thrown back in disarray, incurring losses of nearly 4,000 men. The defeated French then fled the battle to the fortress of Gaeta, north of Naples. Cordoba followed the retreating enemy and attempted to take Gaeta by storm, but was thrown back and compelled to besiege the fortress.

With the French army bottled up behind its defensive works in Gaeta, the Spanish and their allies overran Louis XII's Neapolitan provinces and established control over the duchy. Having gained possession of the kingdom, Cordoba offered the French surrender terms, which were quickly accepted. The Treaty of Blois was signed on 22 September 1504, with Louis agreeing to abandon his claims to Naples for a large indemnity, while retaining Milan and the County of Asti. The Valois intervention into Naples had been costly to the king in terms of lost soldiers and equipment, spent treasure and the erosion of his dominance and presence in European affairs.

Under the terms of the treaty Louis XII agreed with the Spanish, Genoa was to remain under his rule, but in early 1506 the populace rebelled against French occupation and declared the city a republic. The king's soldiers in the city were massacred and an independent regime created. When Louis learned of the loss of Genoa, which was an important commercial and trading centre in north-west Italy, he sent a large army to enforce his rights of inheritance. At the approach of the French troops, the ruling doge fled and the city submitted. To enforce his hold on the city, Louis annexed Genoa directly to his kingdom and appointed a new council to govern it. With the city once again under his authority, the king travelled to Italy, entering Genoa on a large black warhorse dressed in a suit of full armour in a display of power. While in Italy, he also travelled to Milan to renew his bond of homage with the Milanese.

While the French monarch was involved with his interventions in Italy, he grew increasingly apprehensive over his lack of a direct successor. He was 46 years old in 1506 and had no male heir. His marriage to Anne of Brittany had resulted in the births of two daughters, Claude in 1499 and Renee several years later, but no surviving male child. After Queen Anne gave birth in 1502 to a stillborn son, there was little probability Louis would have a direct inheritor. In the aftermath of the king's two serious illnesses in 1504 and the following year, plans for the succession of the king's cousin, Francis of Angouleme, were put in play. A secret nuptial contract was signed with the Angouleme branch of the House of Valois, binding the king's oldest daughter in marriage with the heir apparent. To secure the friendship of the potentially hostile Holy Roman Empire, the Valois regime had earlier arranged the marriage of Claude to the son of Philip of Austria. To nullify the agreement, Louis XII summoned the Estates General in 1506 and the representatives voted to void the treaty and authorize the union between Claude and Francis.

In late September 1506, Philip of Habsburg died and was succeeded by his minor son, Charles, Prince of the Low Countries. To govern the strategic lordships, Emperor Maximilian I appointed his daughter, Margaret of Austria, to head the ruling regency council and serve as guardian for Charles. Margaret proved to be an effective and intelligent regent, utilizing her powers to forge a friendly relationship with Louis XII. They soon discovered a common adversary in the Republic of Venice, whose westward expansion had occupied counties where the French and Austrians both possessed claims. Through the intervention of Margaret in 1508, her father and the French king arranged the formation of the League of Cambrai, directed against halting the aggression of the Venetians. The league comprised France, the Papacy, the Holy Roman Empire and Spain, who called for the return of all lands taken by the Venetian Republic. The new pope, Julius II, agreed to join the league to advance his rights to Italian territories that the Venetians had recently seized. The College of Cardinals had elected the experienced and politically skilled Cardinal Giuliano della

CHARLES II.
(Image from the National Library of France and is a reproduction by scanning of a bidemensional work from the Saint Marin Abbey of Tours, France and considered in the public domain)

PHILIP II AUGUSTUS.
(Coronation of Philip II Augustus of France – British Library. The work is in the Public Domain in its country of origin and other countries and areas, where the copyright term is the author's life plus 70 years or less)

LOUIS XI. (This work is in the public domain in its country of origin and other countries and areas where the copyright term is the author's life plus 100 years or fewer)

LOUIS XII. (This work is in the public domain in its country of origin and other countries and areas where the copyright term is the author's life plus 100 years or fewer)

FRANCIS I. (This work is in the Public Domain in its country of origin and other countries and areas where the copyright term is the author's life plus 100 years or fewer. This work is in the Public Domain in the United States because it was published or registered with the U. S Copyright Office before 1 January 1926)

HENRY IV. (This work is in the Public Domain in its country of origin and other countries and areas where the copyright term is the author's life plus 100 years or fewer. This work is in the Public Domain in the United States because it was published or registered with the U. S. Copyright Office before 1 January 1926)

LOUIS XIV. (This work is in the Public Domain in its country of origin and other countries and areas Where the copyright term is the author's life plus 100 years or fewer. This work is in the Public Domain in the United States because it was published or registered with the U. S. Copyright Office before 1 January 1926)

NAPOLEON. (This work is in the Public Domain in its country of origin and other countries and areas where the copyright term is the author's life plus 100 years or fewer. This work is in the Public Domain in the United States because it was published or registered with the U. S. Copyright Office before 1 January 1926)

LOUIS XII LEADING HIS ARMY INTO BATTLE. (This work is in the Public Domain in its country of origin and other countries and where the copyright term is the author's life plus 100 years or fewer. This work is in the Public Domain in the United States because it was published or registered with the U. S. Copyright Office before 1 January 1926)

FRANCIS I AT THE BATTLE OF MARIGNANO 1515. (This work is in the Public Domain in its country of origin and other countries and areas where the copyright term is author's life plus 100 years or fewer. This work is in the Public Domain in the United States because it was published or registered with the U. S. copyright Office before 1 January 1926)

LOUIS XIV AT THE SIEGE OF MAASTRICHT 1673. (This work is in the Public Domain in its country of origin and other countries and areas where the copyright tern author's life plus 100 years or fewer. This work is in the Public Domain in the United States because it was published or registered with the U. S. Copyright Office before 1 January 1926)

NAPOLEON AT THE SIEGE OF TOULON 1793. (This work is in the public domain in its country of origin and other countries and areas where the copyright term iis the author's life plus 100 years or less)

NAPOLEON AT THE BATTLE OF FRIEDLAND 1807. (This work is in the Public Domain in its country of origin and other countries and areas where the copyright term is the author's life plus 100 years or fewer. This work is in the Public Domain in the United States because it was published or registered with the U. S. Copyright Office before 1 January 1926)

CORONATION CEREMONY OF NAPOLEON. (This work is in the public domain in its country of origin and other countries and areas where the copyright term is the author's life plus 100 years or fewer. This work is in the Public Domain in the United States because it was published or registered with the U. S. Copyright Office before 1 January 1926. Painting by Jacques-Louis David is on display at the Louvre Museum in Paris)

Rovere to the throne of St Peter in 1503 after the death of Pope Pious III, and as Julius II he proved to be a shrewd, self-serving politician and capable military commander, who was determined to enlarge papal territory.

After the creation of the League of Cambrai, Louis XII vigorously prepared his forces for the war against the Republic of Venice. In mid-April 1509, he crossed the Alps and travelled south to Milan to make final preparations for the clash with the Venetians. While the king was in Milan with his 20,000 infantry, including 8,000 Swiss pikemen, and over 2,000 heavy cavalry, Pope Julius II made the opening move in the campaign by demanding the evacuation of all Venetian soldiers from his claimed papal lands. The pope's ultimatum was ignored by Doge Leonardo Loredan, and with a just cause thus established, Louis XII personally led his massed army forward against the Republic of Venice in late May. After crossing the Adda River, Louis turned his troops south towards the town of Pandino, 20 miles east of Milan in the Lombardy region. The commander of the doge's army, Bartolomeo Alviano, was compelled to push south to block the advancing Louis from cutting his lines of communications. On 14 May, the French clashed with the Venetians at the village of Agnadello. As the Venetian artillery opened fire on the French, a soldier shouted at the king to take cover, to which Louis XII was said to have replied: 'No cannon ball can kill a king of France; if you are afraid stand behind me.' The Venetian troops held the high ground with a fortified line of trenches, forcing Louis to send his infantrymen charging up the hill into their opponents, overwhelming them, as the enemy cavalry fled the battlefield. During the fierce and bloody fighting, nearly 10,000 Venetian troops were killed or captured. Following the battle, Louis ordered a Te Deum to be sung at Notre Dame in Paris in celebration of his victory at Agnadello.

In the wake of the Republic's defeat, the doge's troops were compelled to abandon the towns of Bergams, Crema and Cremona, which were taken by Louis XII's forces, while the Romagna area was abandoned and seized by Pope Julius II.

The successful French campaign against the Republic of Venice had checked the territorial ambitions of the doge, but the unifying bond of the League of Cambrai soon dissolved as its members began acting in their self-interest. In 1510, the pontiff negotiated a separate peace agreement with Doge Loredan, then turned his diplomatic and military initiatives against Louis XII to isolate and force him from Italy. Julius II arranged a treaty of cooperation with the Swiss Confederation to deny the French access to its mercenary soldiers, while obligating them to provide a force of infantrymen should hostilities erupt in northern Italy. He further offered to cede Naples to King Ferdinand of Spain to detach him from the league.

Pope Julius II renewed the war with France in the spring of 1511, ordering a naval expedition to attack the regime's occupied seaport in Genoa. The attack was thwarted by the fortification's defenders, but the pope remained undeterred in his quest to drive the French out of Italy. In May 1511, he moved against the Duchy of Ferrara to separate Duke Alfonso d'Este from his alliance with the French. The duke sent appeals to Louis, asking for military intervention in his fight against the pope. In response, Louis dispatched an army to Ferrara to reinforce d'Este's war effort. The fighting continued inconclusively for over a year until a new commander, Gaston de Foix, Duke of Nemours, arrived to lead Louis XII's army to victory, forcing the pontiff to withdraw his soldiers to Ravenna. After Julius II was driven out of Ferrara, he organized the Holy League with the Spanish and Doge Loredan to force the French from Italy, while King Henry VIII of England joined the alliance in a bid to expand his territorial holdings in northern France.

Threatened by the armies of the Holy League, de Foix reorganized his forces to contend with the mercenary Swiss troops in the north of Italy, the Spanish and papal soldiers in the south and the Venetians in the east. The Swiss launched the league's first attack, taking the town of Bellinzona, while the Venetians laid siege against Brescia. In February 1512, de Foix advanced over the Po River to Brescia, ordering the garrison commander there to submit. When de Foix did not receive a reply, he unleashed his assault early on 18 February, leading 12,000 infantrymen and horse soldiers against the town. By the afternoon, Brescia was occupied by the French, who mercilessly ravaged the town. The sack of Brescia was a brutal and cold-blooded act of vengeance against the residents and troops of the Holy League for their refusal to surrender, with over 8,000 killed.

Following the slaughter at Brescia, Gaston de Foix re-formed his army and advanced against the papal and Spanish forces in Romagna. Waiting for reinforcements from the Holy Roman Empire, the Holy League's troops withdrew to Ravenna. The French then broke off their campaign in Romagna and followed the allies toward Ravenna. On 11 April, Louis XII's troops collided with the league force along the Ronco River near Ravenna. The league's soldiers were positioned in front of the unfordable Ronco, with the cavalry in the rear and along the wings, while the infantry occupied the front lines. The French were aligned in an arc opposing their enemy, with the foot soldiers in the middle and horsemen on the flanks. Duke Alfonso d'Este was present with a contingent of his Ferrarese troops supporting the French. Louis' army had approximately 23,000 men, while the allied force totalled 21,000 under the command of Ramon de Cardona, Viceroy of Naples. The battle began with artillery barrages from the French and

Spanish guns lasting several hours. De Foix's cannons pounded Cardona's lines of trenches, inflicting heavy casualties. When the Duke of Nemours repositioned some of his cannons to fire directly on the enemy's cavalry, the horse soldiers charged into his front but were repelled by the French. As the Spanish horsemen retreated, the French commander ordered his infantry to charge the Holy League's lines, reaching their entrenchments in a bloody and fierce melee. As the fighting raged, de Foix sent several artillery pieces across the river to open fire on the rear of the Italian-Spanish infantrymen, while his cavalry crashed into the allies' lines. Hard pressed by the French assault, Cardona's men began fleeing the battlefield, leaving their dead and wounded behind. The allies sustained casualties of over 9,000, while the French lost more than 7,000 dead and wounded. During the battle, Gaston de Foix was killed leading a cavalry charge against the retreating Spanish, and his loss became a serious blow to the war effort of Louis XII.

The Holy League's defeat at Ravenna served as a catalyst to motivate Emperor Maximilian of Austria and the Swiss Confederation to officially join the pope's coalition. In May 1512, a sizable Swiss army led by Cardinal Matthaus Schiner crossed the Alps into northern Italy to unite with the forces of Doge Loredan near Verona. While the Holy League was reinforcing its forces, Louis XII appointed Lord Jacques of La Palice as the new commander-in-chief of his army, replacing de Foix. When the allied army turned west from Verona and advanced towards Milan, La Palice was compelled to abandon eastern Lombardy. The league's army, led by Francesco della Rovere, Duke of Urbino and Schiner, quickly occupied Ravenna and Bologna and began to march against Milan. La Palice's troop strength had been greatly reduced by the losses at Ravenna, disease and desertion, and he was hard pressed by the allied army. After garrisoning the towns occupied by the French, La Palice evacuated Milan at the end of May and was soon back in southern France in the province of Dauphine. After the retreat of the French, the citizens of Genoa and Milan revolted against their French garrison troops and seized control. In December 1512, Massimiliano Sforza, son of Ludovico, was acknowledged Duke of Milan and reigned over the duchy for the following three years.

Meanwhile, in France, Louis XII had to counter the escalating threat of King Henry VIII of England's invasion to recapture his lost Duchy of Gascony in south-western France. When the English joined the Holy League, King Henry had pledged to launch an attack against Louis' kingdom in support of the alliance and to win the pope's promised backing in gaining the Valois crown. In late June 1512, the English fleet sailed to northern Spain with 6,000 soldiers for a combined attack against Gascony. When

Henry's army landed in Spain, King Ferdinand II's troops were not prepared to participate in the campaign, resulting in a prolonged delay. With the incursion temporarily postponed, Louis took the opportunity to strengthen his defences in Gascony and prepare his soldiers for the anticipated assault. He sent La Palice to Gascony with several thousand veterans of the Italian wars to reinforce his army. The Spaniards continued to vacillate through the summer months, and by October it was too late to launch an invasion, causing Henry VIII to recall his army to England and the danger to Louis temporarily abating.

In February 1513, Pope Julius II died and the College of Cardinals elected as pope Giovanni de Medici, who took the name of Leo X. After the death of the driving force behind the Holy League and the anointment of a pro-French pontiff, the power and unity of the alliance against Louis XII began to weaken. The French king's position improved further when Ferdinand of Spain abandoned the Holy League and signed a separate peace agreement with the Valois regime. By the spring of 1513, the French monarchy had secured its borders and felt strong enough to resume its quest for possession of Milan. In the meantime, the troops of the Swiss cantons remained in Milan protecting the rule of Duke Massimiliano. The duke's reign was proving unpopular with the Milanese, and threats of rebellion were beginning to spread. In May, the French monarch appointed Louis II of La Tremoille to lead his invasion force, and after assembling 1,200 cavalry and 11,000 footmen at Lyons, he crossed the Alps into northern Italy, capturing Asti and Alessandro before making a rapid advance towards Milan. As the powerful French army approached the city, the inhabitants rebelled against the excessive taxation and brutal policies of Massimiliano. The Swiss troops were unable to contain the rebels and the city soon surrendered to the French. While La Tremoille was overrunning Milan, the fleet of Louis XII sailed into the harbour of Genoa to relieve the French garrison, which had been holding out in the citadel. The fresh royal troops rescued their stranded compatriots and forced the Swiss soldiers to surrender the city.

Following the defeat of the Swiss Confederation's troops in Milan, the survivors withdrew to the formidable fortress at Novara to await the arrival of relief forces from the cantons. Soon after his capture of Milan, Louis of La Tremoille left a strong garrison to hold the city and pursued Sforza and the Swiss troops to Novara. La Tremoille's French artillery began to batter the defences, while the infantry guarded against sorties from the garrison. As the French continued to invest Novara, the Swiss Confederation sent a relief army of over 4,000 soldiers to break the siege. When the Swiss rescue force neared the citadel, the French commander pulled his troops out of their siege lines and advanced to attack them. After marching through the day, La Tremoille made camp for the night and posted his sentries. During the rainy night, the Swiss launched a surprise attack, catching the French unprepared. La Tremoille's startled men rushed into the escalating battle, but his infantry was crushed without cavalry support. After their defeat at Novara, the Valois troops and the garrisons from the French-occupied towns withdrew across the Alps to the Dauphine. Meanwhile, in Genoa, the residents again revolted, compelling the French garrison to flee as the doge was restored to power.

Henry VIII of England remained a member of the Holy League, and in April 1513 negotiated a treaty of alliance with Maximilian I of Austria for a two-pronged attack against France. The English fleet crossed the Channel in June, landing in the Pale of Calais with more than 30,000 soldiers, who joined the waiting mercenaries. In late July, Henry led his forces out of Calais, heading for the French fortress of Therouanne. When Louis was informed of the English advance, he sent a large army led by Louis of Piennes to shadow the invaders, but with orders not to attack them. When Henry's troops reached Therouanne after an eleven-day march, the citadel's northern defences were besieged, but the southern walls remained uninvested, allowing the French to receive reinforcements and supplies. When Emperor Maximilian joined the English army with his Habsburg soldiers, he insisted Henry besiege the southern side, and three days later troops moved to blockade the area. The English and imperial forces pressed their attack, but Louis' men continued to repel their sorties and resist the bombardments.

In the meantime, to the south of Calais, Louis XII was assembling a large army to drive the allies out of France. He reached the town of Amiens in mid-August to personally direct the attack. When the garrison commander at Therouanne requested provisions and supplies, Louis sent a train of wagons escorted by 2,000 cavalry to the fortress. On the morning of 16 August, the relief train was attacked by a force of 1,000 knights led by Henry VIII near the village of Guinegate. The French, under orders not to engage the enemy, began to fall back, but their advance guard was assailed by Henry's cavalry. After a brief clash, the French horsemen turned and fled, with Henry and his mounted knights in close pursuit. As the Frenchmen rode away, they dropped their heavy armour and lances, leading this brief encounter to become known as the Battle of the Spurs because their spurs were the only objects the French used during the fighting. After the French failure to resupply Therouanne, the garrison held out several more days before surrendering on 23 August. Henry VIII and Maximilian agreed to destroy the fortification in reprisal for the garrison's prolonged resistance, razing it to the ground.

After their destruction of Therouanne, the English monarch and the Holy Roman Emperor resumed their campaign, advancing against Tournai. When the allies reached the outpost town, the governing council attempted to negotiate with Henry, but he refused to offer terms. Tournai was besieged, with its walls battered by the allied siege guns. After six days of resistance, the town's leaders submitted to Henry.

While the English and imperial forces were moving through north-western France virtually unimpeded, Louis XII was threatened in the southern part of his realm by an invasion into the Duchy of Burgundy by the Swiss Confederation. In August 1513, a Swiss army of 15,000 infantry and 1,000 imperial cavalry sent by the Habsburg emperor, Maximilian, marched into the duchy. The French forces, too weak to confront the allies, retreated to the stronghold at Dijon. The Swiss and their imperial allies laid siege to the town in early September. By the middle of the month, the walls were breached and the French governor, Louis of La Tremoille, asked for terms. The Swiss leader demanded Louis XII give up his claims to Milan and Asti, order the garrisons still in occupied Italian towns to surrender and pay a large indemnity. Acting in the name of the king, the governor agreed to the stipulations, effectively ending the French realm's occupation of Italy.

Meanwhile, across the Channel, Louis XII's Scottish ally, King James IV, had invaded England to compel Henry VIII to return home to defend his realm. During the Scots' advance south, they clashed with an English army at Flodden Field on 9 September 1513, during which James IV was killed and his forces defeated. James and Louis had earlier agreed to an alliance against England, but the Scottish king's defeat ended Louis' belief that Henry would have to abandon the French war to protect his kingdom against his northern neighbours.

The new year began in great sorrow for Louis XII with the death of Queen Anne on 9 January at Blois. The king, who was suffering from gout, mourned deeply for the loss of his trusted advisor and true love. Shortly after his wife's death, he told his courtiers to make her vault big enough for them both, for before the year was over he would be with her. Following an extended mourning period, Anne's body was taken to Paris for burial at St Denis. The marriage between the king and Duchess of Brittany had resulted in the birth of eight children, but only two survived into adulthood, Claude and Rene. Serving as French queen, Anne took an active role in the governing of the kingdom, and due to her influence with the king, the Duchy of Brittany maintained a degree of independence. Through the encouragement of Queen Anne, Louis XII and the papacy were reconciled, and her death provided the opportunity for peace with England. Two weeks after the death of Anne, negotiations were opened with the English regime for the marriage of Louis to Henry VIII's sister, Mary Rose. While the talks continued, the two kings agreed to honour a temporary truce. Under the terms negotiated by France and England for the marital union between the two kingdoms and the end to the war, the French king pledged to make a large remuneration payment and accept the loss of the towns already occupied by the English in the Artois region, while Henry agreed to recall his soldiers to England and abide by the status quo. A formal marriage ceremony took place by proxy in August 1514, with Mary finally arriving at her husband's court in October. The actual wedding ceremony was then performed on 9 October at the town of Abbeville, north of Paris.

Despite his setbacks in Italy, the French king remained unwavering in his quest to expand his kingdom into Milan, and preparations were soon underway for a new campaign. However, as soldiers and supplies were assembled, Louis' health deteriorated rapidly from the effects of gout and the stresses of his rule. King Louis XII died in Paris at the Tournelles Palace on 1 January 1515, at the age of 52 and after a reign of sixteen years. His body was embalmed and laid in state for ten days. On 11 January, the king's remains were taken to Notre Dame for the funeral Mass, and the next day the body was moved to the Basilica of St Denis. The coffin remained in the church overnight, and the following morning was carried to the crypt of the French sovereigns. With Louis XII having died without a direct male successor, under Salic Law his cousin, Francis of Angouleme, was acknowledged as King of France.

Selected Sources

Baumgartner, Frederic J., *Louis XII*
Butler, Mildred Allen, *Twice Queen of France*
Castries, Duc de, *The Lives of the Kings and Queens of France*
Knecht, R.J., *The Rise and Fall of Renaissance France 1483–1610*
Knecht, R.J., *The Valois – Kings of France 1328–1589*
Masson, Gustave, *Medieval France*
Potter, David, *A History of France 1460–1560*
Romier, Lucien, *A History of France*

Francis I

In October 1524, King Francis I assembled an army of more than 26,000 soldiers in southern France, marching into northern Italy to resume his quest for possession of the Duchy of Milan. When the French neared Milan, the defending Spanish and Austrian troops of Emperor Charles V abandoned the city, withdrawing to the fortified stronghold at Pavia, allowing Francis to occupy Milan uncontested. To secure his hold on the Milanese duchy, the king advanced against Pavia to destroy the enemy's forces there. He ordered several assaults by his soldiers against the strong defensive works, but they were thrown back with many men killed or wounded. Unable to take the citadel by storm, Francis laid siege to Pavia to compel the garrison's submission. As the siege continued into the winter months, the imperial and Spanish troops launched several sorties but were beaten back in fierce and bloody fighting. By late February 1525, the allies' food and other supplies were nearly depleted and a desperate attack was ordered. In the early morning of 25 February, the garrison mounted a powerful sortie, catching the French unprepared. Francis attempted a counter-attack, but his men were unable to break through the fortified line of the German mercenaries, Spanish pikemen and arquebusiers. During the melee, the French suffered over 8,000 casualties, and Francis I was captured leading a cavalry charge.

Francis was born on 12 September 1494 at the castle of Cognac in south-western France, the second child of Louise of Savoy, wife of Count Charles of Angouleme. The healthy infant's father was a member of a minor branch of the ruling House of Valois, while his mother was the daughter of the Duke of Savoy. Less than two years after his birth, Francis' father died and he inherited his properties under the guardianship of Louise. Francis had been born into the subordinate wing of the Valois dynasty and seemed to have little chance of succeeding to the French throne. In 1498, the King of France, Charles VIII, died unexpectedly without a direct heir, and the French throne was claimed by Louis of Orleans as the closest male relative. Upon his assumption to the French monarchy, Louis XII was childless, and his cousin, Francis, became the heir apparent. As the recognized successor, he was taken under the protection of the king, who provided him with a household, the title of the Duke of Valois and a castle at Amboise. Under the direction of Louise of Savoy, renowned scholars were employed for the education of Francis and his older sister, Margaret. The two children were taught Spanish, Italian and Latin, also studying history, geography, mathematics and religion under the watchful eye of their mother. The young Francis was trained to fight with the weapons of a knight and became skilled in archery and horsemanship. He enjoyed hunting and spend hours stalking deer and wild boar, while taking part in numerous jousting tournaments. As the heir became older, he was described by contemporaries as being particularly tall, at over 6 feet, with a solid body frame and imposing physical appearance.

By 1510, King Louis was still without a direct heir and began to prepare for the succession of his cousin to the French throne. To provide a direct line for Francis' future assumption of the realm, the king arranged the marriage of his recognized heir to his daughter, Claude of France. The wedding took place on 18 May 1514 in the chapel of Saint-Germain-en-Laye near Paris, under an atmosphere of grief following the death of Queen Anne four months earlier. The ceremony was performed without the usual pomp and grandeur of a royal marriage, the traditional majestic feast that followed the service being replaced by an ordinary dinner. In spite of the sombre wedding, it created a firm bond between Francis and the royal family to secure his future acceptance as monarch. He was now widely acknowledged as the dauphin and played an increasingly significant role in the governing of the kingdom. The marriage with the eldest daughter of the king was purely a political manoeuvre, engineered by Louise of Savoy for her son to claim his birthright. In the wake of the nuptial ceremony, Francis displayed no interest in his wife, abandoning her after the ritual to go hunting with his many friends. He considered Claude fat and less than attractive, with her hunched back and poor eyesight. Despite arranging the Angouleme family's merger into the Valois dynasty, Louise of Savoy refused to attend the wedding.

Francis continued to ignore Claude, leaving her at Saint-Germain and travelling to Paris with his boisterous cohorts. He spent his nights gambling, drinking and engaging in numerous sexual encounters. As the dauphin remained in Paris, ignoring Claude, Louis XII devised a plan to replace him as heir by arranging his marriage to Mary Rose Tudor, sister of Henry VIII, in anticipation of producing a male successor. After negotiations with the English regime, Mary was married to the French king by proxy on 13 August 1514. During a violent October storm, Mary crossed the English

Channel and landed at Boulogne, where she was greeted by Francis, who was substituting for the sickly king. He escorted the queen through the pouring rain to Abbeville, where she finally met Louis. On 9 October, the formal wedding ceremony was performed and Francis' future succession to the French crown was left in question.

The dauphin displayed no concern about the birth of a new heir, telling his friends he had nothing to fear. On 5 November, Mary was anointed queen at the Basilica of St Denis, with Francis carrying the consort's crown to the high altar. A month-long celebration followed the coronation, with martial games, dancing and lavish banquets. Francis enthusiastically participated in the festivities, always dressed in elaborate clothing embroidered in gold and silver. As the Christmas season approached, the king became seriously ill from the effects of gout and fatigue, taking little part in the administration of the kingdom. By late December he was nearing death, and Francis made ready for his unchallenged succession to the throne. Louis XII's health continued to deteriorate, and during the early morning of 1 January 1515 he died. Before his death, he called Francis to his bedside, telling him to prepare to rule France for his time to die had come. After the announcement of Louis XII's death, Francis I was immediately acknowledged as king by the French lords, churchmen and subjects.

After his death, Louis XII's body was embalmed and laid in state at the royal palace before burial at St Denis. Now holding the reins of power, the new king began forming his government, naming several members of Louis' old regime to his council and placing two of his supporters in the important posts of chancellor and constable. King Francis created a new atmosphere of change and transformation, but nepotism and bribery for government offices continued to be widespread.

On 18 January 1515, the 21-year-old Francis I departed from Paris for Rheims and his coronation as king. Upon reaching the city, he was greeted by Archbishop Robert de Lenoncourt and other prelates and escorted into the cathedral. As was customary, the king spent the evening in the cathedral, offering prayers of thanksgiving and praise to God before withdrawing to the archbishop's palace for the night. The following morning, he was taken back to the cathedral by two bishops for his consecration, wearing a white gown over a shirt and tunic. The coronation ceremony began with Francis pledging to protect the Church and promising to promote peace in Christendom. The oath was followed by the anointment of the king with holy oil over his upper body by the archbishop. Next he replaced his clothing, changing into his coronation robe of blue embroidered with gold fleur de lys. The archbishop then lifted the crown of Charlemagne and placed it on Francis' head. After the crowning, he was escorted to the throne by the twelve peers of France. With the king sitting on his throne, Archbishop de Lenoncourt shouted three times, 'God save the king!', and after the trumpets and organ blared out, the congregation declared, 'Long live the king!'. The singing of the Te Deum and Pontifical Mass ended the service. King Francis I then returned to the archbishop's palace for dinner with the peers in the great hall in celebration of his assumption of the crown.

The day after his coronation, Francis set out on a brief pilgrimage to enhance the widely held belief that he now held supernatural powers to heal. He travelled to the Shrine of St Marculf at the Abbey of Corbeny, where he was greeted by the monks and escorted to the priory to pray before the relic of the saint's skull, which was believed to have the power to cure illnesses. The next day, Francis 'healed' several victims of scrofula by touching their open sores with his hands. From the abbey, he journeyed to the Shrine of the Black Virgin at Notre Dame de Liesse, offering prayer to the three knights who brought to the church the statue of the Black Virgin, with its believed ability to cure the sick.

Following his visit to Corbeny, Francis travelled the 20 miles back to St Denis to reconfirm the cathedral's special rights and privileges, reinforcing the bond between the Church and monarchy. Remaining at the cathedral, he prepared for his grand entrance into Paris. On the early morning of 15 February, the mayor and alderman of Paris, along with numerous city officials, made their way to St Denis to escort the new king into their city. A large procession of assembled dignitaries then moved into the crowded and jubilant city through the north gate. Riding ahead of Francis were the Grand Master of France and the four marshals of the army, followed by the guard of forty gentlemen pensioners and a large group of musicians, pages and heralds. The king entered Paris mounted on a great warhorse under a white canopy. From his horse, he threw gold and silver coins into the crowd lining the processional route. Francis was dressed in a uniform of silver cloth and wore a white hat beset with many jewels. Riding behind him were members of the royal family and other nobles, all richly dressed. At the rear of the procession were 400 archers, providing protection for the new monarch. The grand column made its way across Paris and ended with a service of thanksgiving at Notre Dame. The archbishop offered thanks to God for the heavenly foresight that brought Francis to the French throne. The celebration continued with a majestic dinner at the Louvre Palace, followed by dancing. After being welcomed by the citizens of Paris, several days of martial tournaments and jousting competitions were held in celebration of Francis' assumption of the throne.

In the aftermath of the celebrations, Francis I spent the next several months consolidating his hold on the monarchy and setting in place a functioning governmental administration. At the time of Francis' succession, France was at peace with its potential enemies and enjoying a prolonged period of economic prosperity. While at Amboise, he had been exposed to numerous stories of the grandeur and magnificence of the Italian cities from returning soldiers, travellers and clerics. Similar to his predecessor, Francis held hereditary rights to the Duchy of Milan through his great grandmother, Valentina Visconti, and was now motivated into enforcing his claims. After securing his reign, he began to make plans for his invasion of Milan, which was currently ruled by Duke Massimiliano Sforza. The two previous French kings had led unsuccessful expeditionary forces into Italy in an attempt to conquer new lands, and Francis was determined to triumph where they had failed.

In preparation for his departure from his realm, the king negotiated peace treaties with neighbouring kingdoms to secure his borders, and an alliance was arranged with the Doge of Venice to militarily supplement his campaign. The king's mother, Louise of Savoy, was named as regent. On 29 June 1515, Francis I departed from Amboise and made his way south to Lyons. The king remained in Lyons for three weeks, completing his preparations. At the end of July, he joined the army at Grenoble and the march into Italy began. Meanwhile, the Duke of Milan, Massimiliano Sforza, formed a coalition with Pope Leo X, King Ferdinand II of Aragon and the Holy Roman Emperor, Maximilian I, to defend Italy against the French invasion.

Acting on the advice of his marshals, Francis ordered his army to cross the Alps into northern Italy by advancing through a small pass not usually used because of the danger of rockslides. The French vanguard moved through the pass unchallenged, emerging into the plain of Piedmont, and was soon followed by the king at the head of his troops. After reaching the Po Valley, he turned his forces east and united with his Venetian allies at the city of Lodi, south of Milan. As the allies resumed their march to Milan, Francis was approached by envoys from the Swiss, offering to withdraw from the war for the payment of 1 million crowns and the pledge to pay a subsidy to each canton. Under the terms of the agreement, Francis would be allowed to recruit troops from the Swiss Confederation to reinforce his army.

Francis accepted the proposal, but when the provisions of the treaty were presented to members of the Swiss Confederacy, the western cantons accepted the terms and abandoned the war, while the troops from the eastern and central cantons moved out with flags flying to fight the French.

On 13 September, the 15,000 Swiss soldiers from the eastern canton departed from Milan in support of the Milanese, led by Cardinal Matthaus Schiner. Meanwhile, the French king established his encampment near the town of Marignano and sent scouts to make a reconnaissance of the area. As Schiner's troops advanced near the French camp on a hot and dry day, they created a large cloud of dust, warning their opponents of their approach. Francis quickly established a fortified defensive position, with trenches and artillery sites. The battle began in the late afternoon, some 7,000 Swiss pikemen deploying into a square formation and charging at the French, breaking through the first line of infantrymen, who were guarding the artillery pieces. As the French front threatened to break, the German mercenaries hired by Francis advanced into the fray, pushing Schiner's soldiers back in savage hand-to-hand fighting with swords, spears, lances and daggers. Francis, dressed in full armour and mounted on a large warhorse, led his cavalry into the melee just as a second column of Swiss entered the battle. The king and his horsemen made charge after charge into the enemy's front, but were repeatedly repelled. The fighting continued into the night, with both armies refusing to fall back. By midnight, the French and Swiss were too exhausted to continue the battle and both sides withdrew to their camps. Under the light of the quarter moon, Francis repositioned his troops into an extended single line, while praying for the arrival of his Venetian allies in the morning.

At daybreak on 14 September, the battle resumed with 8,000 Swiss infantrymen charging into the French defences. The troops of Cardinal Schiner broke through, overwhelming the French infantry, while the left flank began to collapse and the king's troops started to retreat. As the Swiss gained the advantage, 12,000 allied soldiers finally arrived on the battlefield. The reinforced French now outnumbered their enemy, and Schiner's troops began to abandon the field, giving the victory to King Francis. The French lost over 5,000 men, while more than double that figure of Swiss mercenaries were killed, captured or wounded. The defeated Cardinal Schiner fled, taking refuge with Emperor Maximilian.

Despite his defeat of the Swiss at Marignano and the collapse of Massimiliano Sforza's defences, Francis I offered him generous terms for the surrender of his Duchy of Milan. On 16 September, Sforza submitted to Francis, accepting an indemnity of 94,000 crowns, an annual pension and residence in France. A month later, Francis entered Milan in a triumphant procession, offering thanks to God for his victory at the city's cathedral. After the battle, Francis ordered a medal made in honour of his victory, bearing the words 'I have vanquished those whom only Caesar vanquished'.

The French were welcomed by the inhabitants of Milan. Francis quickly established his government, appointing a governor and ruling council. The city's senate was reformed to now include both Italian and French members. To secure his victory at Marignano and his occupation of the duchy, Francis was eager to reach an agreement with Pope Leo X and gain his support against an attack by the Venetians. Fearful of future French expansions into Italy, the pontiff was willing to negotiate a treaty of peace with Francis. A meeting at Bologna was soon arranged between Leo and the French king. The pope arrived at Bologna on 8 December, and three days later Francis entered the city, with the streets decorated with festive tapestries and lined with cheering crowns welcoming him. He was met by two cardinals and escorted to meet Pope Leo at the papal palace. The king bowed before the pontiff sitting on his throne, then moved forward to kiss his foot in a sign of deference. Following their introductory meeting, Francis attended Mass with Leo X the next day, sitting with the cardinals. After the religious service, the pope and king spent the next few days in lengthy negotiations. The preliminary Concordat of Bologna, signed on 15 December, gave the king the power to appoint French clergy to Church offices, confirmed his right to tithe the priests and restricted their option to appeal directly to Rome, while the Holy See was permitted to retain all money generated in France. During their talks, the pontiff offered the Eastern Empire to Francis if he could force the Turks out of Constantinople. Before leaving Bologna, the king was asked to use his supernatural powers of healing by touch for the scrofula infection, performing the ritual in the papal chapel before the pope. On 15 December, Francis departed from Bologna, returning to Milan satisfied that the papal conference had been a success.

In early January 1516, Francis left Milan for France, leaving a force of 700 cavalry and 10,000 foot soldiers to protect his newly won duchy against an attack by Maximilian. He met Louise of Savoy in Provence, who was accompanied by his wife and sister. Together, they made a pilgrimage of thanksgiving for the king's safe return and conquest of Milan, praying in the cave located in the Sainte Baume mountain range of southern France, where according to legend Mary Magdalene had spent her final years.

The meeting with Pope Leo X had solidified Francis' territorial gains in Italy and dispersed the coalition formed against him. From southern France, he slowly made his way to Paris, touring his kingdom while displaying his royal grandeur to his subjects. He began the triumphal advance through Provence and then along the Rhone River to Marseille, where he entered the city in a grand procession, preceded by 4,000 knights and 2,000 children all dressed in white. He was presented with the keys to the city, while cannons fired volleys of salutes. The next day, the king resumed his journey through Provence, spending three months at Lyons before reaching Amboise in August, eventually arriving in Paris at the beginning of October. Francis I now reigned over a realm at peace, resulting in a period of strong economic activity, with significant increases in the growth of towns, agriculture and commerce.

While Francis I ruled over his kingdom unchallenged, in Vienna, Cardinal Matthaus Schiner continued to plot against French occupation of Milan, finally convincing Emperor Maximilian that the population of the city was ready to revolt against the French occupation forces. In March 1516, the emperor mustered his army and marched into Lombardy, driving Francis' men back into Milan. When 8,000 Swiss mercenaries arrived in support of the French king, the Habsburg emperor withdrew his forces, fearing another defeat. After Francis' Swiss allies had compelled the imperial troops to retreat, the French king and the Swiss Confederation signed a peace treaty. The Valois regime pledged to pay a large indemnity and make annual payments to each canton, while the Swiss agreed not to support the king's enemies and allow him to recruit soldiers from the cantons.

The Holy Roman Emperor, Maximilian I, died on 12 January 1519, causing a disruption in the status quo of European politics and creating a new potential threat against Francis I. Charles of Flanders, who already ruled the Netherlands and Spain, began to aggressively contend for the throne of his grandfather. If he succeeded in winning the crown of the Holy Roman Empire, France would be surrounded on three borders by a powerful potential rival. To prevent the election of Charles, Francis put forward his own candidacy for the imperial throne. The formal voting process had been established in 1356 by Emperor Charles IV with the issuance of the Golden Bull, the imperial decree naming seven German electors to select the new emperor. In the years since its proclamation, the selection process had been subjected to widespread political abuse and misapplication. The French king now dispatched numerous envoys into Germany armed with chests of gold to influence the electors in his favour. However, in June 1519, despite Francis' attempts to buy his election, the electors chose Charles as the next Holy Roman Emperor. This marked the beginning of a longstanding rivalry between Francis I and Emperor Charles V.

Charles of Habsburg was born on 24 February 1500 in the Flemish city of Ghent, the first son of Duke Philip of Burgundy and Joanne of Trastamara. He grew up under the custody of his aunt, Margaret of Austria, in the city of Mechelen in present-day Belgium. Under the guardianship of Margaret of Austria, renowned scholars were named to tutor Charles and he received a broad-based education. When Philip of Burgundy died in 1506, his 6-year-old son assumed his title and lands, with Margaret of Austria appointed to serve as regent for the strategic duchy. Ruling over the turbulent domains of her nephew, the regent's regime grew increasingly unpopular with the magnates and city burghers, and in 1514 they rebelled against her administration. As the revolt grew stronger in favour of the young duke's assumption of power, Margaret was forced to withdraw from the government in early January 1515 and Charles assumed the ducal throne. Through the hereditary lineage of his mother, Charles was the acknowledged heir to the crown of Spain, and when the reigning Spanish king, Ferdinand II, died in 1516, Charles succeeded to the throne, meaning he now held power over Spain, the Low Countries, Navarre, Naples, Sicily and the Spanish colonies in the New World.

The election of Charles V to the throne of the Holy Roman Empire meant he now ruled a vast territorial region, creating a significant new threat to both France and England. In early 1520, the French regime needed an ally to offset the power of the Habsburg Empire, and turned increasingly to Henry VIII of England. Tensions intensified at the French court when the English cardinal, Thomas Wolsey, arranged for Emperor Charles to stop off in England during his voyage to the Netherlands to discuss unfolding events in Europe. As the danger of an Anglo-Habsburg union grew, Francis pressed for talks to open with the English, and negotiations were begun to quickly resolve unsettled issues and guarantee peace between the two realms. The Treaty of London was signed in October 1518, with the English agreeing to return to Francis the seized city of Tournai, in current-day southern Belgium, in exchange for the payment of reparations. Mary Tudor, the 2-year-old daughter of the English king, was pledged in marriage to the Dauphin Francis, and the two kings agreed to meet the following year in English-occupied France.

A shallow valley in the Pale of Calais was chosen as the site for the meeting between the English and French monarchs, and workmen soon began construction to accommodate the expected large gathering. The area lacked any towns to house the participants, so the French and English began transforming the valley into a magnificent city of tents. An army of carpenters, masons and glaziers constructed an encampment of grand palaces, banqueting halls and pavilions, along with sites for jousting lists and chivalrous martial contests. The French labourers built brightly coloured pavilions and refurbished the nearby castle at Ardres for Francis' living quarters. Over 300 tents were erected to house the French participants, with their coats of arms affixed to the outer surfaces. The French king had a pavilion over 60 feet tall built, covered in golden cloth and supported by two ships' masts. The sight of the golden covered tents gave the spectacle the name 'The Field of the Cloth of Gold'.

Before the meeting between Francis and Henry, an agreement was signed on 6 June 1520 reiterating the terms of the Treaty of London, with both parties pledging to honour its stipulations. The kings met the following day, departing from their encampments with 500 cavalry and 3,000 foot soldiers to the sound of cannon fire. When the two monarchs reached the edge of the tournament field with their trusted noblemen, they stopped at the designated location. Francis was magnificently dressed in a silver jacket studded with diamonds, pearls and rubies, with a golden cloak wrapped across his back. At the sound of the trumpets, the kings rode towards each other slowly before charging forward. When they neared each other, they lowered their hats before embracing several times. Drinks of wine were then served and a toast made to the friendship between the two kingdoms.

Martial competitions began on 9 June, with 300 mounted warriors involved in the jousting tournament. During the following seventeen days, the two kings dined together in their splendid temporary palaces and took part in numerous martial contests. The mock warfare comprised jousting in the tilts and fighting an adversary on foot with spear and sword. Both Francis and Henry participated in the jousting events with great enthusiasm, the French king, mounted on his warhorse, charging against his opponents. During the jousting bouts, the Valois monarch received a black eye and bloody nose, but continued to battle his challengers. The nights were occupied with majestic banquets, masquerade balls, music and dancing. On 13 June, wrestling replaced the jousting contests due to rainy weather, and the English king challenged Francis to a bout. Francis agreed to participate, and to Henry's great surprise he was quickly thrown to the floor. Despite his embarrassing defeat, Henry retained his friendly attitude and asked for a rematch, which Francis politely declined. On 23 June, the two monarchs, along with their queens, attended a church service in the chapel, decorated with elaborate wall hangings and statues of various saints, with Cardinal Wolsey singing the Mass. The music was provided by the choirs and organists of the two royal chapels. The final banquet was held the following day, ending with an exchange of gifts. The Field of the Cloth of Gold was a triumphant success, creating a new spirit of friendship between the two old enemies. Nevertheless, the elation was short-lived, the English turning increasingly toward an alliance with Charles V. Shortly after his grand summit with Francis, the English king met Charles at Gravelines, agreeing to hold a conference in Calais and not make a separate treaty with the French regime.

As ruler of Spain, the Low Countries, Austria, Naples and Germany, the emperor of the Holy Roman Empire was a formidable enemy, and Francis became increasingly endangered by the powerful Charles V, who ruled officially as King of the Romans until his coronation as emperor by the pope in Rome. The French king became apprehensive of the emperor's presence in Italy, with his powerful armed forces threatening the Duchy of Milan. It thus became the goal of French foreign policy to keep the emperor out of Italy and occupied in northern Europe. The Valois king employed an army of mercenary soldiers, who in March 1521 invaded the Habsburg providence of Luxembourg on the northern French border. A second agreement was made by French representatives with the ruler of Navarre to attack Spanish-occupied lands. Francis hoped his two incursions into the empire would compel Charles to react to protect his lands, and consequently be a distraction from Italy.

In April 1521, Charles V sent an envoy to meet with the French king, accusing him of arranging the two attacks against Habsburg possessions. Francis strongly denied the accusations, but by the end of the month the emperor's troops had repelled the two invading armies and re-established his rule. Francis' first moves against Charles V to protect his Duchy of Milan had proved unsuccessful, and he now had two hostile forces on his borders. Meanwhile, in Italy, Pope Leo X abandoned Francis and threw his allegiance to Emperor Charles, whom he considered the more beneficial ally. In late May 1521, the pontiff and Habsburg regime signed a secret treaty affirming Charles' rights to the imperial crown and supported his occupation of Naples. The pretext to severing his relationship with Francis soon occurred when the king's troops in Milan pursued anti-French protesters across the border into papal territory. Despite negotiating the agreement in private, Leo's alliance with the Habsburgs was soon made public. When Francis learned of the new anti-French treaty, he retaliated by retaining the papal revenues generated in his kingdom. The king's continued possession of Milan now became increasingly questionable.

As the threat of war escalated, Henry VIII arranged a peace conference at Calais with representatives from the French kingdom and Holy Roman Empire. On 20 July, the envoys of Charles, Henry and Francis met to resolve the danger of war erupting, but no compromise was worked out. Meanwhile, Cardinal Wolsey was holding separate secret talks with the imperial emissary and negotiated an agreement between the two realms against the French. On 23 August, the cardinal travelled to Bruges to sign the treaty with Charles V. Under the agreed terms, England would declare war against France if by the end of autumn Francis I and Charles were still at odds. Discussions between the emperor and France continued but failed to find a resolution.

As the negotiations at Calais dragged on, Charles V sent his formidable army across the border into north-eastern France in late August 1521. The imperialists attacked Mezieres, but were thrown back by the defenders and compelled to lay siege to the strongly fortified town. While the Habsburg soldiers maintained their siege lines, a second force occupied Ardes without resistance. Francis responded to the invasion by mustering a strong force to relieve Mezieres. As the French neared the town, the emperor's soldiers abandoned their siege and withdrew towards imperial territory. During their retreat, they brutally laid waste to the countryside and sacked every town in their path.

With his kingdom now at war with the Habsburgs, Francis sent orders for his generals to attack the forces of Emperor Charles. In northern Italy, his troops marched against the imperial-occupied town of Parma, compelling the garrison to retreat and re-establishing French sovereignty. In the meantime, at Calais, the emperor instructed his envoy to accept the latest French offer. When Francis was informed of the Habsburg proposal, he refused to agree to the terms and prepared to lead his soldiers into battle. On 4 March 1522, he advanced against Charles' forces investing the town of Tournai to relieve the siege. During the journey to attack the Habsburgs, rainy and stormy weather made the roads impassable and many French troops became sick and exhausted. Unable to move forward, Francis was compelled to order a withdrawal. When the French defenders at Tournai learned of their king's retreat, they surrendered. After the failure of his campaign to retake Tournai, Francis became despondent, ordering his men to lay waste to the countryside.

While Francis I was suffering defeats in France, his governing council in Milan had become unpopular with the citizenry, who threatened to rise up against the occupying soldiers. When Charles V sent an army of Swiss mercenaries to reconquer the duchy, the populace joined the imperial forces and expelled the king's troops from several towns in the duchy. In the spring of 1522, Francis sent reinforcements to his Italian army to recover his lost lands. The French attempted to retake the city of Milan, but their attacks against the heavily fortified walls were repeatedly repelled. In April, the local French general made another assault against enemy troops but was routed and compelled to retreat from Italy, leaving the Duchy of Milan in the hands of the Habsburgs. Following his ejection from Italy, King Francis attempted to reopen peace talks with the Habsburg emperor, but his offer was rejected. In the wake of Francis' failed endeavour to revive peace negotiations, Cardinal Wolsey – acting in the name of Henry VIII – signed an agreement with the imperial government in November at Bruges, committing English forces to act in concert with Charles V in a campaign against France. The French king was now isolated and confronted by two powerful adversaries.

In December 1521, Pope Leo X had died and the Papal Conclave elected Adrian VI as his successor. The new pope had been the tutor and close friend of the Holy Roman Emperor, but ruled with strict neutrality in European affairs. As the head of Christendom, he attempted to unite all of Europe in a new crusade against the Turks, who had just seized the island of Rhodes and were encroaching further into Christian lands. To gain Adrian's favour, Francis pledged to participate in the expeditionary force provided Milan was returned to him.

After losing possession of the Milan duchy, Francis prepared his army for another invasion of Italy against the Habsburgs. Although the English and Charles V had agreed to act in concert against the French, Francis took diplomatic measures to restrain Henry VIII's involvement in the conflict. Under earlier treaties with the English, he had agreed to pay a pension to them, but with Henry now an ally of his enemy, the payments were cancelled. The French monarch retaliated further by sending his Scottish ally, John Stewart, to Scotland to harass the English towns along the border region. When Henry VIII loudly protested to the Valois regime, Francis claimed ignorance and the English were compelled to refrain from fully supporting Charles V.

While Francis I was manoeuvring against the English regime, in March 1522 he sent an army reinforced with Swiss mercenaries into Lombardy with orders to restore French dominance. The king's general, Viscount Odet Lautrec, reoccupied parts of the Duchy of Milan, but the city of Milan, led by Duke Francesco II Sforza, repelled the attacks and forced the French to fall back. Unsuccessful at taking Milan, Lautrec relocated his troops to the fortified town of Pavia, opening siege operations. The Italians, led by Prospero Colonna, had followed the French from Milan, and as Lautrec was besieging Pavia they attacked him from the rear. Francis' troops, taken by surprise, were compelled to end their siege and withdraw to Monza. Colonna pursued Lautrec and established a strong defensive position to his rear, reinforced with deep trenches and fortifications. The exhausted and despondent Swiss mercenaries now threatened to mutiny if an attack was not ordered by the French commander. Consequently, on 27 April, the French and their Swiss allies advanced against the Milanese forces behind their fortified position, and were cut down with over 3,000 killed.

Without his Swiss infantrymen, who had abandoned the battle, Lautrec was compelled to return to France and face the wrath of Francis for his unsuccessful campaign.

In late May 1523, Charles V again visited Henry VIII and the two rulers agreed to launch a joint campaign against France. In July, English troops raided the coastline of Brittany and made several brief sorties into the French interior from their stronghold in the Pale of Calais. Despite the possibility of future incursions from Henry, the French monarch remained defiant in his quest for Milan and began assembling an army while making preparations for a further invasion of northern Italy. After again appointing Louise of Savoy as regent during his absence, Francis I made his way from Paris to Lyon to join his army. While he prepared his forces for the Italian offensive, the Constable of France, Duke Charles III of Bourbon, renounced his loyalty to the French crown and in July 1523 formed an alliance with Charles V. The Bourbon duke agreed to lead a rebellion against the Valois throne in exchange for a large cash payment and his marriage to one of the emperor's sisters. They planned to invade France from the south as Francis departed over the Alps on his Italian campaign. The plot by Bourbon and the emperor was soon revealed to the French, and Francis moved quickly to isolate the duke from the Habsburgs. Realizing that his plot had been revealed to the king, Charles of Bourbon fled to the safety of the Holy Roman Empire. While moving to arrest Bourbon's accomplices in France, Francis offered a large reward to anyone who captured the duke.

While Francis remained in France rooting out the plotters, his army, led by Admiral Guillaume Gouffier, Lord of Bonnivet, crossed the Alps and advanced against Milan. Gouffier was raised and educated at the French court and became a favourite of Francis I. He was named Admiral of France in 1517, which gave him total jurisdiction over all maritime affairs and also access to large sources of revenue. In the imperial election of 1519 for the new emperor, Gouffier led the campaign in favour of Francis I and spent large sums of money to secure votes. He fought with the French armies during the Italian wars and took part in the Battle of Marignano.

Gouffier led the French attacks against the defences of Milan but failed to break through the battlements, and imperial troops led by Prospero Colonna forced his withdrawal. Meanwhile, in eastern France, the invasion of the Bourbon duke and Charles V never materialized. As part of the planned three-pronged attack against the French, the English army of 12,000 soldiers advanced into Picardy in late September, commanded by the Duke of Suffolk. He laid waste to many farms and villages, reaching within 50 miles of Paris. When the Habsburg army that was assigned to support the

English campaign failed to appear, the Duke of Suffolk withdrew to Calais. With the allies' planned invasions of France now abandoned, Bourbon was compelled to flee to Italy.

Pope Adrian VI died in September 1523 following a reign of less than two years, and Clement VII was elected to the papacy. Soon after his election, the new pontiff launched a peace initiative to end the war between France and the Habsburg Empire. Francis replied to the papal appeal by demanding the surrender of the Duke of Bourbon, while Charles V requested possession of Burgundy. Both ultimatums were quickly rejected and the fighting resumed. The French army in Italy was now suffering from a lack of support by Paris, with provisions and supplies depleted and low morale among the soldiers. Unable to risk an attack by the Habsburgs, Admiral Gouffier withdrew his army towards the Alps. As the king's troops were crossing the Sesia River in north-eastern Italy, they were attacked by imperial forces reinforced with German pikemen. During the ensuing melee, Gouffier was wounded and his men decimated by the enemy's assaults. The remnants of the shattered army made its way over the Alps to France, leaving Milan in possession of the Habsburgs.

Queen Claude of France died in July 1524 after ten years of marriage, while Francis was preparing for the invasion of Milan. Despite the king's many amorous affairs, the couple had developed a loving relationship, with Francis showing her true affection and care. They had seven children – four girls and three boys – including the dauphin, Francis, born in February 1518.

In July, the Duke of Bourbon again returned to France with an imperial army, but his offensive soon faltered before the walls of Marseille and he was compelled to retreat. With his enemies seemingly in disarray, Francis resumed his quest for the occupation of Milan, and by October a new army was mustered in southern France. Francis took personal command of the troops and began his fourth invasion of Italy. The French king reached Milan late in the month to discover the plague was rampant in the city. He was forced to alter his plans, instead attacking the nearby town of Pavia. On 6 November, Francis besieged the town, which was defended by a garrison of 6,000 German and Spanish soldiers. He ordered his artillery to bombard the massive defensive works, and the cannon fire soon made a breach in the walls. The imperial forces refused to surrender and continued to defend the town, unleashing a determined counter-attack. With his men unable to advance into Pavia, Francis ordered them to pull back and maintain their siege lines. The battle for Pavia continued throughout the winter months, with frequent clashes between the two sides. As the siege wore on, Francis sent a force of 6,000 men south to invade Naples, weakening the strength of his army to a dangerous level.

As the French remained bogged down at Pavia, the enemies of Francis I renewed their war effort against his kingdom. Charles III of Bourbon received financial aid from the Habsburg emperor and purchased the services of a large force of German infantry and cavalry, advancing into northern Italy to join his Habsburg allies at Pavia. The stalemate between the two armies remained into February, with frequent clashes and feints by both Francis and the Habsburgs. When the imperial troops launched a surprise sortie against the headquarters of Francis, they were quickly repelled, and the impasse continued. On 20 February, the Valois monarch's military strength was further weakened when his Swiss mercenaries suddenly abandoned his army and returned to their canton to defend it against an imperial attack. Following the departure of the Swiss, 2,000 German soldiers also deserted Francis, diminishing his power even more, while Charles V's army under Prince Charles of Lannoy was increased with the arrival of additional troops. Outnumbered by the enemy, the French generals counselled their king to retreat, but Admiral Gouffier convinced him to remain and fight.

In the late evening of 23 February, following a powerful artillery bombardment, the imperial forces and their allies advanced against the French in their fortified encampment. Using sappers to weaken the walls during the night, several breaches were made by morning and Prince Charles sent his imperial soldiers rushing into the French camp, with his German allies on his right flank and his remaining Swiss on the left. As his infantry was fighting against the imperial forces, Francis I led his heavily armoured cavalry forward, slamming into the enemy. The French horsemen were now in the line of fire of their artillery and lost the support of the heavy guns. As the king's cavalry continued to engage the Habsburgs, the Spanish arquebusiers entered the battle, shooting at the French with devasting effect. As the 1,000 Spanish fired volleys at the French cavalry, those who fell to the ground wounded were killed by imperial infantrymen armed with daggers. During the desperate melee, two French marshals and Admiral Gouffier were killed, but Francis fought on, refusing to surrender. When the king's horse was killed, he continued to fight on foot, cutting down several Spanish knights. Francis was eventually knocked to the ground, and as a Spanish foot soldier was about to kill him, a lieutenant of the Duke of Bourbon intervened, saving his life. The king refused to surrender to an ally of the traitorous duke, but when the Viceroy of Naples approached him, he offered his sword. Following the king's submission, Charles of Lannoy secured the victory, with over 8,000 French and their mercenary soldiers left dead on the battlefield of Pavia. The remnants of the French army withdrew under Charles IV of Alencon. The scale of defeat at

Pavia mirrored France's devastating loss at Agincourt in 1415, with the loss of many high-born noblemen.

In the aftermath of the Pavia disaster, Francis I was taken to the nearby monastery of Carthusian by the Viceroy of Naples and Charles III of Bourbon. The king still refused to acknowledge the duke, considering him a traitor. Francis was soon moved to the castle at Cremona, where the Habsburg emperor sent an envoy demanding Burgundy's return to its rightful duke, the surrender of the Dauphine province to the empire and the renunciation of all Valois claims to Italy, while Henry VIII was to receive his rightful French lands. Francis swiftly refused to comply with these terms. After remaining at Cremona for three months, the imperialists became increasingly afraid the king would escape his captivity. Francis was transferred to Spain by ship, being imprisoned in the Alcazar in Madrid. For security, he was confined to a small room in the upper floor of the castle, 100 feet above the ground, and guarded by two companies of soldiers. In these harsh conditions, Francis soon became ill with a high fever and was unable to speak, see or hear. After examining the king, his Spanish doctors feared his imminent death. When his sister, Margaret, arrived from France to facilitate negotiations, she took care of Francis and he began to slowly recover his strength. After the king regained his health, he sent his sister back to Paris with instructions to proclaim the dauphin, Francis, king under a regency government ruled by Louise of Savoy. When the decree was presented to the French Parliament, the members refused to honour it. With no chance of escaping and his presence needed in France to prevent internal disorder, Francis I sent word to Charles V accepting his terms. On 14 January 1526, King Francis signed the Treaty of Madrid, which included a new provision authorizing his marriage to Eleanor of Austria, sister of the Habsburg emperor. As part of the agreement, on 17 March 1526, the dauphin and Duke of Orleans, Charles, were exchanged for the king, allowing Francis to return to France. In mid-March, Francis crossed the border into France, weeping as he set foot in his kingdom, and was greeted by the great lords of the realm. He mounted his horse and rode to Bayonne, entering the cathedral there to give thanks to God for his freedom, with Margaret and his mother at his side.

Following his return to the French kingdom, Francis reasserted his sovereignty by assuming control of the government from Louise of Savoy and reinstating his personal rule. Many high magnates had been killed or captured at Pavia and they were replaced on the royal council with friends and allies of the monarch. During Francis' absence in Italy and Spain, the parliament had manoeuvred to increase its dominion and independence.

Now holding the reins of power, the king moved to check the attempted seizure of the government by the legislative members. In July, he summoned the full parliament to convene. Sitting on his throne, he ordered his edict read to the assembled lay peers, nobles and clergymen. Under the terms of the decree, the representatives were forbidden to interfere in state affairs, except regarding law, and any limiting statutes passed during the regency period were revoked. Three week later, the Duke of Bourbon was tried *in absentia* in the Paris Parliament and declared guilty of rebellion, with his lands and possessions forfeited to the realm.

Soon after re-establishing his rule, Francis mounted an aggressive diplomatic initiative to void the Treaty of Madrid, claiming the terms were approved under duress and citing the ill-treatment he was subjected to as a prisoner. Charles V responded by ordering the king's two sons removed from their captivity at a royal palace and confined to a castle prison. When Francis offered to pay a sizable ransom for the release of his heir and second son, the emperor refused.

In June 1526, after his failed attempts to secure the freedom of his two sons for a ransom, Francis I joined the League of Cognac together with Venice, Milan, Florence and Pope Clement VII, with the stated purpose of driving the Habsburg emperor out of Italy because of his continued possession of the French king's children. Charles V had earlier sent Duke Charles III of Bourbon into Italy to secure his lands, but by March 1527 his army had been unpaid for months and was now near mutiny. Bourbon promised his soldiers great riches with the sack of Rome and began advancing against the city. As his men marched south, sacking numerous towns, bandits and deserters joined his ranks, which grew to over 20,000. Bourbon reached Rome on 6 May and his troops launched a savage attack against the 5,000 papal militiamen and the nearly defenceless Roman citizens. However, as Charles of Bourbon led his troops into the fray, he was killed by a shot from a papal arquebusier. Without their commander to maintain some degree of control, the soldiers, shouting 'Kill, kill, blood, Bourbon!', mercilessly unleashed their assaults against the Romans, killing thousands. Pope Clement VII escaped capture, hurrying to the protection of Castel Sant'Angelo, where he was compelled to stay until a ransom was paid. The looters remained in Rome until February 1528, when the outbreak of plague and food shortages forced them to abandon the city.

In early 1528, while the imperial army was pillaging Rome, Francis I sent a military force into Italy in pursuit of the Kingdom of Naples. His army swept across Lombardy and invaded the northern parts of the Neapolitan realm. The French moved through the region, encountering little opposition before besieging the city of Naples. As the king's men pressed forward, their Italian ally, Prince Andrea Doria, abandoned his French allies and joined the forces of Charles V. In September, the prince attacked Francis' troops occupying Genoa and drove them out. While the king's army remained before the walls of Naples, an epidemic of cholera spread rapidly through their ranks, decimating the soldiers, and with the loss of his Italian supporters, the French commander ended the campaign in Italy.

By late 1528, Francis I's ambitions in Italy had again been frustrated, while his two sons still remained prisoners of Charles V in Spain. He then began to search for a peaceful settlement with the Habsburgs. In early 1529, the French monarch's mother, Louise of Savoy, arranged to meet with Charles' aunt, Margaret of Austria, to discuss a possible resolution to the conflict. The two princesses had grown up together in the French court and had formed a close relationship. They met north of Paris at Cambrai on 5 July, and by August an agreement was reached. Under the terms of the Treaty of Cambrai, also known as the Treaty of the Ladies, Francis gave up his claims against the Low Countries and Charles V abandoned his rights to Burgundy for the payment of a large indemnity, while the French king also pledged to marry Eleanor, sister of the emperor. To gain the release of his two sons, he pledged to repudiate his hereditary claims to Italy; once the money for Burgundy was paid, the emperor agreed to release the dauphin and his brother. The French king further approved the transfer of the seized Bourbon properties back to the Habsburgs. The treaty was signed on 3 August, and two days later Francis celebrated the peace in Cambrai Cathedral with his mother and Margaret of Austria.

In compliance with the Treaty of Cambrai negotiated with Charles V, Francis was married in the monastery chapel of Beyries in south-western France to Eleanor on 7 July 1530, and the two long-standing adversaries were now brothers-in-law. At the approach of the wedding date, Eleanor left Spain and was met at the French border by Francis I. She made her official entry into the French kingdom at Bordeaux and was welcomed by city officials and large crowds. On 31 May 1531, she was crowned queen in Paris at the Basilica of St Denis. Eleanor was the favourite sister of the emperor, and Francis utilized her prestige and close association with the imperial regime to promote better relations with the Habsburgs and advance his agenda. However, the king and his new bride were ill-suited to each other, resulting in an unhappy marriage. Francis soon renewed his numerous adulterous affairs with the ladies of the court, developing a special affection and relationship with the Duchess of Etampes, Anne of Pisseleu. Utilizing her close association with the king, Annee acted as his unofficial advisor, influencing his numerous policy decisions. Many nobles and clerics now sought her intervention to utilize her closeness to the king to advance their special programmes. Meanwhile, the marriage between Francis and Eleanor was childless.

In the years following the signing of the Treaty of Madrid, Francis had directed his foreign policy initiatives toward isolating and weakening the power of the Habsburg Empire. In the German regions of Charles' domain, the local lords had become increasingly militant against Habsburg policies, allowing the French monarchy to form alliances in opposition to Charles V's rule. Under the influence of the Valois court, the German magnates established the Schmalkaldic League to expand and protect their regional interests. Francis agreed to back the German rebels to weaken the power of the Habsburg regime and enlarge his presence in their endeavours. He also intervened with financial support for the rebels in Hungary, who were opposing the presence of the Habsburgs. The king's relationship with the German nobles led to diplomatic missions to the Ottoman Empire, encouraging the Turks to attack Charles' eastern borders. To enhance his rapport with England and separate Henry VIII from his continued support of the Habsburgs, Francis openly backed the English king's divorce from the emperor's aunt, Catherine of Aragon, and attempted to influence Pope Clement to gain papal approval for its termination. The foreign policies of Francis were successful in distracting the emperor away from his involvement in France, weakening Charles financially and militarily while depleting imperial resources.

As the French regime pressed its campaign to weaken and isolate the imperialists, by 1536 relations between the Francis I and Charles V had greatly deteriorated, resulting in the renewal of their war. In February, the French invaded the Duchy of Savoy on the south-eastern border of France, which Francis claimed was the rightful possession of his mother. To enforce his inheritance, he assembled an army of over 40,000 soldiers and marched into the duchy. The French quickly overran Savoy, and by the end of March the capital city of Turin had surrendered. With his capture of Savoy, the Valois king was positioned to once again move against Milan.

With Francis again in Italy, Charles V assembled his imperial army to attack the French. On 13 July, the formidable Habsburg forces invaded the French county of Provence, marking the renewal of the Franco-Italian wars. In response to the imperialists' assaults, the king appointed Duke Anne de Montmorency to lead the defence of France. Montmorency was born at the chateau of Chantilly north of Paris on 15 March 1493, the son of William Montmorency and Anne, Countess of Saint- Pot. Through many generations of faithful service to the royal court, the Montmorency family had gained influence, wealth and lands. Anne – so named after his godmother, Anne of Brittany, the wife of French kings Charles VIII and Louis XII – grew up at the French court and was a close childhood friend of Francis. Montmorency was present at the Field of the Cloth of Gold and later served as diplomatic envoy to England. He served in the Italian wars with the French army, participating in the campaigns against Ravenna, Marignano and Pavia, where he won distinction for his leadership and fighting skills. In 1526, he was appointed Grand Master of France, supervising the royal household.

Taking command of the French troops, Montmorency ordered the region of Provence to be evacuated and anything of value to the enemy destroyed. Towns and farmlands were burned and livestock destroyed, leaving a barren land for the invading imperialists. When Charles V entered Provence on 24 July with army of 50,000 men, he found a land deserted and ravaged. In August, he entered the undefended town of Aix and was crowned King of Arles. The imperial forces next advanced against the port city of Marseille, which Montmorency had reinforced with soldiers and artillery. By mid-September, Charles had been unable to break into Marseille and was compelled to abandon his siege. Due to the French scorched earth policy, there was no food for his troops and disease spread rapidly through the army, forcing the emperor to retreat to Spain with his shattered army, ending the campaign. During the withdrawal, over 20,000 soldiers died, with the bodies of men and animals scattered along the roadside.

While Charles V was leading his men into Provence, a second imperial army under the command of the Count of Nassau, William of Dillenburg, invaded Picardy in northern France in July, marching toward Paris. When his forces were detained by the stubborn resistance of the citizen militia at Peronne, and after learning of the imperial withdrawal from Provence, the count retreated across the border to his homeland. As the war continued against the Habsburgs, Francis suffered a painful personal loss on 10 August 1536 when his 18-year-old successor to the French crown, Dauphin Francis, died at Tournon in southern France, after which his younger brother Henry was recognized as heir. The king, who had developed a close association with his eldest son, greatly mourned his death. Conversely, he had maintained strained relations with Henry, whom he considered distant and cold, preferring the company of his youngest son, Charles of Orleans, who was now second in the line of succession.

The conflict with the imperialists continued into 1537, Francis sending troops into Habsburg-occupied Flanders. The Valois troops, under the command of Montmorency, captured the province of Artois in north-western

France and seized many imperial-held towns previously occupied by the French regime. To counter the gains of the French, during the late spring, the Habsburg emperor ordered his forces into Flanders to drive out Montmorency. After several inconclusive skirmishes, a stalemate soon developed, both realms having become war weary. At the intervention of Pope Paul III, a truce was accepted by the warring nations, but this applied only to the conflict in the north, with the fighting in Italy continuing.

While the truce in Flanders was being honoured by France and the Holy Roman Empire, Francis crossed the Alps and seized control of Turin in north-western Italy. The imperialists swiftly counter-attacked, driving the French out of the Piedmont region. In October, the Valois army led by Anne Montmorency and Dauphin Henry attacked the emperor's forces in Piedmont, reconquering most of the province. A standoff then developed, Francis and Charles V signing a truce in mid-November that suspended the fighting in Italy.

In 1538, Pope Paul III personally attempted to mediate a permanent peace between the two belligerents. A peace conference gathered in Nice in June, attended by the pope, the French king and Charles V. The pope conducted a shuttle diplomacy, meeting separately with Francis at his castle and the emperor on board a galley in the harbour. The conferences continued for three weeks but no resolution was found, Francis I being unwilling to abandon his quest for his inheritance of Milan. Despite failing to come to an agreement, the warring rulers conferred at the town of Aigues-Mortes, north-west of Marseille, on 14 July in talks arranged by Queen Eleanor. When the king and emperor met, they embraced each other in friendship. A ten-year truce was quickly negotiated, with France and the Habsburg Empire pledging to defend Christendom and wage war on the Turks in the Mediterranean and Protestant states in Germany. Francis was to retain possession of the Duchy of Savoy and his recently seized Piedmont lands. The French king also agreed to end talks with Henry VIII formulated to forge an alliance against the emperor.

The truce between France and the Habsburg regime continued to be observed, and relations remained friendly. In late 1539, Francis I and Charles arranged to meet in France while the emperor travelled from Spain to quell a rebellion in his Flemish lands. The French king met the emperor at the border, personally escorting him across France to Flanders. As they made their way north through the kingdom, various towns entertained them with grand receptions, banquets, lavish entertainment and tournaments. During their journey, the two rulers renewed their peace talks, but still no permanent resolution was negotiated. Despite the failure to resolve their dispute, the adversaries continued their friendship and pledged to find a permanent peace. In March 1540, Emperor Charles sent a new peace offer to the French regime, proposing the marriage of the king's son, Charles, to his daughter, Mary, with the couple inheriting Flanders and Burgundy. Included in the imperial agreement was Francis' pledge to remove any claims to Italian lands. The Valois king declined the Habsburg proposal and sent an alternative offer, which gave him possession of Milan. The Habsburgs rejected this suggestion but continued the negotiations. By October, no resolution for the succession to the vacant Milanese throne had been found and Charles V ceded the duchy to his son, Philip of Spain, as the threat of renewed war between the two rivals intensified.

During the prolonged period of peace, Francis took the opportunity to rebuild his treasury, military stores and army in preparation for the renewal of the conflict and was confident of victory over the Habsburgs. He launched political initiatives to find allies with the Protestant German warlords and Sultan Suleiman I of the Ottoman Empire. As the French continued diplomatic talks, the emperor sent his fleet to attack the Turks at the town of Algiers, in current-day Algeria, in October 1541. During the voyage across the Mediterranean, the imperial ships were struck by a violent storm destroying most of the fleet and half of the invasion army. To reinforce his offensive against the emperor, Francis sent two envoys to the court of Sultan Suleiman to establish an alliance in opposition to the Habsburgs, but they were intercepted and murdered by agents of Charles V. With the military might of the imperialists weakened by the loss of their fleet and after the killing of his two personal representatives, the French king felt justified in declaring war against the Habsburg Empire.

Upon the dissolution of the Valois and Habsburg detente, Francis I began preparations for the renewal of the war with Charles V. New diplomatic initiatives were undertaken to find allies with the German Protestants, and the army was strengthened with additional troops. In March 1542, the Valois king declared war on the emperor, the French unleashing several sorties against the imperial troops occupying lands in the Low Countries. Meanwhile, an army led by the dauphin advanced across the southern French border and attacked the Spanish-held city of Perpignan. Henry laid siege to the fortification but failed to breach the defensive works and was compelled to retreat.

With his war against King Francis at a standstill, Charles V intensified his negotiations with Henry VIII for a two-pronged invasion of France. In February 1543, an agreement was signed whereby the two allies pledged to attack the Valois kingdom later in the year. Before they could launch their campaign, the French king marched into Flanders, overrunning and occupying several large towns. Charles V was compelled to respond and the Habsburgs advanced against the French, creating another stalemate. While the imperial troops were occupied with the French, Henry VIII sent his forces from the Pale of Calais to support his ally, raiding into the Artois region. At the end of the year, the attacks of the Anglo-Habsburgs and French had achieved little and the war was again at a stalemate.

After their campaigns against Francis failed to force him to pursue a settlement of the war, the English and imperial regimes agreed in late December 1543 to a combined invasion of France, with the emperor advancing toward the west and Henry attacking the Picardy region from Calais. Their goal was the capture of Paris. The two realms mounted their attacks in May 1544, with Charles marching into Luxembourg in the Low Countries, overrunning the duchy and moving on toward Paris, while the English occupied parts of Picardy and laid siege to the port city of Boulogne. When the Habsburgs assaulted Saint Dizier in north-eastern France, the garrison refused to surrender and repelled the repeated assaults of the imperialists, compelling them to besiege the town. The garrison commander finally submitted on 17 August and Charles renewed his march toward Paris, but his invasion had lost its momentum following the delay at Saint Dizier. During the late summer, the French adopted the scorched earth tactic that had previously been successful in Provence. By early autumn, the Habsburg offensive became bogged down, with shortages of money, war supplies and reinforcements forcing Charles to order a withdrawal. Not willing to risk a battle against the imperialists with the English still campaigning to the west, the French king ordered his army not to attack the withdrawing enemy, but closely monitored their movements.

With the emperor retreating, Francis arranged for peace talks to begin with the Habsburgs and English king. The French and imperialists being eager for a quick settlement, the negotiations soon produced the Treaty of Crepy. Under the terms of the treaty, peace between the two realms was re-established, with the status quo honoured. The king's third son, Charles of Orleans, was betrothed to a member of the imperial family, with either Milan or Flanders as the dowry, while Francis pledged to relinquish his rights to Savoy and aid the emperor's campaign against the rebellious German Protestants and the advance of the Ottoman Empire. Francis quickly accepted the treaty, as it gave him the possibility of finally acquiring Milan and ended the threat to his kingdom of a double attack by his two powerful adversaries. Despite the French quickly coming to terms with the

Habsburgs, Henry VIII refused to abandon his siege of Boulogne and the negotiations remained deadlocked.

Meanwhile, in Italy, the conflict was renewed with Francis' army advancing against imperial-held towns, capturing several and seizing Nice, while the Habsburg and Spanish troops moved into Piedmont toward French-occupied Turin. In January 1544, the French army led by Count Francis of Enghien laid siege to the town of Carignano south of Turin. When the emperor sent a relief force to drive off the Valois troops, Enghien left part of his army to maintain the siege and moved against the imperial and Spanish soldiers. The two armies clashed at Ceresole on the outskirts of Turin on 11 April. The French count deployed his 12,000 foot soldiers along the crest of a ridgeline, with the light cavalry on the right wing and the pikemen and arquebusiers positioned in the center, while the left flank was made up of light cavalry and infantry. The Habsburg army of over 20,000 men commanded by Alfonso d'Avalos occupied a location along a parallel ridge. The imperial front faced the enemy with infantry forces on the left and German pikemen in the centre, while Spanish arquebusiers were on the right. The front of the French comprised pikemen, while troops armed with arquebuses were placed in the second line. The battle began with several hours of skirmishes between the arquebusiers, while the artillery exchanged volleys of cannon fire. As the fighting continued, Count Francis' men pushed forward, soon overrunning the enemy on the right and in the centre, but on the left wing Avalos' soldiers gained the advantage, driving the French back in a fierce melee. With his left flank threatening to break, Enghien led his heavy horsemen charging into the Habsburg forces and overwhelmed them, securing victory for the French. Nearly 2,000 Frenchmen were killed or wounded at Ceresole, while Avalos suffered losses of over 5,500.

As Francis and the Habsburgs were concluding negotiations for the end of their war, the army of Henry VIII finally forced the garrison at Boulogne to surrender. The prolonged siege against the port city's fortifications had delayed the English advance against Paris, denying Charles V's army much-needed reinforcements. Following his occupation of Boulogne, the English king ordered the defensive works to be reinforced and garrisoned with a strong force of troops. As the English strengthened their hold on Boulogne, Francis dispatched an army under the dauphin to drive them from the city. Upon reaching the city, Henry of France unleashed several assaults against the reinforced walls and towers, but his soldiers were beaten back. Unable to take Boulogne by storm, the dauphin was compelled to open siege operations. As the siege dragged on into July, Francis sent a fleet of nearly 250 ships and an army of 30,000 men to raid the southern coastline of England. On 21 July 1545, the French troops landed on the Isle of Wight, destroying several towns before the English rallied and beat them back to their ships. Four days later, the French attacked at Seaford, but were again forced to withdraw. When Francis' fleet encountered English ships near Beachy Head, a brief skirmish took place before the French sailed away. By early September, the Anglo-French war had reached a stalemate and peace talks were once again resumed. Following prolonged negotiations, the Treaty of Ardes was signed on 7 June 1546. Under the terms of the agreement, peace was restored between the two kingdoms, Henry VIII pledging to vacate Boulogne for the payment of a large indemnity in gold.

Throughout the thirty-two-year reign of Francis I, his foreign policy had been directed primarily at the quest for the Duchy of Milan. During his campaigns in Italy, he was exposed to the architecture, art, literature and music of the Renaissance movement. Witnessing the grandeur and beauty of the Renaissance, he brought back to his French court artists, scientists, writers and musicians. When the king led his army into Italy on his first campaign against Milan, he met Leonardo da Vinci, persuading him to relocate to France. A house was provided for da Vinci near the royal castle at Amboise in the Loire Valley, and the great artist spent his last years in the employment of Francis. Through the king's association with da Vinci, the French were able to acquire many of his paintings, including the Mona Lisa. To add to his expanding art collection, Francis sent his agents into Italy seeking to purchase paintings and sculptures in the Renaissance style. Many valuable works of art were presented to Francis as gifts from the papacy and numerous Italian lords. The king's private art collection became the core of the Louvre Museum. Francis was a friend and patron of Renaissance arts and letters, energetically seeking to bring noted artists to work and live at his court.

At the French court, the spirit of the Renaissance movement extended to architecture, resulting in the construction of many magnificent chateaux by Francis and his courtiers. The royal palaces at Blois and Amboise were modified to more closely resemble the French Renaissance style. Under instructions from the king, the massive 440-room chateau of Chambord was built in the Loire Valley under the advice of da Vinci to serve as Francis' hunting lodge. The castle was surrounded by a 13,000-acre wooded park and game reserve. The palace at Fontainebleau south of Paris was rebuilt to provide the king with a stately country estate for hunting, and the new chateau of Madrid was constructed on the outskirts of the city in 1527, the castle being richly decorated inside and out with terracotta embellishments.

Francis I's interest in the Renaissance included music, which played an important role in palace life. He invited the most talented composers, musicians and singers of the age to reside at his court, and they provided music for the Church, royal ceremonies and entertainment. The king extended his patronage to the arts with the sponsorship of noted writers; he was especially devoted to poetry and was an avid author of many poems.

During the reign of King Francis I, the New World was discovered by Christopher Columbus in 1492, sailing for Spain. As the stories of great discoveries spread across Europe, the French king took an interest in the exploration of this new land. Through his financial support for new voyages of discovery, France gained rights to territorial claims in the western hemisphere. Money from the royal French treasury funded part of the voyage of Giovanni Verrazzano to the New World in 1524. After sailing across the Atlantic on his ship *La Dauphine*, Verrazzano explored the coastline from present-day North Carolina to Massachusetts looking for the fabled Northwest Passage to the riches of China. The king also paid for the three voyages of Jacques Cartier to search the region beyond Newfoundland, seeking a shorter passageway to the west. Cartier's expeditions travelled along the coastline of Canada, discovering and exploring the Saint Lawrence River. Before launching his second expedition, Cartier was given the *Grande Hermine* by the king to use as his flagship. The voyages of Verrazzano and Cartier gave the French kingdom valid claims to lands that would be colonized in the following century as New France.

As Francis I continued his foreign policy directed against the Habsburg empire and Henry VIII, his health was beginning to rapidly decline. He was frequently ill with infections and high fever, while suffering from the prolonged effects of syphilis. Despite his weakening state, he governed his kingdom with a firm hand, his rule remaining unchallenged. By early March 1547, the king knew his death was imminent and began to prepare for the succession of Henry, by then his only surviving son. He called the dauphin to his bedside, telling him about his failures and attempting to implant what he had learned of kingship. He counselled Henry to reign as a just and good king and to act in the name of God. In the early morning of 31 March 1547, at the chateau of Rambouillet on the outskirts of Paris, King Francis I died after hearing Mass and kissing a crucifix. On 21 May, the king's coffin was taken to the Church of Notre Dame for a short religious service, and the next morning the long funeral cortege set out through crowded streets to the Basilica of St Denis for the last rites at the traditional burial site of the French kings. On 23 May, the coffin was lowered into the vault.

At the death of Francis I, the dauphin succeeded to the throne of France unchallenged as Henry II. As king, he continued his father's policies against the House of Habsburg, sending his armies against imperial-occupied lands. After a failed invasion of Naples in 1557, France and the Habsburgs came to terms, with Henry agreeing to abandon his claims to Milan, finally ending the prolonged Italian wars. He then became involved in the struggle against the rise of Protestantism in France, enacting the Edict of Chateaubriant, which authorized sweeping repressive acts against non-Catholics. Henry II died in 1559 after being wounded during a jousting tournament, and his eldest son, Francis II, was crowned king. During the rule of the new king, the oppressive initiatives against the Protestants were continued, resulting in the Amboise Conspiracy in March 1560. The Huguenot faction rebelled against the young king in an attempt to seize power, but their plot was quickly foiled by the Ultra Catholics. The sickly Francis II died in December that year and was succeeded by his brother, Charles IX. Under the reign of the new king, who came to throne aged just 10, the real power was exercised by his mother, Catherine de Medici, who resumed and intensified the oppressive measures against the Protestants. In 1574, the young Charles IX suddenly died and the throne passed to his brother, Henry III. As the Religious Wars persisted and the Ultra Catholics became more tyrannical, Henry III deserted them and joined forces with Henry of Navarre, who was the leader of the Huguenots and acknowledged successor to the childless French king.

Selected Sources

Frieda, Leonie, *Francis I – The Maker of Modern France*
Hackett, Francis, *Francis The First*
Knecht, R.J., *French Renaissance Monarchy: Francis I & Henry II*
Knecht, R.J., *Renaissance Warrior and Patron – The Reign of Francis I*
Knecht, Robert J., *The Valois – Kings of France 1328–1589*
Potter, David, *A History of France, 1460–1560*
Seward, Desmond, *Prince of the Renaissance – The Life of Francois I*
Wilkinson, Burke, *Francis in All His Glory*

Henry IV

In 1589, Henry III of France was assassinated, and according to Salic Law, the throne was inherited by his cousin, Henry of Navarre. Despite general consensus that Henry was the rightful successor to the crown, the French Catholics refused to acknowledge him as their king, reigniting the bloody and savage Religious Wars. In the aftermath of four years of fighting between the Catholic League and the Huguenots, Henry denounced his Protestant faith on 25 July 1593 and accepted the Catholic religion at a renouncement ceremony in the Basilica of St Denis in Paris. To further secure his acceptance as king by both the Huguenots and Papists, on 27 February 1594 his coronation ceremony was held at the Cathedral of Chartres with both Protestants and Catholics in attendance. By agreeing to accept the Catholic religion and ceremonially receiving the crown of France from the Church, Henry IV gained widespread acceptance as the rightful monarch of France. He made his triumphant entrance into Paris in March 1594 and was enthusiastically welcomed by the city's war-exhausted population. In September 1595, Pope Clement VIII formally revoked his excommunication of Henry, recognizing him as the lawful king, enhancing his sovereignty and weakening the Ultra Papists' opposition. Henry IV could now begin the process of reuniting a kingdom that had been divided and ravaged by more than thirty years of brutal religious civil war.

Henry IV, the first Bourbon French king, was born on 14 December 1553 at the castle of Pau in the small Kingdom of Navarre. His father was Antoine of Bourbon, Duke of Vendome, who was a direct descendent of Louis IX, which placed his son in the line of succession to the French monarchy in the event the House of Valois failed to produce a son. Henry's mother, Joan, was the daughter of the reigning King of Navarre, Henry II, and heiress to his kingdom. Soon after his birth, Henry of Navarre was baptized with the ceremonies of the Catholic Church by the Cardinal of Armagnac. At an early age, he was taken from his mother by the King of Navarre and sent to the castle of Coarraze to be raised in the Pyrenees as a peasant boy. He received no special recognition or treatment for his position as heir to the Navarre crown. The young prince spent over a year at Coarraze until May 1555, when he was returned to the royal court by his mother after King Henry II died. Under Salic Law, at the death of Henry II, his son-in-law, Antoine, succeeded to the monarchy of Navarre through his wife as sole descendant of the king, and Henry of Bourbon now became heir to the throne. Joan continued to raise her son according to her father's wishes, and Henry was sent back to Coarraze, where he was brought up outdoors with the local peasant children. He ran barefoot with the shepherd boys up the mountain trails, wrestled with them, played their games and ate their food of black bread, beef and cheeses. He developed a robust health and strong physical features that would serve him well in the future during his participation in the French Religious Wars.

At the Navarre court, the academic education of Henry was under the direction of his mother, who employed Protestant tutors for the instruction of her son. Queen Joan had converted to the Protestant faith and was an ardent supporter of the new doctrine. Under the queen's orders, her son was taught the Calvinist religion. In addition to religion, the heir to the Navarre crown was instructed in French and Latin, mathematics, history and the classics. In the summer of 1561, the Queen of Navarre sent her son to reside at the French court, where his education was continued in schools provided by the king.

As the First Religious War erupted between the Catholics and followers of the Protestants, Henry's mother, who had accompanied him to Paris, was compelled to leave the royal court and return to Navarre because of her unyielding Calvinist beliefs, while her son remained with his father. Without the protection and influence of Joan of Navarre, Henry now attended Catholic schools with the other noble children, including the future King Henry III and Henry of Guise. At court he became friends with Henry of Guise, who attempted to influence him to join an arch-Catholic faction against the Protestants. In the future, Henry of Guise would become an arch-enemy of the Navarre prince.

As Henry of Navarre remained at the royal court, he witnessed the governing of the regime and was exposed to the art of compromise and moderation. He was part of the entourage that toured France from 1564 with the young King Charles IX over a two-year period. The prolonged excursion gave Henry a visual education in the diversity of France's geography and the opportunity to experience the realm's different lifestyles and customs. The prince of Navarre also observed the statesmanship and manipulations of the monarchy, as the king's officials administered the crown's decrees. While Henry was in Paris, his father died in 1562 from wounds received during the siege of Rouen, fighting for the French against the Spanish in Picardy. At the time of his father's death, Prince Henry was alone in Paris and was distraught at his loss. He was compelled to suffer the grief by himself, while his mother remained in Pau defending her kingdom against an outbreak of rebellion.

After spending over five years at the royal court, Henry returned to Navarre in February 1567 and was reunited with Queen Joan. Under the direct supervision of his mother, he resumed his education and was instructed in the social graces of etiquette, dancing, arts and music. Renowned masters of arms were appointed for his martial training, Henry mastering the skills of a knight fighting with sword, lance, spear and mace from a charging warhorse. As part of his military education, he was exposed to castle warfare, learning the strategies of laying siege, storming a stronghold and leading his men into battle. Henry was obsessed with hunting, which enhanced his fighting instincts and strengthened his endurance.

The Third Religious War broke out in 1569, and the reinforced royal army, nominally led by the king's 17-year-old brother, Henry of Anjou, marched against the Anti-Papists. On 13 March, the royalists collided with the rearguard of the Huguenots at Jarnac. The Catholic force of 27,000 men was personally led by Marshal Gaspard de Tavannes, who sent his cavalry and footmen charging into the Huguenot troops under the command of Prince Louis of Conde. Prince Louis was unable to repel the advancing enemy and was forced to retreat to Cognac. During the fighting, Conde was unhorsed and taken prisoner. Shortly after his capture, he was killed by an officer of the king's guards. As the acknowledged senior prince of the blood, Henry of Navarre was then given command of the Huguenot soldiers, but Queen Joan would not allow her 15-year-old son to accept the offer. The day after the battle, Joan presented Henry to the assembled troops, where he took an oath on his honour and soul never to abandon them. He remained with the army as the religious adversaries continued the civil war with appalling brutality. In Paris, Papist mobs burned Protestant houses and murdered the inhabitants, while Catholic churches were destroyed by the Huguenots. Henry rode with the army and witnessed the barbarism of the war.

In September 1569, the forces of King Charles IX advanced against the Calvinists' castles in an attempt to compel them to seek terms. As the royalists threatened to march against Bearn, Queen Joan and her two children were compelled to abandon the city and take shelter at La Rochelle. Prince Henry soon rejoined the Anti-Papists' army as the nominal head of the troops. As the war resumed, soldiers from Protestant Germany united with the Huguenots, while men from Italy and Spain linked up with the royalists. The king's army now totalled over 30,000 cavalry and foot soldiers, while the Anti-Papists could put 25,000 men into the field.

The Huguenots, now led by Admiral Gaspard II de Coligny, laid siege to the town of Poitiers but were unable to penetrate its defences, and in September abandoned their attack after a six-week campaign. The young prince of Navarre served with the Anti-Papists, gaining an education in leading soldiers into battle. As the Protestants turned south, they collided with the king's forces near the town of Montcontour on 3 October 1569. The royalist army, led by King Charles IX's brother, Henry of Anjou, was made up of 7,000 infantry and 7,500 cavalry, while the Huguenot force comprised 13,000 foot soldiers and 6,000 horsemen. The battle began with a clash between the advance guards, with the Protestants hard-pressed to hold their line and compelled to call for reinforcements. During the fierce fighting, Admiral Coligny led a cavalry charge to stem the advance of the enemy, but was driven back as Henry of Anjou sent his reserves into the melee. The king's Swiss mercenaries then charged into the anti-Catholics, overrunning them and securing victory for the Valois crown. After four hours of fighting, the Huguenots were compelled to retreat, leaving over 4,000 casualties on the battlefield.

Following the defeat of the Huguenots at Montcontour, Admiral Coligny withdrew his battered forces into south-western France, where he was able to recruit replacements. With his army reinforced, the admiral moved north into the Loire Valley toward the small village of Arnay-le-Duc on the road to Paris. During this campaign, Henry of Navarre remained with the Huguenots and continued his military education with his exposure to the operations of the army against the Catholics, learning military tactics and leadership. On 25 June 1570, the Protestants clashed with a much larger Papist army led by Marshal Charles II Cosse, Duke of Brissac. The Huguenot forces comprised approximately 2,000 cavalry and less than 3,000 infantry, while Cosse commanded 13,000 French and Swiss troops. The armies were deployed along rolling hills, with a stream between them. Cosse's men initiated the fighting, advancing to cross the stream, but despite repeated assaults were thrown back by the Protestant arquebusiers and cavalry charges. After his soldiers failed to break the enemy's front, the marshal attempted to outflank Coligny's line, but was again repulsed. The unsuccessful attack against the Protestant flank ended the fighting, with Coligny withdrawing to the town of La Charite on the road to Paris. The inconclusive battle at Arnay-le-Duc convinced King Charles to agree to the Anti-Papists' demands, and the Treaty of the Peace of St Germain was signed on 8 August 1570, ending the Third Religious War. The agreement was highly favourable to the Protestants, who gained additional concessions from the Valois regime. Under the terms of the treaty, the Huguenots were granted the rights to freely practice their religion and hold public office, and possession of four fortified towns was conceded to them. Included in the agreement, Charles IX acknowledged Queen Joan of Navarre and Henry as his loyal relations. Following the signing of the treaty, the Huguenot forces were disbanded and Prince Henry returned to his mother's court in Navarre. Henry's participation in the campaign gave him experience in positioning artillery pieces for battle, sending out reconnaissance patrols, selecting terrain to gain an advantage over the enemy and constructing a fortified position with trenches, obstacles and barricades.

The Treaty of St Germain resulted in nearly two years of reconciliation and peace between the royalists and Huguenots. After the signing of the treaty, Queen Joan and Prince Henry departed from the royal court, returning to Bearn to restore order following their long absence during the Third Religious War. Charles IX was a weak and sickly king, the power behind the throne being his mother, Catherine de Medici. While Henry stayed in Navarre, rumours spread in the court that Admiral de Coligny was negotiating the marriage of the prince to Queen Elizabeth of England. An alliance between the English and French Protestants through the union of Henry and Elizabeth would constitute a great threat to the reigning Valois regime. To counter this danger, Catherine de Medici proposed the marriage of her daughter, Margaret, to Prince Henry of Navarre. When the proposition was presented to Joan of Navarre, she had little interest. Coligny was in favour of the idea and used his influence with the Queen of Navarre to gain her approval, suggesting it would produce a lasting and stronger reconciliation with the French crown. After nearly two years of negotiations, the nuptial agreement was finalized and signed on 11 April 1572. Under the terms of the accord, Henry and Margaret were to retain their present religion, and the Cardinal of Bourbon would perform the marriage ceremony as the uncle of the prince, not as a priest.

Shortly after the marriage treaty was signed, Charles IX invited Queen Joan to travel to Paris and take part in the planning and preparations of the wedding. She willingly agreed and spent three busy weeks in Paris involved with the crafting of the arrangements. When the queen returned home, she was exhausted and confined to bed with a high fever. Joan had been in poor health for several months, and now her strength deteriorated rapidly. Queen Joan died on 9 June 1572, sparking gossip that she had been poisoned by agents of Catherine. Henry was not with his mother when she died and had been slow in making his way to Paris, unaware of her serious illness.

After the death of Joan, there were rumours in Paris spread by the Huguenots that the marriage between Henry, now King of Navarre, and Margaret had been cancelled due to fear of his assassination by the Catholics. When Admiral Coligny spoke out in favour of the nuptial union, the opposition of the Protestants was diluted and Henry entered Paris on 7 July for the ceremony. He was greeted by Catherine de Medici and Charles IX, who welcomed him warmly to the family. The official announcement of the marriage was made on 17 August, and the following day the ceremony took place at Notre Dame, followed by a Mass attended by Margaret but not Henry. Four days of festivities followed, including a grand ball at the Louvre Palace, theatrical performances and a masquerade ball.

Despite the outward appearance of reconciliation between the religious factions, tensions remained high and the danger of violence continued to escalate. Queen Catherine now became concerned about the Valois regime's sustained rule, fearing the Huguenots would stage a rebellion overthrowing her son or the Guise supporters would dethrone the king to take control of the monarchy. Meanwhile, the Guises warned the Parisians to prepare for an outbreak of violence, distributing weapons, and the city was ready for an eruption of carnage. To limit the risk of hostilities, Catherine devised a plot to murder the recognized leader of the Huguenots, Admiral de Coligny. Under the influence of his mother, Charles IX supported the plan and, using his name, arrangements were made for the assassination. On the morning of 22 August, a member of the Guise faction fired two shots from his arquebus, hitting Coligny twice, but the wounds were not fatal. The Protestants then rose up in anger, vowing vengeance.

With the admiral's life in danger, the Huguenots petitioned Charles IX to reinforce the security of his house, which he agreed to arrange. The king ordered his brother, Henry of Anjou, to send additional guards to Coligny's dwelling. The Duke of Anjou dispatched the Gascon commander, Cosseins, who was a personal enemy of the admiral, to lead the detachment of French and Swiss soldiers. Around four o'clock in the morning, Henry of Guise accompanied by a large escort arrived at Coligny's house, and with the troops of Cosseins stormed through the front door, breaking into the admiral's bedroom. He was struck in the head by the butt of a gun and thrown out of the window to the ground. A crowd of men in the street rushed to the admiral's body, mutilating it before dragging him through the streets and throwing the remains into the Seine to ignite the St Bartholomew's Day Massacre.

Close to dawn on 23 August, Charles XI sent a messenger to Henry of Navarre requesting a meeting. Henry quickly dressed and was taken to Charles' palace. While waiting to see the king, he met Louis, Prince of Conde. Together they entered Charles' room, where he was standing with Queen Catherine and his brother, Henry of Anjou. The king, with a dagger in his hand, moved forward toward the King of Navarre and Conde, threatening to stab them, but his mother intervened to prevent their murder.

Meanwhile, royal soldiers were ransacking the Louvre Palace, killing the Huguenot noblemen who had attended Henry's wedding, while the Catholic mob rioted in the streets of Paris, murdering every Protestant they could find. As Henry and Louis of Conde remained prisoners of the French regime, the massacre went on for several days, spreading to some of the outer regions of France. By the end of the violence, more than 3,000 Huguenots had been killed in Paris and 7,000 more in the provinces.

The days immediately following the massacre were dangerous times for Henry of Navarre. When the French king demanded his brother-in-law accept the Catholic religion, he initially refused, but pledged to follow orders in every other way. Charles IX responded by threatening to kill Henry unless he became Catholic, compelling him to agree. Henry was further forced to expel the Protestant ministers from Bearn and appoint a Catholic lieutenant general for his realm. At the demand of the king, Henry participated in the royal siege of the Protestant stronghold at La Rochelle in May 1573. Throughout his ordeal at court, he maintained a cheerful attitude and enjoyed the company of many friends, but was always under the watchful eye of Queen Catherine and her two sons, who could order his imprisonment or death at any time. Remaining in Paris, Henry occupied his days hunting and playing tennis and other sports, while engaging in numerous amorous affairs with the ladies of the court. He spent four years as the virtual prisoner of Charles' regime.

King Charles IX died on 31 May 1574 and was succeeded by his brother, Henry of Anjou. At the time of his brother's death, Henry III was in Poland reigning as sovereign. After the news of Charles' death reached him, he gave up the Polish throne and returned to France. When Henry of Navarre was presented to the new French king by Catherine de Medici, he was greeted as a friend and given his freedom from confinement. Despite the friendship of the king, Henry of Navarre's movements were still closely monitored by the Queen Mother.

After staying in the hostile environment of the Valois court for four years, Henry of Navarre decided to leave Paris. He devised a plan to escape by first disappearing during the night, throwing the palace into a panic when the royal guards could not find him. After waiting several hours, as the queen's men searched for him, he quietly entered the palace, telling Catherine and her son that he would always be their faithful servant. Hoping to have thrown the queen off-guard, he left the palace at dawn on 3 February 1576, riding west towards Poissy with his faithful guards. On 7 February he reached Alencon, where 250 local supporters joined his militiamen. The King of Navarre continued travelling west until reaching Saumur.

While Henry remained in Saumur, the Catholics and Protestants came to terms, ending the Fifth Religious War by signing the Edict of Beaulieu. The Huguenots had assembled an army of over 30,000 men in the vicinity of Paris, threatening Henry III's regime. The presence of the large armed force convinced King Henry and his mother to negotiate with the Anti-Papists. Under the terms of the edict, the Protestants were given the freedom to worship in France, with the exception of Paris, and law courts were now to have an equal number of Catholics and Huguenots to try cases involving the Anti-Papists. The previously confiscated property of the Protestants was to be returned and the king denounced the St Bartholomew's Day Massacre. After the signing of the agreement, Henry of Navarre repudiated his Catholic faith and returned to the Protestant Church, which gained him support from many of the Huguenot warlords. The treaty was highly unpopular with the Catholics, whose uprising against the monarchy allowed Henry of Guise the opportunity to become the leader of the opposition party. Under the leadership of Guise, the Sixth Religious War erupted towards the end of 1576.

The citizens of Peronne in Picardy were the first to rebel against the terms of the Edict of Beaulieu when the Protestant Henry of Conde was reappointed to the province as royal governor. Unwilling to be ruled by a 'heretic', the residents formed the Catholic League to resist the Huguenots and maintain the rights of the Church of Rome. Under the leadership of Duke Henry of Guise, the Catholic League developed into a serious threat to the French monarchy, receiving subsidies from Spain and the support of the Holy See to conduct a campaign to discredit Henry III's regime. The league accused the king of being too tolerant of the Anti-Papists. Under attack by Henry of Guise and his brother, Henry III now willingly allowed the Leaguers to increase their influence over his kingdom and his policies against the Protestants. In 1577, the king became head of the Holy League, but the power remained in the hands of Henry of Guise and his brother, Louis, Cardinal of Lorraine.

Under the terms of the Treaty of Beaulieu, Henry of Navarre had been appointed royal governor for Gascony in south-western France. Taking the reins of power, he established his governing council in Bearn. He spent little time in the town, being occupied travelling throughout the province executing the crown's will and justice. Poverty was widespread in Gascony due to the effects of the religious wars and the resulting political instability. Henry introduced a policy of moderation and patience, slowly gaining the support of the Catholics and Protestants. To secure his province against internal rebellion, he established loyal garrisons in strategic towns and pressed upon his people that they were all subjects of the king and under his royal authority.

While Henry of Navarre travelled through Gascony solidifying the peace and his government, in Paris Henry III established the Catholic League throughout his kingdom and reinforced his army for the renewal of the religious wars. On 16 January 1577, he disavowed the Edict of Beaulieu, after which fighting between the Huguenots and Papists soon broke out. The royal forces quickly gained the initiative, and throughout the year slowly overwhelmed numerous Huguenot towns. When the Protestant stronghold at Languedoc surrendered in September, peace negotiations were begun and a treaty was soon signed. The resulting Edict of Poitiers eliminated many of the concessions earlier granted to the Anti-Papists, who lost the freedom of worship, while the Catholics pledged to abolish their Holy League. In the Huguenot provinces, the royal-appointed administrators lost most of their independent rule, Henry of Navarre claiming he was now governor in name only. Despite supporting the Edict of Poitiers, fighting in the provinces erupted again as Anti-Papist warbands terrorized the countryside, leaving many towns in ruins.

Soon after the signing of the Edict of Poitiers, Henry of Navarre left the Gascony court and returned to his chateau at Nerac. The Renaissance-style chateau had been built by Henry's ancestors and was a favourite residence of his father, who created a magnificent park along the river. Here he was occupied with the pleasures of a country gentleman, hunting in the surrounding thick woodlands, playing his favourite game of tennis and pursuing numerous romantic affairs. Henry of Navarre frequently attended parties and balls and was a much sought-after guest.

In early October 1578, Queen Catherine travelled to Nerac with Margaret to reconcile her daughter's marriage to Henry. The south-west region of France remained in turmoil following the Treaty of Poitiers, and the Queen Mother wanted to bring peace to the populace by initiating a new royal policy toward the Protestants. However, the journey to Nerac with Margaret served as a ruse to permit Catherine to collect information in secret for the best policy to pursue the Huguenots. Margaret had no desire to leave the grandeur of Paris for a provincial court and had no interest in reuniting with her husband, while Henry shared her feelings. At his Nerac court, he had numerous mistresses and greatly enjoyed his unencumbered life. While Margaret remained with Henry at his small country palace, Catherine was negotiating with the Anti-Papists and Catholics in Gascony. The Protestants presented a long list of demands, which were swiftly rejected. The King of Navarre intervened, proposing a policy of moderation, which enticed the Huguenots to reduce their ultimatums. In spite of showing a willingness to restrain their demands, they insisted upon freedom of worship and possession of additional towns. The Queen Mother agreed to give the Huguenots fifteen more towns, but refused to grant them self-determination of religion. The Protestant delegates agreed to the proposed conditions, and on 21 February 1579 the Treaty of Nerac was signed.

Catherine de Medici was satisfied with her treaty and soon departed from Nerac for Paris, leaving her daughter with Henry. Margaret became mistress of the house and completely refurnished the interior in the latest style, with large tapestries and mirrors, while new cooks took over the kitchen, preparing a wide variety of rich foods. The result of Margaret's changes was a household of ceremony and pomp, which Henry of Navarre strongly disliked. They now lived separate lives, with their own numerous amorous affairs. Despite having little contact with her husband, when he became seriously ill with a high fever at the town of Eauze, Margaret left Nerac and rushed to his bedside, remaining with him for seventeen days while he recovered his health.

The towns occupied by the Huguenots under the terms of their recent treaties with the royal court were for only a limited time period and by the spring of 1580 they were due to be returned to the Catholics. The Anti-Papists refused to abide by the conditions of the agreement, and on 28 May made preparations to besiege the town of Cahors in south-west France. Henry of Navarre was given command of the Huguenot army and advanced against the Catholic-occupied town. Cahors was defended by a strong garrison and protected on three sides by a river. The inhabitants were pro-Catholic and strongly supported their garrison. Henry launched his attack during a violent storm, sending his men to place small bombs at a gate protecting the bridge crossing the river to Cahors. When the bombs exploded, the Catholics assumed the sound was from the raging storm, allowing Henry's soldiers to break through the gate into the town. The Papist troops quickly rallied, and with support from the residents, who had been issued weapons, fought the Protestants in the streets for four days before surrendering. Henry of Navarre personally led his men in the fighting, encouraging them to victory.

The Battle of Cahors was the only significant encounter of the Seventh Religious War, and in late 1580 peace talks began in the town of Fleix. An agreement was soon signed, with the Huguenots only gaining a six-month extension for their possession of the castles granted in the Treaty of Nerac. In November 1583, the time period for the Protestants' occupation of the towns granted under several edicts was about to expire. Negotiations between the Anti-Papists and Catholics had been held in Paris, but to little effect. As the talks remained at an impasse, Henry of Navarre captured the Catholic-held town of Mont de Marsan. The French king countered by occupying three other towns and ending the peace conference, sending the King of Navarre's delegation back to Gascony. Henry III soon had second thoughts about his decision, and quickly reinstated the negotiations, while withdrawing the royal troops from the recently seized regions to return to the status quo.

As the negotiations to resolve the religious conflict continued, in June 1584 the acknowledged heir to the French crown, Francis of Anjou, died; under Salic Law, Henry of Navarre now became the successor to the throne. After six years of marriage, King Henry III and Queen Louise had no children, and there was little likelihood they would provide a male inheritor. The Papists, led by Duke Henry of Guise, strongly opposed the King of Navarre's assumption of the French monarchy and transformed the Catholic League to defend their religious interests. Henry III refused to support the radical league's policies and attempted to convince his brother-in-law to return to the Church of Rome. Despite the monarch's personal interventions, Henry of Navarre refused to accept the Catholic faith, knowing it would mean the loss of his Huguenot allies, while the Papists would likely still remain his enemy. To maintain peace with the Anti-Catholics, Henry III extended the date for the return of their castles to Catholic control by two years and granted several additional concessions to counter the growing popularity and power of the Catholic League. In spite of the French king's personal involvement, his initiatives only further alienated Henry of Guise's followers.

In 1585, Pope Sixtus V succeeded to the papal throne, increasing tensions in France further by excommunicating Henry of Navarre, declaring him incapable of ruling over France. The Huguenots reacted to the papal bull by accusing the pontiff of heresy and calling him a liar. With the danger of war's renewal escalating, the Catholic League recruited three new armies to oppose King Henry of Navarre and the Protestants. Henry of Guise led an army on the kingdom's eastern border to defend against marauding bands of mercenary troops sent by German princes in support of the French

Huguenots. A second military force was dispatched to deal with the Anti-Catholics in Gascony, while a third was deployed to protect Paris.

Independent of the king's approval, the Catholic League began launching attacks against Protestant strongholds. The Leaguers quickly overran many Anti-Papist towns to gain near total control of the area north of the Loire. The Catholic forces under the command of Henry of Guise were becoming renowned for their fighting skills and a growing threat to the reign of King Henry III, as the Duke of Guise actively pursued a change in the French monarchy under his family's rule. To gain Catholic League support, Henry III was compelled to sign the Treaty of Nemours, which ended the crown's policy of fostering religious tolerance and compromise with the Huguenots, resulting in the reduction of sympathy between the warring factions. Acting in the name of her son, Catherine de Medici had negotiated the treaty with representatives of the Guise faction and the agreement was signed on 13 July 1585. Under the terms of the treaty, all prior edicts were voided, the Huguenots were dismissed from royal offices and the Church of Rome was acknowledged as the only religion in France.

As Franc moved closer to the outbreak of war, Henry of Navarre left Gascony and established his new headquarters in Saintonge province to direct the Protestant war effort. Under Henry's orders, the Huguenots seized twenty Catholic-held towns, strengthening their rule over the region. The Papists' forces in the southwest of France were led by Anne, Duke of Joyeuse, and as he moved his royalist army to intercept Henry's advancing troops, he clashed with the Protestants near the village of Coutras on 20 October 1587. Henry of Navarre deployed his troops along a hilltop, with his left flank shielded by a river and his right blocked by dense woodlands. He arrayed his artillery on the summit of the hill and the infantrymen were placed behind the line of cannons. As the morning sun broke over the horizon, Joyeuse launched his assault, sending his foot soldiers up the hill toward Henry's position. The Protestants' artillery and arquebusiers opened fire on the approaching Catholics, decimating their ranks and driving them back. The Catholic forces were routed, with over 2,000 dead and most of the army's commanders killed, including the Duke of Joyeuse. In the wake of his victory at Coutras, Henry returned to his Navarre kingdom, remaining there for nearly a year involved with hunting and his new love affairs, while King Henry III and Henry of Guise fought for the throne of France in the War of the Three Henrys.

In May 1588, Duke Henry of Guise travelled to Paris seeking reconciliation with the king. The negotiations quickly broke down and, fearing for his life, Henry III fled to Chartres. The warring parties resumed their talks, and the king was forced to grant additional concessions to the Catholic League and name only a Catholic as his heir designate. To ratify the agreement, the Estates General was summoned to Blois in December. Supporters of the Catholic League dominated the assembly and the king made little progress in reasserting his authority. Under the influence of the league, the delegates voted to reduce the powers of the king in favour of Henry of Guise. With all his options exhausted and the fear of a Guise coup escalating, Henry III was forced to protect his monarchy by arranging the assassination of his rival. On 23 December, at the chateau of Blois, the royal bodyguards – known as the Forty-Five – stabbed the duke to death as the king looked on. The murder of the duke's brother, Cardinal Louis of Lorraine, and the arrest of numerous leaders of the Catholic League followed on the next day. The bodies of the Duke of Guise and his brother were burned and their ashes scattered.

In the aftermath of the murders, rioting by the Catholics erupted in Paris. Large groups of Papists marched through the streets of the city, denouncing the king and calling for his overthrow. A Catholic council was formed and governed Paris, while repudiating the king. With his rule now reduced to a few towns in the Loire Valley, King Henry III was forced to summon Henry of Navarre to confer at the chateau of Plessis-les-Tours. On 13 April 1589, Duke Henry rode to the chateau with a small escort, and during his meeting with the king he forged an alliance against the Catholic League. At the conference, the French king disavowed the recent decrees of the Estates General and agreed to recognize his brother-in-law as his successor designate, while Henry of Navarre pledged to support freedom of religion in the kingdom.

Following his conference with the monarch, Henry took command of the combined armies and marched against the Catholic League supporters in Paris. As he led the siege of the capital, a young monk named Jacques Clement gained access to Henry III at his court in St Cloud through a forged letter of introduction. He claimed to have a secret message for Henry, and as he approached him drew a knife from his sleeve, mortally stabbing the king in the lower abdomen. Henry cried out: 'This wicked monk has killed me; kill him!' The assassin was quickly slain and his body burned, with the ashes thrown into the Seine. Before dying, King Henry commanded his courtiers to acknowledge Henry of Navarre as his successor, ending the Valois line of sovereigns and beginning the reign of the House of Bourbon.

When the Duke of Navarre reached St Cloud, the king was already dead and he was recognized as Henry IV, heir to the French crown, by the courtiers. Despite the acclamation of his rule by the court, Henry's acceptance as king was mostly in name only throughout France. To calm fears, on 4 August he issued a proclamation promising to retain the Church of Rome in his kingdom and limit the Huguenots' freedom of religion to the edicts already granted by the Valois monarchs. Many of the Catholics still rejected Henry IV as their king, with large parts of the army refusing to fight for a heretic. To press his inheritance rights, the new king mustered his depleted army and marched into Normandy – the 'bread basket of Paris' – to threaten the capital's food supply. The royal forces had declined to less than 7,000 troops, and a defeat now by the Catholics would likely mean the end of Henry's monarchy. The king faced a formidable task of quelling the danger of the Catholic League's army, which had received thousands of new volunteers, while the Cardinal of Bourbon had been named King Charles X by the Papists.

The Catholic League now held power over the north and east of France, as the people rallied to its struggle against the 'usurper' Henry IV. Although the Cardinal of Bourbon had been appointed French king by the Catholics, he served only as a figurehead for the Duke of Mayenne, Charles of Lorraine, who held the real reins of power. Charles, the second son of Francis of Guise and Anna d'Este, was born on 26 March 1554 at Alencon. During his youth, he was closely associated with the royal court and was a supporter of the king's brother, Henry of Anjou, the future King Henry III. In 1572, he left France and served with the Christian army fighting the Turks in Greece. When the Duke of Anjou was elected to the throne of Poland, Charles accompanied him to Warsaw. Charles remained away from France for only a brief period before returning to join his brother in the war against the Huguenots. In 1577, he led a Catholic army in Poitou that defeated the Protestants. Charles was named governor for Burgundy and promoted the cause of the Catholic League in his province. When Henry of Guise was assassinated at the chateau of Blois in December 1588, Charles became head of the Catholic party and continued the war against Henry of Navarre.

Meanwhile, outside the borders of France, Philip II of Spain had ambitions for the French crown, while neighboring Savoy and the Low Countries sought to expand their territories into Henry IV's realm. Fearing a larger and more powerful Catholic-ruled France, the Protestant realms of England and the Netherlands threw their support behind Henry IV, sending troops and money for his war against the Papists.

To defend his rule, the French king advanced his army into Normandy, gaining control of Dieppe and establishing his headquarters for the fight against the Catholics of Charles of Lorraine. Henry constructed a fortified position near the village of Arques, south of Dieppe, to repel the attack of the Catholic League. Henry deployed his troops along a hillside, with pikemen and arquebusiers in the trenches and cavalry in the rear. Henry commanded an army of approximately 1,200 mounted men and 4,000 infantry, including a detachment of Swiss pikemen, and faced a much larger force of over 20,000 soldiers led by Duke Charles of Mayenne. The Catholic forces appeared near Dieppe in mid-September 1589, and after making a reconnaissance of the Huguenots' deployment unleashed their attack against Arques on 21 September. In the early morning mist, a large detachment of hired German pikemen performed a ruse by shouting to Henry's Swiss mercenaries that they would not fight against fellow Protestants, but once they were allowed to enter the Huguenot camp the Germans attacked those inside, overrunning the first line of the anti-Papist defences. With his front in danger of collapse, Henry IV led his cavalry in a charge against Charles of Lorraine's horsemen on the flanks, driving them back in a fierce encounter with swords and pistols. As the Catholic League's mounted troops withdrew, the Huguenot pikemen advanced, with their artillery blowing large gaps in Mayenne's infantry formations, which also pulled back.

Unable to defeat Henry IV at Arques, the Catholics withdrew to attack Protestant-occupied Dieppe, but were again thrown back. Mayenne abandoned the campaign on 6 October. Shortly after the Catholic retreat, Henry's army was reinforced with additional royalist troops and 4,000 English soldiers from Queen Elizabeth I in support of her Protestant friends. After defeating the Catholics near Arques, the French king moved his reinforced army, now comprising over 15,000 men, toward Paris in a bid to capture the city before Charles of Mayenne arrived to strengthen the garrison. Henry reached Paris on 31 October, ahead of the Papists, and stormed the outer districts on the left bank. The cold and wet weather had made the Seine impassable, and when the Catholic army arrived on 2 November, Henry was compelled to abandon the attack against the capital and return to his campaign in Normandy.

With the Catholic army remaining in Paris, the Huguenots unleashed attacks against towns in Normandy, occupying many of them in a lightning campaign. As the Protestants continued to expand the lands under their authority, elsewhere in the provinces the Catholic warlords and their people began to renounce their support for the puppet king, Charles X, declaring for the Bourbon regime of Henry IV. Henry aggressively adopted and promoted a religious policy of tolerance and moderation that set the foundation for his acceptance as monarch by all French factions. Paris, however, remained a stronghold of support for Charles X and was the ultimate military objective of the Huguenot war effort.

In the spring of 1590, King Henry resumed his campaign of conquest, storming numerous Catholic-controlled towns in the vicinity of Paris to deny reinforcements and supplies to the city and force the Catholic League's army into a decisive battle. In March, the royalist troops were 40 miles east of Paris, preparing to invest the town of Dreux, when Charles of Mayenne's forces, newly reinforced with Spanish soldiers from Flanders, moved from the capital to relieve the siege. The two armies clashed on the plain of St Andre, near the town of Ivry, on 14 March. Henry IV had been reinforced with further English troops sent by Queen Elizabeth and now commanded over 8,000 pikemen and arquebusiers plus 3,000 mounted soldiers armed with swords and pistols, while Duke Charles had 15,000 infantry and 4,000 cavalry. The Huguenot troops were deployed along a line facing their enemy. After an artillery exchange, the French king led his cavalry in a charge against the Catholic horsemen. The Huguenot mounted soldiers galloped into the centre of the Catholic League formation, first firing their pistols before drawing their swords and crashing into the duke's troops, driving them back all along the line. Meanwhile, Henry's arquebusiers fired volley after volley into Mayenne's pikemen. The Papists, under heavy pressure, broke and fled the battlefield, leaving behind nearly 4,000 dead. Charles of Mayenne escaped with the remnants of his shattered army towards Paris, with the royalists in close pursuit and continuing to assail the enemy, leaving the bodies of Catholics scattered across the countryside.

The defeat of the Catholic League at Ivry weakened the defences of Paris, and in mid-May Henry IV returned to besiege the city, his 15,000-strong force blocking all access. The Catholics' field army had been battered and the city's stock of provisions and supplies was inadequate to withstand a prolonged siege. Although Henry's soldiers were denied entry into Paris, the beleaguered city suffered greatly with over 13,000 inhabitants dying of starvation. As the Catholic garrison continued to hold the king's forces in check, Duke Charles of Lorraine was in Flanders negotiating with Philip II of Spain for the intervention of a Spanish army, led by Alexander Farnese, Duke of Parma and governor of the Low Countries. An agreement was arranged and Farnese was sent with 14,000 men to relieve the siege of Paris. The Spanish duke united his army with that of Mayenne, which had been augmented with fanatic Catholic citizens who had risen up against the 'heretic' troops of Henry IV. Now opposed by more than 25,000 soldiers, Henry lifted the siege and withdrew to spend the winter in northern France.

From his headquarters in the north, the French king sent envoys to Queen Elizabeth's English court and the German Protestants seeking reinforcements, war supplies and financial aid for the war against the Catholics. During the winter months, Huguenot soldiers mounted attacks against the Papist towns surrounding Paris, slowing the flow of troops and supplies into the capital. In April 1591, Henry IV's men stormed the city of Chartres after a siege of two months. The capture of Chartres reduced the supply of grain to Paris and was a major loss to the city, as the Protestant ring around it continued to tighten. As a result of his winter diplomatic initiative, by the summer King Henry's army was augmented with English, Dutch and German anti-Papist troops. Meanwhile, across France, Huguenots launched independent campaigns against the Catholics, expanding the territory under Henry's rule as the offensive against the Catholic League gained momentum.

As Henry IV continued his conquest of Papist-occupied towns in northern France, the Catholic League became beset with internal discord in Paris. The more liberal and conservative factions openly fought against each other for control of the ruling council. Support for Duke Charles of Mayenne fell to a new low, allowing the extremists to secure power and push their campaign for a strong Catholic monarchy. Through the summer months, dissent worsened, and in November the radicals murdered three opposition leaders in the so-called Seize of Paris. The Seize was a council of sixteen members, whose goal was to establish a weak monarchy which they could dominate. As the Seize continued to take power, the Duke of Mayenne surrounded the council in the Bastille in December, dissolving it and placing moderates in the government.

While the Catholic parties fought against each other for control of their administration, Henry IV opened a new campaign for the conquest of Normandy. The Huguenots occupied many Catholic League towns before advancing against the strongly defended city of Rouen. The garrison had been recently reinforced and its defensive works strengthened. When King Henry called upon the Catholic troops to surrender, the defenders replied they would rather die than accept a heretic as king. The residents of Rouen paraded in the streets, carrying white candles in support of the Church of Rome and in opposition to the Protestants. The siege wore-on until 24 February 1592, when the Huguenots were compelled to withdraw following a sortie by the garrison, which overran many of their defensive positions.

Meanwhile, Henry IV took 7,000 cavalry and moved out to intercept the fast-approaching forces of the Duke of Parma before his army of 29,000 men could relieve the siege. He clashed with Farnese at Aumale, near the

Bresle River in north-east Normandy. Leading his horsemen, Henry boldly charged into the enemy. As the royalists fought the Catholic mounted troops, Farnese sent a unit of light cavalry to attack Henry's flanks. With his escape route threatened, Henry was forced into a fighting retreat. During the withdrawal he was wounded in the lower abdomen by a bullet from an arquebusier, but despite the pain he made his way back to his army. The king had to be carried in a litter for several days, but soon recovered from his wound.

Meanwhile, the commander of the garrison at Rouen led a sortie from the town, charging into the besieging Huguenots, destroying most of their supplies. Farnese reached Rouen soon after and forced the Protestant troops to abandon their siege. With Henry's men now falling back, Farnese advanced to Caudebec to attack him, but became trapped by Protestant troops on an island in the Seine during April and May 1592. When his outer works were taken by the Huguenots, Farnese was compelled to force a crossing of the river. He collected all the flatboats and ferries along the river bank and, after positioning his artillery to cover the passage, directed his soldiers to the far bank. During the battle, the Duke of Farnese was wounded, dying from his injuries in early December.

Following the clash at Caudebec, Henry IV led his army against Mayenne, who took command of the Catholic forces after Farnese was wounded, and became trapped at Yvetoland. During the fighting against the Papists, the Protestants inflicted over 3,000 casualties on their opponents. The recent clashes against the Catholics had left Henry's army exhausted and his supplies depleted. He attempted to renew his campaign in north-western France, but with little success. During the remainder of 1592, the forces of the Catholic League continued to fight with the royalists for possession of towns and territory, but with inconclusive results.

The year ended with the Protestants increasingly doubtful of achieving final victory against the Papists. In January 1593, the leader of the Catholic League, Charles of Mayenne, summoned the Estates General. Many of the assembled members had become war weary, disliked the dependence on foreign nations for money and soldiers and strongly opposed the growing influence of Spain in French affairs. The delegates were eager to resolve the war peacefully, prompting the assembly to reopen peace talks with Henry IV. The king, also desirous of achieving a reconciliation, agreed to send a delegation to the assembly. The representatives gathered in May, when it soon became apparent that the king's Protestant beliefs were the major issue prohibiting the Catholic party from accepting his reign. The members of the Catholic faction acknowledged that under Salic Law

Henry IV was the lawful heir to the French throne, but they could never accept a heretic as their sovereign. It was now apparent to Henry that the only pathway to peace was through renouncement of his Protestant faith. On 25 July 1593, at the Basilica of St Denis, the king entered the church dressed in all white satin and formally repudiated his religion, accepting the Church of Rome's teachings. To augment his acceptance and legitimization as king of a united France, Henry IV's coronation ceremony was performed at Chartres Cathedral on 25 February 1594 before the gathered Catholics and Huguenots. The anointment service had been temporarily delayed until a substitute for the sacred oil used in the ceremony could be located. The urn used to consecrate most of the French kings since 496 was in the Catholic League's possession at Rheims. After searching the churches, the monks at St Martin in Tours discovered an alternative, which they claimed was even older and more sacred than the chalice at Rheims.

With the sacred oil now in the possession of the Church, Henry travelled to Chartres for his crowning as king. After entering the church, Henry solemnly walked to the altar, surrounded by six lay and six spiritual peers of France, and kissed the sword of Emperor Charlemagne. He then lay prostrate before the altar as the Bishop of Chartres prayed over him and anointed his head and body with holy oil. The sceptre was given to the king by the great lords of France, after which the bishop took the crown from the altar and placed it on the monarch's head as the congregation shouted, 'Long live the king!' Drums, bugles and fifes then played, while cannons and musketeers fired volleys and courtiers threw gold and silver coins to the audience. This was followed by a High Mass and the singing of the Te Deum. The coronation service ended with a grand banquet. Following over thirty years of religious wars, the king could now begin the process of unifying his battered kingdom under his rule.

Following Henry IV's anointment as King of French, towns across the kingdom revolted against their Catholic lords and accepted him as their overlord. Paris remained non-submissive, and in early 1595 a student attempted to stab the king with a knife, but Henry quickly moved aside, avoiding the attacker and suffering only a minor wound. Henry's conversion to the Church of Rome convinced many members of the Catholic League to end their religious war and acknowledge him as their sovereign. To secure the allegiance of the great French warlords of the Catholic League, he issued grants of titles, government offices and money in exchange for their pledges of obedience and support. The king personally negotiated with many of the Catholic fortified towns to gain their acceptance of his reign. In the regions that refused to agree to his rule, the citizens rebelled against their local officials and gave their loyalty to the throne. By the end of 1595, most of northern France was under the authority of the king's government. Henry IV's position as a Catholic and king was further strengthened in September 1597 when Pope Clement VIII revoked his excommunication and recognized him as the lawful ruler of France. The Protestants in the south of the realm were disappointed by his acceptance of the Catholic Church but remained loyal, and their beliefs were solidified when the regime issued the Edict of Nantes in 1598, which confirmed their rights of religious liberty.

In the early morning of 18 March 1598, King Henry IV rode quietly into Paris, and after nearing Notre Dame Cathedral was greeted by a large crowd, which cried out, 'Long live the king!' He entered the cathedral to attend a Mass of Thanksgiving presided over by the archbishop. Following the sermon, the service ended with the singing of the Te Deum. The king then announced a pardon for the city and issued a proclamation granting a general amnesty. The news was greeted with wild cheers from the assembled citizens, church bells ringing out across Paris. That afternoon, the Spanish garrison marched out of the city and Henry peacefully reoccupied what had been the centre of the Catholic League's power.

With most of France recognizing his monarchy and Philip II still a threat to his reign, Henry IV declared war against Spain in January 1595. The Spanish king had relentlessly supported the Catholic League in its war against the Huguenots, providing troops, war supplies and money. After receiving the news of France's call to arms, Philip II immediately began preparations to invade France. During the summer of 1595, Henry was attacked on five separate fronts, with the greatest danger coming from the east. As 12,000 Spanish and Catholic League soldiers led by Don Fernando of Velasco and Charles of Lorraine, the Duke of Mayenne, moved into the Franche-Comte region of eastern France, the king took command of his forces and advanced against them. On 5 June, while making a reconnaissance of the enemy's position with his scouts, he encountered the army of Velasco and Charles of Lorraine. When several of his men and his marshal, Charles de Gontaut, Duke of Biron, were surrounded, Henry charged forward with his escort and clashed with the Spaniards. In the ensuing melee, the king was nearly killed several times by bullets from the musketeers, but as the battle continued his men drove the Spaniards back. As the remainder of his army arrived, Henry led his troops into the fray, chasing Velasco and Lorraine from the field. The Spanish forces were withdrawn by Velasco, having suffered heavy casualties, while the French incurred less than 3,200 dead and wounded. After the decisive French victory at Fontaine-Francaise,

Philip II was compelled to pull his army back from the region, allowing the king to bring the whole of Burgundy back under his rule. The Spanish continued to occupy towns in northern France, but over the next year, Henry's troops were slowly able to drive the invaders out of Picardy. The war now became a fight for the border towns and strongholds.

In early November 1595, Henry led his army into north-western France near the border with the Low Countries to besiege La Fere. The fortified town was the supply depot for the artillery, munitions and war supplies utilized by the Spanish soldiers in France, and its capture would be a significant loss to them. The stronghold was surrounded by marshlands and defended by a large garrison. The French maintained the siege through the winter, but the Spanish retained possession of the fortress. In March 1596, the Austrian governor of the Low Countries marched his forces against the besiegers, but was repelled by King Henry's men. After his failure to relieve the garrison, the governor seized the French-occupied city of Calais on 17 April. Henry refused to abandon his attack at La Fere, allowing the Spaniards to take several additional towns. Finally, on 22 May, La Fere surrendered, freeing the French troops to rebuild the defences of the border provinces.

While Henry IV was defending the borders of France against invasion, roving bands of brigands attacked isolated towns in the south-east of the kingdom, killing many men and raping women. As the marauders ravaged the countryside, the inhabitants of the village of Croc rose up against the plundering of their farmlands and the excessive taxation of the nobles in the Croquants Revolt. The Croquants supported Henry IV against the Catholic League and the warlords who supported it. Under increased pressure from the crown for additional funds to finance the war against the Catholics and the invading Spaniards, the lords pressed their subjects for more tax. To repel the attacks of the brigands and magnates, the some 20,000 peasants – armed with muskets and pikes – advanced against the bands of Leaguers and Spaniards, In the aftermath of inconclusive fighting, the peasant soldiers dispersed, ending their uprising. The peasants swore allegiance to the king and received his pardon and pledge to investigate the abuses of the nobles and tax collectors. Henry carried out several reforms in support of the Croquants, reducing their taxes and the confiscation of their crops and stock for non-payment. Despite the disbandment of the farmers, the kingdom remained under threat of assault by the bandits, even in regions free of Spanish and Catholic League forces.

Henry IV was hard pressed to find new sources of revenue to finance his war against the Spanish incursions into France. Several attempts were made to find more money from the nobles, but were largely unsuccessful. While the king remained in Paris with his mistress, Gabrielle d'Estrees, the Spanish seized Amiens and spent three days sacking the capital of Picardy. When informed of the Spanish occupation of Amiens, the king shouted to his courtiers: 'I will have that town back or die!' He managed to borrow money from the magnates of Rouen and made plans to retake Amiens. The king assembled his army near Amiens and laid siege to the town. While the investment continued, troops of King Philip II attacked several French-occupied towns but were unable to capture any of them. During the siege of Amiens, the French king reorganized his army, creating a permanent military force. He put the troops of Picardy, Champagne and Gascony on a permanent basis, along with the regiments from Piedmont. Each battalion comprised veteran musketeers and pikemen. In July 1597, Henry was back at Amiens with his soldiers and on the seventeenth of the month fought alongside his troops to repulse a sortie by the town's garrison. When Philip sent a relief force toward Amiens, Henry led his men, beating them back. Finally, on 25 September, the town surrendered to the French king.

By 1598, the Spanish invasion into France was in shambles as Philip II's war effort faltered on every front. In the Low Countries, Dutch forces continued to overpower Philip's troops, while the Spanish ally, Duke Charles Emanuel of Savoy, had been defeated by the French. The Spanish king suffered a disastrous loss when a large naval force sailing for Ireland was destroyed by violent storms. After the Spanish army failed to hold any of Henry IV's territory, the leader of the Catholic League, Charles of Lorraine, agreed to acknowledge King Henry as the rightful monarch of France. The Duke of Mayenne's acceptance of the king's reign caused many of the Catholic League's extremists to also recognize the kingship of Henry. On 2 May 1598, envoys from Philip II of Spain and Henry IV signed the Treaty of Vervins, which had been negotiated under the sponsorship of Pope Clement VIII's legate. Under the terms of the agreement, the Spanish recognized Henry IV as King of France and withdrew their soldiers from his territory. The Spanish king also pledged to end his support of the Catholic League. The city of Calais and fortress at Risban, which had been recently captured by Spanish troops, were returned to the crown, and the French kingdom was to retain its borders of 1559.

By 1598, the French king still had no direct successor to his throne. Henry and Queen Margaret had been separated for many years, with no prospects of reconciliation. When a search was made of the available European princesses for a suitable wife, Henry showed little enthusiasm, preferring to continue his romantic liaison with Gabriella d'Estrees, with whom he had a relationship for many years. It was only after the sudden death of his mistress in 1599 that Henry began to consider marriage to Marie de Medici, the daughter of the Grand Duke of Tuscany, Francesco I. Marie was born in Florence at the Pitti Palace on 26 April 1575, the daughter of Grand Duke Francesco and Archduchess Joanna of Austria. She had five sisters and one brother, but only Marie and her older sister, Eleonora, survived into adulthood. Marie was raised at the Pitti Palace, where she received a well-rounded education, studying reading, writing, science, mathematics and philosophy. She was trained in the arts by local Florentine artists, while learning to play the lute and guitar.

Henry IV had earlier conspired to find favourable conditions that allowed him to divorce Margaret and marry Gabriella, but his mistress's premature death turned his attention to Marie. A delegation was sent to Rome to secure a divorce from his wife, while negotiations for the marriage were finalized with the Duke of Tuscany. The legal separation was granted by Pope Clement VIII in September, after which the marriage ceremony between the king and Marie took place by proxy on 5 October. While Henry IV always treated Marie with great tenderness, respect and love, he continued his many amorous relationships with the women of the court, finding a new mistress in Henriette d'Entragues. Nevertheless, in 1601, Marie gave birth to the dauphin, Louis, who was acknowledged as the heir to the French throne. The marriage with Marie resulted in five additional children – two sons and three daughters.

Henry IV had survived several assassination plots during his reign. In 1602, a new conspiracy was organized by the French governor of Burgundy, Charles de Gontaut, Duke of Biron. The duke had previously served the king faithfully and well as a general and civil administrator, but was ambitious to create an independent lordship and conspired with Duke Charles Emmanuel of Savoy and the new King of Spain, Philip III, to achieve his goal. Shortly after the signing of the Treaty of Vervins in 1598, Henry IV's court sent the duke on a diplomatic mission to Brussels, where he became involved with agents from the Spanish kingdom and Charles Emmanuel for the overthrow of the French monarchy and the break-up of the kingdom into independent provinces. After seizing control of France, Biron was to be appointed Duke of Burgundy. Under the scheme devised by Biron, the Spanish would send a formidable military force into France from Flanders, while the duke attacked from the east. The plotters planned to assassinate Henry and the dauphin, while acknowledging as king Caesar Bourbon, the illegitimate son of Henry and his mistress, Henriette d'Entragues. He would then reign over a greatly reduced France. Henry IV had been warned of the duke's conspiracy and closely monitored his movements. Eventually, in 1601, Charles of Biron was arrested at Fontainbleau on orders from the king. Put on trial and found guilty of treason, Biron was beheaded at the Bastille in Paris on 31 July 1602.

As the result of years of religious wars and internal strife, the French economy was in chaos, with many citizens suffering in poverty. To return the nation to prosperity, Henry IV appointed Maximilian of Sully as his Minster of Finance. Sully quickly introduced a series of reforms to revive the stagnant economy. Under Sully's plan, government expenditure was greatly limited, commerce received favourable treatment from the regime, a powerful mercantile programme was put in place and the expansion of agriculture was encouraged with the introduction of new planting methods and crops. With the king's approval, the taxation system was reformed to a more equitable basis, while the burden on the peasants was reduced. To facilitate growth in commerce, the transportation system was revamped by numerous public works programmes, which constructed new roads and canals. To open new markets for French goods, King Henry sponsored the exploration and settlement of Canada, which resulted in a vast new empire under French authority. Under Sully's direction, economic conditions improved throughout the realm and the crown's financial budget returned to a surplus.

While Henry IV was involved with the economic recovery of his kingdom, he assembled his army for a campaign against the Duke of Savoy, Charles Emmanuel. In 1588, the ambitious Duke Charles Emmanuel had occupied the Marquisate of Saluzzo, which was under the protection of Henry IV. With peace now established with Spain, King Henry began preparations to regain his lost territories. As part of the Treaty of Vervins, the Saluzzo region was to be returned to the French regime, but Charles Emmanuel retained possession of the area despite repeated demands for its restoration. The Duke of Savoy negotiated with royal courtiers and arranged a plot to poison the king, but the conspiracy failed. As the duke continued to defy the French monarchy, Henry invaded Savoy. He besieged several of the duke's towns, French artillery pieces battering the fortifications and blowing large gaps in them, forcing the garrisons to submit. During the winter offensive, large parts of Savoy were overrun by Henry IV. With the intervention of Pope Clement VIII, a peace treaty was signed at Lyons on 17 January 1601, which ceded all the duke's lands bordering the Rhone River, along with the eastern province of Bresse and communes of Gex and Bugey, to the French in lieu of Saluzzo.

At the beginning of the seventeenth century, the Habsburg family controlled Spain, most of present-day Germany, the Low Countries and parts of Italy. When the Habsburg emperor, Rudolf II, occupied the German Duchy of Cleves-Julich, which was strategically located on the border with France, Henry IV became threatened by the proximity of his enemy. The French king began preparations for war with the Habsburgs, launching a diplomatic search for allies to confront the emperor. The quest resulted in the concept of the Grand Design, which he envisioned as the formation of a league of kingdoms devoted to keeping the peace by their unified front actively checking the aggression of the Habsburgs. Henry soon found a supporter of his plan in the ageing Queen Elizabeth I of England, who was being challenged by the Spanish. In 1603, Henry sent an envoy to England to form the framework of the Grand Design, meeting with the newly crowned King James I, who like his predecessor favoured the undertaking. The plan for this league of united European nations comprised six hereditary regimes, five elective states and four republics. Delegates from each realm would meet in a senate to peacefully resolve problems.

In 1607, the Duke of Cleves-Julich-Berg died without an heir. Bordering on both France and Habsburg lands, maintaining friendly relations with the duchy's new ruler was vital to both regimes' security. Henry supported the governing of the duchy by two Protestant principalities, Brandenburg and Neuburg, and threatened to intervene with his army to guarantee their possession of Cleves-Julich-Berg. In opposition, the intensely Catholic Habsburgs sent their army to seize Julich to ensure it was governed by followers of the Church of Rome.

In the wake of the occupation of the duchy by the Habsburgs, Henry IV spent the autumn of 1609 preparing his forces for a spring campaign against the emperor. Envoys were dispatched to the German regimes to unite them against Rudolf II, while the Dutch Protestants also agreed to send troops. The French eventually mustered an army of over 30,000 men for the offensive, with King Henry personally serving as commander.

Before departing on his German campaign, the king named his wife as regent, with a council of fifteen advisors, to rule France. Queen Marie had not been formally crowned by the Church, and before leaving for Germany, the king decided to hold the ceremony to ensure the regime would follow her orders. A coronation service of great splendour and pageantry was held at St Denis in May 1610, and three days later Queen Marie made her grand entry into Paris. During a gala party that night at the Louvre Palace, the king was gloomy and pessimistic, telling his courtiers: 'There is something here which gravely troubles me but I do not know what is the matter.' Several months before the coronation, Marie had a dream that her husband had been murdered, and she became increasingly concerned for his safety, which added to the despair of the royal court. As preparations for the war were finalized, Henry remained in a fog of depression.

The following evening, 14 May, Henry ordered his coachman to take him to the Arsenal to visit his finance minister, Sully. After bidding Marie farewell, he entered the royal coach with several noblemen and departed from the Louvre for the ride through the streets of Paris. The carriage was drawn by eight horses, with the king protected by several walking footmen and a few outriders. The carriage's leather curtains were pushed back enabling the king to view the crowds gathered along the streets as he slowly made his way to the Arsenal.

At the end of 1609, rumours had spread rapidly through Paris that the Huguenots were preparing a repeat of the St Bartholomew's Massacre for the Catholics, to take place on Christmas Day. The king was alleged to know about the plot, but dared not interfere for fear of incurring the wrath of the anti-Papists. Among the numerous people who believed in this account of the king's complicity in such a scheme was an ardent Catholic follower named Francis Ravaillac, who had been a schoolmaster and had also been in a debtors' prison. While in confinement, he had visions and suffered from mental illness. In late 1609, Ravaillac had been in a crowd watching the king ride through the streets of Paris when he shouted to the monarch: 'Sire, in the name of our Lord Jesus Christ and the Virgin Mary, may I speak to you?' As he pressed forward toward the king, the royal guards pushed him back. Ravaillac then returned to his residence in Angouleme, where he heard a rumour that King Henry was threatening to depose the pope.

As the rumours about the king's plot against the pope continued, Ravaillac returned to Paris, where he was told by a group of royal soldiers that if war was declared against the papacy, they would gladly fight with the king. Ravaillac considered Pope Paul V as God's representative on Earth and was determined to protect him by killing Henry IV. He stole a knife and waited for the opportunity to assassinate the king. In the early morning of 14 May 1610, Ravaillac was at the main gate to the Louvre, waiting for the king to leave the palace. When Henry finally departed in the early evening, he followed him. As the coach reached Rue St Honore, it was forced to halt by two slow moving carts. Taking advantage of the delay, Ravaillac climbed on the carriage and, reaching through the open window, stabbed King Henry with his knife. Bleeding from the wound, the king cried out, 'I am wounded', whereupon the assassin quickly struck him again, killing Henry.

Ravaillac made no attempt to flee and was arrested by an officer of the king's guard. Henry was taken to a room at the nearby Hotel de Retz, where attempts were made to revive him. Queen Marie was escorted from the Louvre, but by the time she arrived the king was showing no signs of life. The news of King Henry's assassination spread rapidly through Paris, leaving citizens shocked in their grief. Shops were closed and crowds gathered demanding vengeance against the regicide. In the provinces, the reports of Henry IV's death caused great gloom and despair. During his reign, Henry had brought peace and an expanding economy to France, giving its people hope for the future. He was remembered as a king who loved his subjects and worked for their betterment.

After the seizure of Ravaillac, he was tried by the Parliament of Paris and sentenced to death. During his interrogation, the assassin expressed his belief that the French king was preparing to attack the papacy and that he had acted because Henry had not brought the Huguenots back to the true Catholic faith. During Ravaillac's execution, which lasted over an hour and was brutal, his body was dismembered and burned. Throughout the execution, he was said to have prayed to God and then cried out with horrible screams.

In the aftermath of his death, Henry IV's body was embalmed and dressed in white satin before it was moved to the large reception room in the Louvre Palace, where it lay in state. According to the king's wishes, his heart was given to the Jesuits to be placed in their college. An effigy was made from wax and wicker showing the king wearing the royal crown, and this was placed close to the coffin. On two occasions each day, servants placed plates of food before the casket, which symbolized the continuance of the French kingship. Crowds of French subjects passed the coffin in reverent silence, while a hundred masses each day were said at Notre Dame and the realm's churches. On 25 June, the 9-year-old King Louis XIII visited his father's casket, sprinkling it with holy water. Four days later, Henry's remains were transferred to Notre Dame, through streets with houses and buildings draped in black cloth, where the funeral Mass was held with great ceremony and pomp. Following the funeral, the casket was moved to the Basilica of St Denis and buried in a tomb. The body remained in the vault until the French Revolution, when it was disinterred and destroyed by rioting Paris mobs.

In the wake of the assassination of King Henry, Louis was anointed king, with his mother, Queen Marie, serving as regent. The policies implemented by the regent were soon unpopular with the magnates, resulting in an uprising in 1614. Three years later, the king removed his mother from power, exiling her to Blois under house arrest, and ruled the kingdom with the advice of several of his favourites. In February 1619, several nobles banded together and threw their support behind Queen Marie, rebelling against Louis XIII. With his reign threated, the young king mustered his royal army and marched against his mother at Blois. As the his forces moved toward Blois, Louis opened peace talks with Queen Marie. An agreement was soon arranged, and under the terms of the treaty the Queen Mother was given the district of Anjou as governor and pledged to reconcile with her son. Their accommodation lasted only until the next year, when Marie was again in revolt with her followers. In August 1620, with his regime in danger of seizure, Louis XIII's army of more than 3,000 men, led by Louis II of Bourbon, was sent against the rebel troops, defeating them at the Battle of Ponts-de-Ce. Marie was compelled to submit to her son, but was compensated with a seat on the royal council, where Louis could keep a watchful eye on her, allowing him to take full control of the council. With the Queen Mother no longer a threat, Louis moved against the still-recalcitrant Protestant nobles, defeating their army and imposing his sovereignty.

When Cardinal Armand-Jean de Richelieu was appointed chief minister by Louis XIII in 1624, he directed the policies of France toward the break-up of Spanish-Habsburg hegemony in Europe and the establishment of royal absolutism in France. The king renewed hostilities against the Spanish regime, bolstering his offensive by negotiating an alliance with England while continuing to battle the Protestants in France. When the succession to the vacant crown of the Duchy of Mantua was disputed, the king, on the advice of Richelieu, sent his army into northern Italy to occupy Savoy. In 1635, Louis intervened in the Thirty Years' War, occupying Artois and Roussillon. Louis had married Anne of Austria in 1615, and following his death at the age of 41 in 1643, his eldest son was acknowledged as successor to the French crown, reigning as King Louis XIV.

Selected Sources

Briggs, Robin, *Early Modern France 1560–1715*
Castries, Duc de, *The Lives of the Kings and Queens of France*
Gisserot, Jean-Paul, *The Family Trees of the Kings of France*
Knecht, R.J., *Renaissance Warrior and Patron – The Reign of Francis I*
Knecht, R.J., *The Rise and Fall of Renaissance France 1483–1610*
Maurois, Andre, *A History of France*
Pearson, Hesketh, *Henry of Navarre*
Russell, Lord of Liverpool, *Henry of Navarre*
Sedgwick, Henry Dwight, *Henry of Navarre*
Seward, Desmond, *The Bourbon Kings of France*
Seward, Desmond, *The First Bourbon – Henry IV of France & Navarre*

Louis XIV

On 5 September 1651, Louis XIV reached the age of majority and the regency rule of Queen Anne of Austria was officially ended. Two days later, the king declared his assumption of the French throne to the gathered deputies at the Paris parliament. From the parliament, he made his way to St Chapelle and attended Mass with the peers of France, governmental officials and council members, offering thanks to God for his kingdom. Following the religious service, Louis XIV returned to the chamber of the assembly, where he addressed the members. The king announced: 'I have come to my parliament to tell you that in accordance with the law of my state, I am going to take upon myself the management of my government and I hope the goodness of God will grant that this will be with piety and justice.' The governing administration of the regent had grown increasingly unpopular over the constant demands for more taxes, and the delegates now looked to the new regime of the king to bring peace and prosperity. Under the sixty-four-year reign of King Louis XIV, the Kingdom of France would rise to new heights of power, glory and expansion of its borders, while becoming the centre of European culture, music and arts.

King Louis XIII and Queen Anne had remained childless for nearly twenty-eight years until late 1637, when the queen became pregnant. Nine months later, the king was informed that his wife was in labour at the Chateau Saint-Germain. The great lords and ladies of the realm made their way to the palace for the birth. The queen's ladies of honour and women of the royal family were present in the delivery room, while the high noblemen and princes of the blood were in the next chamber. Anne had a difficult labour, and for a time her life was in danger. Around midday on 5 September 1638, the midwife held up the baby and shouted out: 'It is a dauphin!' Shortly after the delivery of his son, the king arrived at the queen's bedside, and with the gathered lords and ladies gave thanks for the new heir to the crown of France. As reports of the dauphin's birth spread from the palace to Paris, the kingdom erupted in mass celebrations, with the ringing of church bells, firing of cannons, dancing in the streets, fireworks and religious services of thanksgiving. The people of France received the delivery of the dauphin as a sign of peace and a better future. While the French realm rejoiced at the birth of the dauphin, the king's brother, Gaston of Orleans, and cousin, Henry II of Conde, had no reason to celebrate, their likelihood of sitting on the throne having greatly diminished.

Dauphin Louis spent the next four years under the custody of a governess and was cared for in the royal household. Shortly after the death of Louis XIII in May 1643, the queen met with the French first minister, Cardinal Jules Mazarin, and arranged to have the final testament of her husband set aside, which had omitted her from the newly created regency council. She had been in the shadows of the king's reign and was now eager to lead a new government in the name of her son. To gain approval from the Paris parliament, Anne came to the legislature with the boy-king to have the testament voided. After first attending Mass at the nearby St Chapelle, the queen and Louis returned to parliament, where he told the members: 'I have come to testify my affection and my good will toward my parliament.' The queen also spoke to the deputies, assuring them she would be happy to have their counsel at all times. When the parliament was asked to approve the appointment of Queen Anne as regent for the remaining minority years of the king, the delegates granted the request, permitting her to establish the ruling administration.

With the approval of Queen Anne, Cardinal Mazarin resumed the foreign policies of Louis XIII, continuing the French war against Spain and the German Habsburgs. Under orders from the regency council, Louis XIV's army was sent into the Spanish Netherlands to break the siege of the town of Rocroi. Led by Louis II of Bourbon, on 19 May 1643 the French relief force of 23,000 men destroyed the enemy's formation of elite infantry by unleashing a spirited cavalry charge, breaking through their lines and inflicting over 8,000 casualties to end the siege. In France, the victory at Rocroi was considered a good omen for the reign of the new king, and also secured the power of Queen Anne. The Spanish defeat signalled the beginning of the decline of its golden age and the rise of French power.

Under the reign of Queen Anne, taxes were raised to fund the war against Spain, leading to the French peasants and merchants becoming increasingly impoverished, while the nobles had little influence over her government. To counter the royal administration's unchecked spending, the high magnates turned to Louis II of Bourbon, who was young, ambitious and a highly talented and successful military commander after his recent victory at Rocroi. As the French lords led by Louis II of Bourbon began to openly defy Anne's decrees, the towns and peasants looked to the Paris parliament as their protector against the increased taxes, the assembly's members becoming increasingly hostile to the registration of new revenue edicts by Louis XIV's government. As the requests for new taxes continued, the parliament began openly threatening the regime of Anne, proposing a reduction in the powers of the monarchy.

In the meantime, Louis XIV remained in the household of the queen, who was responsible for his care. During his early years, the king received little education from his governesses and was occupied playing games, attending church services and listening to stories. He greatly enjoyed performing mock military manoeuvres with the other children of the court, leading his troops into battle. Louis loved to hammer his toy drums, attempting to duplicate the music of the Swiss guards. With his kingdom at war against Spain, he was exposed to talk about the army and battles at the royal court. When Louis reached his seventh birthday, he was removed from the custody of the queen, with Mazarin appointed as the supervisor for his education.

Under the direction of Cardinal Mazarin, the king received a practical education rather than a scholarly one. The cardinal appointed a governor for Louis and several teachers were hired to instruct him in reading and writing, mathematics, the Spanish and Italian languages, drawing, fencing, equestrianism and dancing. The quality of the academic tutoring was poor, and as a result the substance of the king's education was inadequate. Upon reaching the age of 12, Louis had learned to write and read French, while acquiring some Spanish and Italian. The emphasis of his instruction tended toward military studies, being trained in the martial skills of horsemanship, fencing and hunting. He received training in the battle tactics and weapons of a seventeenth-century warrior king, practicing with the sword, spear, lance and mace, while learning to shoot the musket and attack an enemy from a charging warhorse.

At the royal court, several priests contributed to Louis' religious education, while the Queen Mother took an active-role in the formation of his beliefs about God. From Anne of Austria, he was exposed to the ways of a pious life. When she visited churches, convents and monasteries and met with the bishops and abbots, her son accompanied her, participating in the services and ceremonies. It was Anne's goal for her son to become a great Christian king.

During 1647, Queen Anne's war against the Spanish in the Low Countries was going badly, with enemy forces retaking numerous French-occupied towns, so Mazarin decided to take the boy-king and his mother to the front to bolster the morale of the soldiers. On the way to visit the army, the royal entourage stopped at numerous towns, where Louis was welcomed by the notables and large cheering crowds. At each gathering, he patiently listened to the speeches of the local dignitaries as they talked at length about their loyalty to his crown. Despite the presence of the king at the frontier, additional French towns and villages were captured by the Spanish, while France's army in Catalonia – led by the king's cousin, Louis II of Conde – was compelled to withdraw after persistent attacks by the Spaniards. The court next travelled through Normandy, visiting Dieppe, where the queen and Louis XIV were met by wildly welcoming crowds. By August, the king was back at Saint-Germain following his successful political promenade. Numerous courtiers noted that the king now seemed more serious and unassuming after his experiences at the front.

In November 1647, Louis XIV became seriously ill with smallpox. There was no known cure for the disease and the king's life was in danger. He began to feel ill on 10 November with a high fever, and the queen became increasingly worried about his health. Two days later, the illness was diagnosed as smallpox by the court physicians. During the following few days, the fever continued unabated and Anne's anxiety escalated. Eventually, the fever broke and boils spread over his body, which was a sign of his improvement. Louis seemed to slowly recover until 21 November, when his fever suddenly returned and he fainted. He regained consciousness nearly an hour later, feeling stronger as the day wore on. The following morning, the illness again became more severe and the doctors did not expect him to recover. As Louis struggled to regain his health, political parties began to form around his younger brother, Philip of Anjou, and his cousin, Prince Louis II of Conde, to succeed as the new king. Around midnight, Louis' high fever began to ease and the pockmarks returned. During the next few days, Louis' health steadily improved; he had survived the disease, but was scarred with pockmarks for life.

The royal government, led by Mazarin and approved by Queen Anne, had continued the conflict against the Spanish in the Netherlands and the German Habsburgs in the east. The war was opposed by the parliament of Paris, whose representatives had grown increasingly rebellious, while the king's subjects still suffered under the heavy tax burden. However, the French armies then began to turn defeat into victory, gaining the initiative on several fronts. In south-east France in the Spanish-held Roussillon region and along the Rhine, Louis II of Conde defeated enemy forces and advanced the French war effort. On 20 August 1648, the Prince of Conde drew the imperial army of Archduke Leopold into battle at Lens in Flanders, outmanoeuvring him and encircling his Spanish infantry. The French unleashed an attack from all sides, compelling the enemy to surrender, with over 3,000 killed or wounded and a further 5,000 captured. When Louis XIV was informed of the great victory at Lens, he cried out that 'the members in parliament will be quite unhappy about this', indicating he realized his legislative assembly was filled with deputies who were not pleased with the success of their king.

In the aftermath of the French victory at Lens, the Peace of Westphalia was signed with the Austrian Habsburgs. Under the favourable terms of the treaty, Louis XIV was ceded the bishoprics of Metz, Verdun and Toul, plus parts of Lorraine and Alsace. The agreement also confirmed the 1555 Peace of Augsburg, giving each state the right to determine the religion of its subjects. The war had depleted the finances and resources of the Habsburgs, limiting their future ability to expand into the territory of Louis XIV.

The victories gained by France on the battlefield were largely ignored by the king's subjects and members of the parliament of Paris, who were only interested in the oppressive taxes imposed by his regime to pursue the war. By 1648, the parliament had become increasingly belligerent, refusing to register into law the new edicts of Mazarin. In the wake of the victories by the French army, the government of Queen Anne and Cardinal Mazarin were emboldened to apprehend three representatives of the parliament who had spoken out strongly against the tax increases. When the residents of Paris learned of the arrests, they broke out in rebellion, throwing up barricades across the city, marking the beginning of the Parliamentary Fronde (the French word *fronde* meaning 'sling', the Parisian mob using slings to smash the windows of Mazarin's supporters).

The rioting crowds seized control of the city, with the exception of the royal palace, which was defended by the French and Swiss guards. The Paris assembly was considered the defender of the city's residents, who rioted against the imprisonment of the three deputies. Confronted by the citizens' escalating uprising, Cardinal Mazarin released the prisoners, to the wild cheers of the demonstrators. In September, the royal court withdrew from Paris to the village of Rueil and sent Louis II of Conde with the army to restore order and the rule of Louis XIV. Supported by his veteran soldiers, Conde attacked the insurgents, and after several skirmishes the leaders of the Parisians agreed to discuss a peace agreement. A treaty was quickly negotiated and the king and his entourage returned to Paris, but tensions between the two factions continued high. The violence in the streets soon resumed, the Parisians breaking into the royal palace and demanding to be taken to Louis. They were led to the king's bedchamber, where he pretended to be asleep. After viewing the apparently sleeping Louis, the rebels quietly withdrew, leaving the royal family badly alarmed. The shaky Peace of Rueil continued, the king remaining in the palace under the watchful eye of his guards, ending the Parliamentary Fronde.

Prince Louis of Conde's intervention to quell the Paris mobs and his recent victories against the Spanish had created a wave of popular support, and he was now resolved to size the throne of France. When Louis II moved to take power, Queen Anne ordered his arrest on 18 January 1650. Following the seizure of Conde, the loyalists advanced against the insurgency, and in early February the 11-year-old Louis XIV travelled to Normandy to participate in the campaign against the dissidents. He spent three weeks moving through the provinces with the queen, encouraging his subjects to defend the throne. The tour of Normandy was the king's first exposure to the battle against the forces opposed to his reign. Later in the year, Louis inspected his troops at the siege of Bellegrade in eastern central France. During his stay at the encampment, rebels on the fortress walls recognized the king and cheered him before firing their muskets at him, killing an officer standing nearby.

Meanwhile, the allies of Louis II flocked to his revolt against the ruling regime, with Henry, Viscount of Turenne, taking command of the uprising. With the support of the Parisians, Henry moved to rescue the imprisoned Conde and his younger brother, Armand, Prince of Conti. Lacking adequate military resources to attack the royalists, he secured aid from the Spanish army in the Netherlands. When the Spanish marched into northern France, the peasants rallied to the king and with the local royal forces halted the invaders. After his defeat, the Spanish general retreated back to the Netherlands. Following the withdrawal of his allies, Turenne and his Frondeurs resumed the war against the king but he was overwhelmed at the Battle of Rethel on 15 December 1650. By April 1651, the royalists had regained power as the rebellion of the nobles collapsed.

In the meantime, during the Second Fronde, Louis XIV was compelled to remain in Paris in an environment of continued intrigues and counter-alliances with the noble parties. Anne was able to find numerous allies among both factions, who gave enough support to keep the monarchy in power, while Mazarin was in Germany arranging financial and military aid. On 5 September 1651, Louis XIV reached the age of majority and the regency regime of Queen Anne officially ended. The throne's government now carried the name and full power of the king, which added authority and effect to its edicts.

In January 1651, Cardinal Mazarin ordered the release of the Prince of Conde in a show of peace with the insurgents. As the royalists continued to expand their territorial holdings across the kingdom, Louis II of Conde again became the leader of the rebels and renewed the alliance with King Philip IV of Spain. Under Louis II's command, the rebellion was rejuvenated and the uprising spread to the provinces in south-western France as they declared their allegiance to Conde. To prevent the further spread of the revolt and reimpose his kingship, Louis XIV mustered a small army and marched to confront the new uprising in the provinces, while recalling Cardinal Mazarin from his mission to Germany. When the first minister retuned at the head of a mercenary army and united his troops with the royalists, Philip IV sent soldiers from the Netherlands to reinforce the uprising of Conde, marking the beginning of the Spanish Fronde.

During the period between 1650 and 1653, Prince Louis II controlled much of Paris through his alliance with the parliament, while leading his soldiers in the revolt against King Louis XIV in pursuit of the French crown. In May 1651, Viscount Henry of Turenne abandoned his allegiance to Conde and became reconciled with the king's regime. He was placed in command of the royal army with the rank of marshal and prepared to move against the Fronde. With the approval of the king's council, the French marshal led his troops into north central France to attack Conde. He first encountered the insurgents at a bridge near the village of Jargeau on 28 March 1652, disrupting the advance of the enemy soldiers. After this brief skirmish, he led his forces north toward Compiegne and intercepted the Frondeurs near Bleneau on 7 April. Turenne's 15,000 men clashed with Conde, beating him back and compelling his troops to withdraw toward Paris. The two armies collided again in July at Saint-Antoine in Paris, near the Bastille, where Conde's soldiers sortied out of their defensive works to attack the royalists. The rebels soon became trapped against the walls, only being saved from destruction by volleys from the fortress' cannons.

While Turenne's army defended the Bourbon monarchy, Louis XIV remained with the royal court, travelling about the countryside and staying at loyal towns. When the Paris parliament sent an embassy to the king with a list of demands for peace, he tore up the document without reading it. Following the Battle of Bleneau, the rebel warlords attempted to negotiate a favourable peace agreement with the king but he told their ambassadors to talk to Mazarin, knowing they had been forbidden by Conde to meet with him. As the insurgent leaders continued their revolt against Louis XIV's reign, he developed a personal and intense resentment of them, blaming the dissidents for the misery now suffered by his subjects.

As the royal government began to recover its footing, coupled with its recent military victories, Louis II of Conde's popularity and control over the conspiracy began to wane. In Paris, differing political parties developed and civil war soon erupted between the nobles and Parisians. With anarchy threatening to erupt in the city, a delegation of members from the parliament arranged a meeting with the king and his advisors, pledging their loyalty and support if Mazarin was dismissed from the government. To save his kingdom from the horrors of civil war, Louis XIV agreed to the proposal and the cardinal was sent into exile in Germany. On 20 October 1652, the royal court returned to Paris in triumph. Under the terms of the negotiated agreement, the rebel lords gave their pledge of loyalty to the crown and the king asserted his authority over the Paris legislative assembly. The leaders of the revolt were forced into exile, with Prince Louis II of Conde fleeing to the Spanish Netherlands to continue serving against the Bourbon monarchy in the army of Philip IV, ending the Parisian phase of the Fronde. When the king was fully restored to power over his kingdom, he recalled Mazarin from exile in early 1653. The return of the cardinal signified Louis XIV's acknowledgment as King of France, the end of the French Fronde and the beginning of absolute rule.

Following the end of the war between the Bourbon crown and the Frondeurs, the royal regime ruled over most of the kingdom unopposed, with Cardinal Mazarin at the head of the king's council. Louis XIV's long-neglected education was renewed and his military training continued. During the Fronde, the king had frequently travelled with his army fighting the Spaniards and was exposed to the planning, preparations and execution of a successful campaign. The king attended commander briefings, visited the men in their trenches, ate army food and spent the nights sleeping under the stars. He was described by contemporaries as having grown into adulthood; tall, handsome, muscular and presenting an imposing royal air and majesty. Louis now routinely attended meetings of the cardinal's council, becoming familiar with the art of diplomacy and the administration of the French government. He regularly travelled with his army and frequently took command of his soldiers.

In the early morning of 7 June 1654, the Bishop of Beauvais, Nicolas Choart, knocked on the door of the French king's chamber, saying: 'We seek Louis XIV of that name, son of the great Louis XIII, whom God has given us as King.' After entering the room, the bishop gave the 15-year-old Louis a container of holy oil and the king dipped his finger into the bowl, making the sign of the cross, while Choart recited a prayer. After dressing, Louis was led to the palace gate, where a long procession waited to escort him to the Cathedral of Rheims for his coronation. The streets of the city were lined with richly dressed residents as the king passed by.

He entered the nave of the cathedral, walking up the choir, and as the organ played he knelt at the high altar. Before the altar, Louis promised to defend and observe the rights of the Catholic Church. After the assembled peers, nobles and commoners accepted Louis as king, he took the coronation oath. The bishop then blessed the royal sword and handed it to the king, who kissed the blade and promised to use it in God's service. The king was then anointed seven times with holy oil, which was believed to have been used in the baptism of Clovis, first King of the Franks. Louis was next dressed in a long, wide-sleeved tunic and cape. He knelt again and the bishop anointed the king once more before placing a ring on the third finger of his left hand, signifying his marriage to the Kingdom of France. The Bishop of Beauvais now took the crown of Charlemagne and placed it on the head of Louis XIV. Wearing the crown and carrying the sceptre, the king was led to the throne of Dagobert, where the French peers paid homage. After the bishop cried out, 'May the king live forever!', the doors of the cathedral were opened and the gathered crowd cheered the anointment of their monarch. While the king remained in the cathedral, a Te Deum was chanted and the Mass celebrated. Louis XIV's final act in the service was to go to confession and receive communion. Following prayers, he walked in procession down the church to the open west door to be hailed as king by his subjects, as the organ played and the bells rang out.

The Treaty of Westphalia, signed in October 1648, had ended the Thirty Years' War with the Austrian Habsburg regime, but the conflict between Spain and Louis XIV's kingdom had remained unresolved. Cardinal Mazarin, hard-pressed to recruit additional soldiers and provide adequate provisions for the French war effort, was now compelled to seek the intercession of the English Commonwealth and sent envoys to Oliver Cromwell asking for his military aid. The negotiations produced an agreement, which provided France with English troops and supplies in exchange for the port of Dunkirk on the Strait of Dover. In 1652, Philip IV renewed the French war and appointed Prince Louis II of Conde as the commander of his military forces in the Spanish Netherlands. With the approval of the Spanish crown, Conde unleashed an invasion into northern France from Flanders with the objective of capturing Paris and reigniting the civil war. As Conde advanced to the French border, Viscount Henry of Turenne was named to lead Louis XIV's troops in the campaign against the rebels. Meeting with the king, Viscount Henry was ordered to march from Paris and drive the Spanish out of France. The two armies clashed in August as the Spanish were besieging the town of Arras near the current-day border with Belgium. The French relief army led by Henry of Turenne attacked the

Spanish two hours before dawn, catching them unprepared. Henry overran the enemy's lines and compelled them to retreat. Conde quickly re-formed his troops and counter-attacked. As the Spaniards moved forward, Turenne repositioned his cannons to the high ground to beat them back with large losses. Louis XIV was present at the battlefield viewing Turenne's lines of assault, the enemy's defensive works and the fierce fight between the rival armies.

In the aftermath of his defeat at Arras, Louis II of Conde was forced to suspend his campaign and fall back to his encampment in Flanders. The French under the command of Henry of Turenne were unable to follow up their Arras victory and the conflict reached an impasse, with neither side able to force a resolution. In May 1656, Marshal Turenne attempted to gain the advantage by besieging the town of Valenciennes in the Spanish Netherlands. As the Spanish continued to man their defensive lines, the governor of the Netherlands, Don Juan José de Austria, sent a relief army to aid the garrison at the end of June. On 16 July, the reinforcements, led by Louis II, attacked Louis XIV's besiegers and compelled them to withdraw. Over the next two years, the war against Spain remained at a stalemate, with only sporadic clashes.

In the early summer of 1658, a French army of 15,000 troops was joined by 6,000 English soldiers from the Commonwealth for a campaign against Spain. At the end of May, Turenne and his English allies besieged the port city of Dunkirk. A Spanish army of 14,000 men, supplemented with a corps of French Fronde rebels led by Louis II of Conde, was sent to raise the siege. The local countryside had recently been flooded, compelling the Spanish troops to deploy on the dunes by the sea. On 15 June, after five artillery salvoes by Turenne, the French infantry attacked Conde's defences in the centre and on the right, while his cavalry charged against the unprotected left flank of the Spanish army, which had become exposed by the retreating tide. After crashing through the left, the French attacked the centre position held by John of Austria, overwhelming his troops. During what became known as the Battle of the Dunes, 1,300 Spaniards were killed or wounded and more than 4,000 taken prisoner. The victory at the Dunes was followed by the French capture of Dunkirk, which broke Spanish resistance. After his victories, Turenne advanced to capture further towns and fortifications, including Gravelines, Ypres and Oudenarde. Louis XIV travelled with his men, motivating and encouraging them with his presence, as his troops marched through the Spanish Netherlands.

During the reign of Louis XIV, the Spanish throne had been repeatedly defeated by the French, and now – after forty years of warfare – was financially ruined. King Philip IV's government was in need of a prolonged period of peace to rebuild its finances and was anxious to negotiate a settlement with King Louis. The Bourbon regime agreed to talks, resulting in the Treaty of the Pyrenees signed on 7 November 1659, ending ten years of war between the nations. Under the terms of the agreement, the French border with Spain was set at the natural barrier of the Pyrenees, while Louis XIV expanded his kingdom by annexing the Roussillon region in present-day south-east France, towns in Flanders and the Flemish province of Artois, in addition to numerous fortifications on the border with the Spanish Netherlands. The treaty also required the Spanish king to recognize and confirm all French gains in the 1648 Peace of Westphalia. Cardinal Mazarin honoured the terms of the treaty with Oliver Cromwell and transferred the port of Dunkirk to the English Commonwealth. A provision in the treaty providing for the marriage of the king to Maria Therese, daughter of Philip IV, with a further clause requiring the Spanish princess to renounce all of her claims of inheritance to her father's empire.

Louis XIV was despondent at the prospects of his forced marriage for political reasons to a foreign princess. He had recently begun a romantic relationship with the niece of Cardinal Mazarin, Maria Mancini, and preferred to marry her. The couple were compelled to part in the courtyard of the Louvre Palace. During the following days, Louis wrote to Maria telling of his endless love, while Cardinal Mazarin threatened to resign if the Spanish marriage was cancelled. Louis realized that, for the betterment of his kingdom, the marriage to Maria Therese must take place. On 6 June 1660, Louis XIV and his mother, Queen Anne of Austria, travelled to the chosen neutral site at the uninhabited island of Pheasants on the border between France and Spain to meet King Philip IV of Spain. At the island, Anne was reunited with her brother after forty-six years at the French court. Three days later, the marriage ceremony was performed by Bertrand d'Echaux, Bishop of Bayonne, and the 21-year-old Louis XIV of France was united with his first cousin, Maria Therese. The wedding service was held at the small church of St Jean de Luz, where Louis saw his bride for the first time. She was dressed in a veil of purple velvet embroidered with fleur de lys over a white dress, with a royal crown on her head. After the ceremony, Cardinal Mazarin noted with pleasure that the Spanish had yet to make payment on the dowry, which if it continued would give France a claim to the Spanish Netherlands. The next day, Louis and his wife began the journey to Paris in slow stages, stopping at numerous towns before reaching the castle of Vincennes, where they remained for a month. On 26 August 1660, the king and queen made their grand entrance into Paris through an imposing arch. Louis, mounted on a horse, and Maria Therese, riding in a golden coach, made their way through streets lined with cheering crowds. When they reached the Hotel de Beauvais, Louis removed his white plumed hat and bowed to his mother on the balcony. The welcoming parade was followed by three days of celebrations.

During their twenty-three years of marriage, Maria Therese became devoted to her husband but lacked the political skills and intellect to play a meaningful role in the ruling of the kingdom. The queen remained faithful to the king, but Louis would take numerous mistresses and engage in frequent brief love affairs. The marriage of Louis XIV and Queen Maria Therese resulted in the birth of three sons and three daughters, including the Dauphin Louis, born in 1661, but none would survive to reign over France. Following the death of Maria Therese in 1683, Louis XIV was married in a private ceremony to his mistress, Frances Aubigne, with a few close friends in attendance. Due to the wide disparity in their social status, the marriage was never openly acknowledged and she did not become queen. Shortly after the nuptial service, Frances was given an apartment at Versailles across from the king's rooms, and each day he spent several hours with her. She exerted considerable political influence over Louis and was one of his closest and trusted advisors. Frances Aubigne was born on 27 November 1635 at Niort in western France, where her father was incarcerated in prison for conspiring against Cardinal Richelieu. After her father's release in 1639, the family relocated to the island of Martinique, where Frances resided for eight years before returning to France. Soon after relocating, both of her parents died and Frances was raised by a wealthy aunt, who provided for her care and education. At the age of 16, she married the poet Paul Scarron, who had many friends and sponsors at the royal court. When her husband died, Frances received his pension through the intervention of the Queen Mother. Through the contacts of her husband, she knew many nobles at court and was named governess for the children of a princely family. At the royal palace, Frances was introduced to Madame de Montespan, the secret mistress of the king. In 1669, Montespan placed her second child by Louis XIV under the care of Frances, and through him she was brought to the attention of the king. After his illegitimate children with Montespan were legitimized, Louis named Frances as caretaker for them. Louis grew to know Frances well during their conversations concerning the education and health of his children, and he became increasingly attracted to her. In 1674, he rewarded her with a large cash gift, which she used to purchase the Maintenon property. The following year, Louis have her the title Marquise of Maintenon. When the king's official mistress left court in 1680, Maintenon was appointed her replacement.

The health of Cardinal Mazarin had steadily declined in recent years due to the stresses of the Franco-Spanish War and the debilitating effects of gout. Before his death on 9 March 1661 at Vincennes Castle, the cardinal advised the young king to rule without an appointed first minister and to create an advisory council. When Louis was informed of Mazarin's death, he broke out in tears at the loss of his guide. The day before Mazarin's death, Louis announced that he would govern alone and serve as his own prime minister. He began his personal administration by dismissing his finance minister, Nichols Fouquet, from his advisory board on charges of embezzlement. To fill the vacant office, John Baptiste Colbert was appointed superintendent of finances. Colbert quickly discovered it was not easy to fund the many requirements of the absolute king. He served the regime with loyalty and ingenuity, providing the money needed to fund the king's many wars, building projects and pleasures. The swift decisions of the young king left no doubt that he was the power in the kingdom and signalled that the era of absolute monarchy had begun in France.

With the government of France now under his unchallenged rule, Louis XIV had by 1667 restored peace and prosperity in his realm, while the fiscal policies of Colbert had filled the regime's coffers. As a result of his father's and the first minister's wars, France had become the dominant military power in Europe, and the king adopted aggressive measures to expand his supremacy. Louis first moved to secure his borders along the Rhine and in the Spanish-controlled Netherlands. In September 1665, Louis' father-in-law, Philip IV, died without paying the dowry for his daughter's marriage in compliance with the Treaty of the Pyrenees. The failure to make the required payment nullified Maria Therese's earlier rejection of her rights of inheritance. In numerous Spanish possessions, the eldest child, either male or female, possessed the right of inheritance, making the French queen the legal successor to her father's lands in the Spanish Netherlands and Franche-Comte.

Prior to claiming his wife's inheritance, Louis XIV rebuilt his army, assembling a powerful military force. Before launching his attack against the new King of Spain, Charles II, he sent envoys to negotiate treaties with England and the United Provinces (Dutch Republic) to ensure their continued neutrality. Meanwhile, the king reformed and reorganized his army, introducing regimental uniforms, standardized artillery pieces and portable pontoon bridges. The French soldiers were now paid regularly and fed routinely from mobile field kitchens, which increased their morale. Schools were created for the artillery and the training of junior officers. The pike was eliminated from his army's weaponry and replaced with the musket, expanding the army's firepower, while the field artillery was enlarged and corps of engineers formed. The new equipment for the army was paid for with funds amassed by Colbert. The kingdom's military forces had grown to 80,000, with more than 50,000 employed in the campaign against Spain. By 1667, Louis XIV was ready to enforce Maria Therese's inheritance rights.

In May 1667, the French army led by Marshal Henry Turenne invaded the Spanish Netherlands. The outer Spanish defences were quickly overrun and most of the border fortifications occupied, while the French moved against the major city of Lille. On 10 August, the vanguard of the French army reached Lille and began to besiege the city. On the following day, Louis XIV arrived to take personal charge of the siege operations, with an artillery battery deployed to fire salvoes against the defenders. An artillery exchange began, lasting several days before the French infantry were sent against the Spanish, taking the palisade and continuing their attack to seize additional defensive works. On 28 August, under mounting pressure, the Spanish garrison commander agreed to surrender terms and Louis XIV entered Lille in triumph. Soon after his victories over the Spanish, Louis XIV wrote to the Archbishop of Paris: 'It is from the hand of God that I receive these happy successes.'

As the king and Turenne led the troops in the conquest of eastern Flanders, the reconciled Prince Louis II of Conde commanded a second French army in the Franche-Comte, defeating enemy forces in three weeks and occupying the region for the Bourbon crown. The French citizens celebrated the king's victories, with Te Deums ringing out across the realm in thanks to God. The apparently quick and easy successes of Louis XIV created a growing atmosphere of apprehension in the European kingdoms, who began to fear for their independence. When Spain elected to give Portugal its independence to concentrate its war efforts against the French throne and the league of England, Holland and Sweden was formed to check French expansion, Louis XIV decided to end the war with Spain and negotiate a peace treaty. On 2 May 1668, the Treaty of Aix-la-Chapelle was signed, giving Louis his conquests in the Spanish Netherlands while the Franche-Comte was returned to Spain, ending the War of Devolution. The additions of Flanders greatly strengthened northern France's defences and enhanced the prestige and power of Louis XIV's regime.

By 1670, the Kingdom of France had surpassed Spain as the dominant military power in Europe and was recognized as the centre of European arts and culture. As a means of displaying his wealth and success, Louis XIV ordered the palace at Versailles enlarged into a magnificent chateau. In 1623, King Louis XIII had a small hunting lodge built at Versailles, later enlarging it into a palace. Louis first visited Versailles in 1641, and later as king utilized the residence for hunting. He went to the palace frequently, and in 1661, after his victory in the War of Devolution, began a major transformation of the chateau. He envisioned the palace as a home for the royal family and his court, servinge as the centre for the regime's government. Throughout the 1670s and early 1680s, several thousand masons, smiths, carpenters and glazers laboured at Versailles. The structure was encased on three sides, overlooking the massive gardens built by Andre de Notre. Versailles now contained 2,300 rooms, including seven apartments for the king located in the centre and seven for the queen in the south wing. Special salons designed by Hardouin Mansart were added, including the War Room (depicting the regime's victories in the Dutch War), the Hall of Mirrors (paying tribute to France's political and economic successes) and the Peace Room (showing the benefits of peace brought to Europe by Louis XIV). In 1682, Louis moved the royal court to Versailles. The refurbished palace established the benchmark for opulence and splendour throughout the European courts.

As well as the king promoting baroque architecture, he was a patron of music and dance. He used the forms of art to promote his quest for personal glory. The king gave artists unlimited resources to create numerous works, and among the many beneficiaries in music were Jean-Baptiste Lully and Michel-Richard Delalande. The king's chosen composers wrote musical pieces for the regime's suppers, royal festivals, parties, ceremonies and celebrations, playing an important role in life at court. He was an enthusiastic sponsor of opera, stage productions and ballets, which were frequently performed at Versailles. Orchestral music was an integral part of all public appearances, official receptions and for Louis XIV's personal enjoyment. The French court became the most emulated in Europe and set the standard for grandeur. Louis sent his agents to Italy with instructions to purchase only the best treasures available, as a means to display his power and wealth. He was also a passionate builder, having numerous projects under construction simultaneously.

The French king was a zealous patron of ballet, frequently appearing in court performances. After his appearance as Apollo in the 'Royal Ballet of the Night', he was hailed as the Sun King. In 1661, he established the Academy of Royal Dance at the Louvre, where ballet masters were appointed to train dancers for court performances. The Academy of Opera was later formed to produce and perform ballet. The king also began the practice of designating an official mistress. The chosen women were usually members of the court who temporarily aroused the king's passion. During his reign, Louis had numerous designated mistresses, but also had many brief amorous affairs. Through his many relationships, he fathered sixteen illegitimate children, who were recognized as part of the royal household.

The victories of the French army during the War of Devolution had only partially fulfilled Louis' goals of territorial expansion, and he considered the alliances negotiated against him by the United Netherlands, England and Sweden as breaches in his treaties with them. The Dutch had also continually interfered with French maritime commercial trade, giving Louis just cause to prepare for war. The French regime spent two years reorganizing, reequipping and enlarging its military power for the coming conflict with Holland. Envoys were sent to isolate the United Netherlands from its allies. The King of Sweden and numerous German princes were paid large subsidies for their pledges of neutrality, while King Charles II of England became allied with the French crown. With his plans and preparations completed, the French army, led by King Louis, crossed the Rhine on 12 June 1672 to invade the United Providences. The Dutch forces were unable to contain the French, and their border fortifications were soon compelled to submit. By the end of June, Amsterdam was under siege by the king's men. With their defences unable to stop the French advance, the Dutch government ordered the protective dykes surrounding the city opened, and Amsterdam was soon an unassailable island. The year ended with Louis' army occupying numerous border towns and strongholds, but the Dutch retaining control over Amsterdam.

With much of their nation under French occupation, the United Netherlands offered Louis XIV peace terms which ceded him the Rhine fortifications already lost, the Dutch Flanders and a sizable war indemnity. The proposal was quickly rejected by the king, who countered by demanding the subjugation of the whole country. The French demands were rebuffed by the Dutch government, but with its army shattered and the province under siege, the residents of Amsterdam rebelled against their regime, electing Prince William III of Orange as their stadtholder. In a bid to repel the French invasion, William opened talks with the Holy Roman Emperor, Leopold I, and numerous independent German princes to create an alliance. Confronted by the new coalition, Louis reduced the number of soldiers in Holland and sent reinforcements to strengthen his defences along the Rhine. In early 1673, the French launched a campaign into the Netherlands to capture the strategic Dutch city of Maastricht, which was located along the Meuse River and controlled communications between Germany and the Netherlands.

Louis arrived before the walls of Maastricht in June with 45,000 soldiers and surrounded the city. The king had recently named Sebastien de Vauban as his chief engineer, and under his direction the French miners dug a series of parallel lines along the fortification's walls, with each one moving closer to the stronghold. Louis closely monitored the excavations, encouraging his men in their dangerous and arduous work. After thirteen days of tunnelling, the French king ordered an assault against the outer walls on 18 June. Louis' men battered the defensive works for a week before finally breaking through, and by mid-August the Dutch governor agreed to surrender.

As the Dutch war effort faltered, Spain entered the conflict along with Denmark, Mainz and Trier in support of Prince William III. To oppose the new expanded coalition, Louis XIV was compelled to vacate much of his occupied Dutch lands and fall back to the more secure border fortifications. From their fortified bases, the French renewed their offensive campaign, Louis sending Conde to deal with William of Orange and the English forces in Flanders while he took command of the attack against Franche-Comte, reconquering the lost province. Marshal Turenne was ordered to take a third army and advance against the Germans along the Rhine. Turenne unleashed a devastating attack against the imperial forces in the Palatinate Electorate. During the campaign in Germany, the marshal was struck by a cannon ball while making a reconnaissance, and his death had a demoralizing effect on the army. Nevertheless, over the following two years, the armies of Louis XIV regained most of the lost territory in the Spanish Netherlands and Holland, where the king led many of the siege operations.

The French resumed their attack in 1677, moving against the fortified town of Valenciennes. With the king leading the army, Vauban threw up his lines of trenches against the walls, and as the royalists drew closer to the defensive works, a heavy cannonade hammered an opening. With the fortifications breached, over 40,000 French troops stormed into the stronghold, forcing it to surrender. After taking Valenciennes, the towns of Cambrai and Saint-Omer were targeted. Cambrai was besieged on 22 March, with 7,000 local peasants forced to dig trench lines around the defences. Eight days later, the French artillery opened fire. By 3 April, an opening in the walls had been made and the French charged into Cambrai, forcing the governor to surrender. Within days, Saint-Omer also fell. As his campaign gained momentum, the king's brother, Philip of Orleans, led the French troops against the town of Cassel, overwhelming the defenders and seizing the stronghold for Louis, while capturing over 2,500 prisoners.

In October 1677, Mary Stuart, niece of King Charles II of England, married William of Orange, creating a possible avenue for her husband to claim the English throne. With the two former enemies now united against France and the realm blighted by poor harvests and revenue shortages, Louis XIV mount a massive attack against the United Netherlands to compel them to seek peace terms. After meeting with his advisory council, the king ordered an assault against the cities of Ghent and Ypres. On 1 March, the

French besieged Ghent with an army of 60,000 men. Several days later, Louis arrived to take personal command of the investment. As trenches were dug around the stronghold, on 8 March the city government agreed to surrender, the Spanish garrison troops giving up the citadel two days later.

Following the taking of Ghent, Louis led his army west to besiege Ypres. Vauban began excavating trenches toward the citadel, the artillery battered the walls and French troops reconnoitred the countryside to guard against surprise enemy attacks. After a week's bombardment, Louis sent his troops forward during the night of 25 March, quickly forcing the garrison commander to submit. The capture of Ghent and Ypres, coupled with French military victories along the Rhine, compelled the Spanish and Germans to negotiate a peace settlement. Meeting in the Dutch town of Nijmegen, talks led to an agreement whereby Louis gained control of Franche-Comte, additional lands in the Spanish Netherlands and the imperial County of Artois. The seized town of Maastricht, along with the Principality of Orange, were returned to Stadtholder William III. The French crown pledged to withdraw from several occupied regions in northern Flanders, while Emperor Leopold I retained his conquered city of Philipsburg but had to accept French occupation of Freiburg and Kehl on the right bank of the Rhine. The Dutch War strengthened France's borders with the Netherlands and to a lesser degree with Germany, while consolidating the kingdom's position as the foremost European power.

After safeguarding his northern borders, Louis XIV directed his war initiatives toward gaining a more protected boundary line to the east. To acquire fortifications in Germany, the king began the phase of his reign known as the Reunions. The French government was ordered by Louis to begin a legal campaign to utilize the numerous local parliaments and law courts to assert France's sovereignty. When the German princes refused to accept King Louis as their overlord, the French army enforced the courts' rulings. The French gained control over Alsace and the surrounding regions without resorting to military force. Louis dispatched his envoys and legal representatives into German lands to energetically search the treaties and records for further justifications to claim additional towns and strongholds. The royal agents examined old title deeds and found validations for pursuing French rights for the regions around Falkenburg, Velden and Germersheim. Through bribery and diplomatic conspiracies, Louis gained control of the fortified city of Strasbourg.

As the French continued to 'legally' take command of additional princedoms and independent cities during the Reunions offensive, the rival European kingdoms grew increasingly hostile. Louis XIV had occupied lands formerly claimed by Spain, Holy Roman Emperor Leopold I,

Stadtholder William III, Sweden and numerous German princes. France's rivals were preoccupied with the Turkish invasion of Austria to respond to Louis' expansions into their territories. As the French continued their aggrandizement, in the summer of 1683 the imperial army led by John Sobieski of Poland defeated the Ottoman Empire's forces in the Battle of Vienna, ending the threat to Vienna and Central Europe. With his acquisitions seized since 1679 now at risk of being challenged, Louis XIV demanded they be recognized as lawful and rightful French properties. To enforce his claims and solidify his possessions, he sent armies to ravage the Spanish Netherlands. When the French advanced into his lands, King Charles II of Spain responded by declaring war to begin the War of the Reunions.

During the following year, the French armies advanced into Flanders, plundering a wide area before seizing the formidable stronghold at Luxembourg. In August 1684, Louis XIV offered the Spanish favourable peace overtures, pledging to vacate many of his recent conquests. The Spanish king had failed to re-form the alliance against France and was thus compelled to accept the terms. With the Holy Roman Empire bogged down with war against the Turks in the Balkans, the Habsburg emperor agreed to acknowledge Louis' conquests in exchange for a twenty-year truce. The brief war crowned four years of French annexations against the Germans and Spanish. The truce left in its wake a growing tide of opposition and discontent at Louis XIV's hostilities and appropriations that would produce negative consequences, as strong anti-French alliances were beginning to form. Nevertheless, when Louis XIV signed the Truce of Ratisbon, the French kingdom was larger and more powerful than it had ever been and the king was at the height of his greatness.

The balance of power began to shift away from France after the death of the Elector of the Palatinate. In danger of losing a vital and strategic ally, Louis XIV promoted the candidacy of the pro-French Elizabeth-Charlotte, Duchess of Orleans, who possessed valid rights to the Palatinate. Despite the king's intervention, the pro-imperial Prince of Pfaltz-Neuberg, Philip William, was chosen as elector by Pope Innocent XI, who acted as arbitrator. While the controversy was being debated in Rome, international pressures mounted with the death of the Elector of Cologne, Maximilien-Henry. The elector had been a loyal follower of the French and it was vital to Louis XIV's presence along the Rhine that a friendly archbishop succeed to the electorate. The French king advanced the candidacy of Cardinal von Furstenburg, while with imperial sponsorship and financial support, the House of Wittelsbach favoured the young brother of its duke, Joseph-Clement. The Archbishopric of Cologne was under papal jurisdiction and Pope

Innocent XI was empowered to appoint the new prince-bishop. To support von Furstenburg's election and influence the pope's decision, Louis moved his soldiers close to the Cologne border, while Emperor Leopold responded by sending imperial troops to oppose the French. France's relationship with the Vatican had been strained over several issues, which Louis now offered to negotiate in exchange for the selection of von Furstenburg. Leopold had recently mounted a successful military campaign against the Turks and used his newly won favour with Pope Innocent to promote his candidate. In September, the pope finally announced the selection of Joseph-Clement as Prince-Bishop of Cologne. The French political position soon deteriorated further when Leopold's army stormed the Turkish-held city of Belgrade and settled the war in the Balkans with the sultan.

During the reign of King Henry IV, the French Huguenots had been granted religious liberty when the king signed the Edict of Nantes on 13 April 1598. In 1685, Louis XIV revoked the proclamation and began to implement a succession of anti-Protestant laws. The repeal of the edict created a wave of hostility and resentment among the Protestant German princes, who now looked to Emperor Leopold for protection. The emperor's imperial army had recently driven the Turks out of Hungary. The victory increased the emperor's prestige and power, propelling him to the centre of the growing movement to resist the French campaign of territorial expansion along the Rhine. In early 1686, the Habsburg regime became the catalyst for the formation of the League of Augsburg among the German princedoms and Spain. In March of that year, Frederick-William of Brandenburg-Prussia agreed to join the emperor to check the French conquests along the Rhine. While Louis XIV's forces were challenging the members of the new league, in November 1688 William III, Stadtholder of Holland, assembled his army and invaded England. He rapidly overcame the resistance of King James II, and by December was in London to seize control of the English kingdom. William soon threw his forces into the fray against Louis.

In late 1688, the princes from Germany and envoys from England and Holland gathered at Augsburg to expand their alliance to ensure the restoration of the borders established at Westphalia in 1648. The French armed forces and economy had significantly deteriorated during the past several years of hostilities against the allies, and the king was not in an advantageous state to fight a prolonged war of attrition. In order to force a quick resolution with England, Emperor Leopold and the German princes, Louis sent his armies into the Electorate of Cologne, forcibly installing Cardinal von Furstenburg as prince-bishop. After occupying the electorate, Louis offered to settle the conflict in exchange for his annexation of the

Palatinate and the terms of the Truce of Ratisbon made permanent. When the emperor did not respond, King Louis unleashed his men across the Rhine into the Palatinate, while a separate army led by the dauphin besieged Philipsburg. The French invasion signalled the beginning of the War of the League of Augsburg, which would last for the following nine years. The war developed into the first truly global conflict, with fighting between the English and French colonists in North America, Africa and Asia as well as the main hostilities in Europe.

Louis XIV had needed a quick display of French military might along with the capture of several strategic strongholds and fortified towns along the Rhine to convince the allied powers to accept his peace terms. By the end of October 1688, the fortress at Philipsburg had surrendered, while the French troops in the Palatinate soon overran the electorate's defenders. Despite the ease of the king's victories, the emperor and the league's members refused to negotiate, beginning preparations for a counter-attack in the spring.

While the conflict along the Rhine continued, on 10 July 1690, a French navy of seventy-five warships defeated the combined Anglo-Dutch fleet of fifty-six vessels at Beachy Head off the coast of south-east England. To distract King William III from supporting his allies in Germany, Louis planned to cross the Channel and invade England, restoring James II to his throne. In early 1692, the deposed James II was at Cherbourg with an army preparing to attack England. On 19 May, the French naval forces escorting the invasion army were attacked by a combined Anglo-Dutch fleet off Cape Barfleur. The fighting lasted throughout the day and into the night, with the French naval captains manoeuvring to engage the enemy. Louis XIV's ships escaped the engagement with only minor damage, but the allies clashed with the French fleet again off Cherbourg, sinking three ships. On 24 May, twelve more French vessels were destroyed along with most of the transports, ending James II's attempt to regain the English monarchy.

Meanwhile, the French armies were able to hold the allies in check in Germany and Holland. Louis XIV now mounted a diplomatic campaign to break the League of Augsburg, but the anti-French coalition remained united, despite the efforts of Louis' envoys to sign separate peace treaties. Over the following three years, French armies waged a victorious war in the Spanish Netherlands, defeating the league's troops in numerous encounters. In May 1692, the king joined his army in Flanders and led an attack against the great fortification at Namur, located in present-day Belgium. The citadel positioned at the confluence of the Meuse and Sambre rivers was the most challenging in the Spanish Netherlands, and had been recently reinforced by Dutch engineers. While part of Louis' massive army of 130,000 men protected the approaches to Namur, the remainder of his forces besieged the city on 30 May, quickly taking the outer defensive works. Vauban led the engineers as they dug their trench lines and slowly moved closer to the walls. The fortress garrison of 5,000 Spanish troops held out for over a month but surrendered at the end of June. Louis' victory at Namur was his last personal success on the battlefield; after participating in the following year's operations, he turned over command of the army to his marshals.

After Louis returned to Versailles, Marshal Francis-Henry, Duke of Luxembourg, was appointed supreme commander of the French forces. He assembled his 80,000-strong army and marched into Flanders to resume the war against the allies. After making contact with the enemy, he constructed a strong defensive front near the town of Steinkerke in current-day Belgium. In the early morning of 3 August, the vanguard of King William III, who had recently been appointed leader of the allied war effort, attacked the French lines. As the remainder of the English and Dutch forces rushed forward into battle, William's initial assault broke through Luxembourg's defences. When the allies charged against the second fortified position, the main body of French troops entered the fray, driving the Dutch back. At the critical moment, Luxembourg threw the French Guardsmen of the Royal Household into the fight, as William III's soldiers withdrew en masse. French casualties at the Battle of Steinkerke were over 8,000 killed, wounded or captured, while the allies' sustained losses of 10,000.

The French forces led by Marshal Francis-Henry remained in the Netherlands, and almost a year later, on 29 July 1693, clashed with William III again at the town of Neerwinden. The allied army of English, Dutch and Spanish troops was attacked by the French, with savage house-to-house fighting in the town. The allies were driven back, but mounted a counter-attack to recapture lost ground. Following a second failed assault by the French, Luxembourg realigned his men and, with his cavalry leading the charge, broke King William's defences, securing victory. Despite the French army's continuing success in the Spanish Netherlands and Germany, the allies remained determined to continue the war. As France pressed the conflict against the Grand Alliance, Louis XIV stayed with his court at Versailles, directing the war effort and negotiating to diplomatically break the League of Augsburg.

While Louis pursued his campaigns against the coalition, French troops continued to occupy their defensive works at Namur. In early July 1695, the army of the Grand Alliance, led by William III of England and Maximilian II of Bavaria, advanced against the strategic Belgian fortress.

The allies besieged the town and sent troops forward to seize the reinforced defences. By 18 July, the English, Dutch and German soldiers had captured the outer fortifications and attacked the inner works, assaulting the strongly entrenched French troops and pushing them back. The remaining 13,000 French troops were compelled to withdraw to the citadel, where they held out until 1 September, when the garrison commander surrendered, having suffered 8,000 casualties, while the allies lost over 12,000 men.

As the conflict dragged on with no conclusion in sight, the French king ordered his field marshals not to launch large-scale offensives but to secure their conquests, as secret negotiations were underway. In 1697, with the allied nations preparing for a large campaign in Flanders, Louis pressed ahead with diplomatic negotiations to reach a peace settlement, offering fresh concessions. The financial cost of the war, widespread famine and economic dislocation drove all the participants to seek an agreement. In England, William III was under growing pressure from his parliament to find a resolution, forcing him to pursue serious peace talks with the French envoys. In September 1697, the Treaty of Ryswick was signed between France and England. This was followed in October by a settlement between Louis and Leopold of Austria, the German princes and the remainder of the league's members. Under the terms of the treaty, Louis XIV agreed to acknowledge William III as the lawful English king and accept the emperor's candidates for the Electorates of the Palatinate and Cologne, while abandoning his territorial gains since 1680, with the exception of the strategic fortification of Strasbourg on the Rhine. The War of the Grand Alliance resulted in a shift of the European balance of power away from the dominance of the French kingdom towards the rise of the English and German regimes.

In the aftermath of nine years of war against the Grand Alliance, the French economy was impoverished, with thousands dying of starvation and disease. To restore prosperity to his kingdom, Louis XIV needed a prolonged period of peace, but events in Europe were rapidly escalating toward the renewal of conflict after the death of the Spanish king, Charles II, and the dispute over the rightful successor to the throne of Spain. When Charles II of Spain was born in 1661, he inherited syphilis and epilepsy from his father and was expected to die during childhood. Despite the anticipation of his early death, the king lived for thirty-nine years. During his reign, he had taken two wives but failed to produce any children. In late 1700, knowing he was dying, Charles signed a will bequeathing his Spanish possessions to his great nephew and King Louis' grandson, Duke Philip of Anjou. Under the terms of the will, if for some reason the French crown declined the appointment, the document named the second son of Emperor Leopold I as the new Spanish king. Louis XIV knew war with the emperor would break out if his grandson accepted the offer, and France would have to fight the powerful coalition of England, the Holy Roman Emperor and the Dutch, with Spain as its only ally. Nevertheless, on 16 November 1700, Louis XIV announced to his assembled court that the Duke of Anjou was to be the successor to the Spanish throne, reigning as Philip V, igniting the War of the Spanish Succession. The alliance between England, Holland, the Holy Roman Empire, the Electorate of Hanover and various lesser German princes was signed in September 1701. To oppose the formidable union, Louis negotiated an offensive alliance with Spain, Portugal, Bavaria and Victor Amadeus II, Duke of Savoy. In December, King Philip V departed from the Duke of Maine's palace for Spain, a caravan of over 2,000 carriages slowly making its way south. When Louis made the announcement of his grandson's selection as Spanish king before the gathered court, he had told him: 'Be a good Spaniard, that is your first duty now but remember that you were born a Frenchman and so maintain union between the two nations, that is the way to make them both happy and keep the peace in Europe.'

The War of the Spanish Succession first flared in northern Italy, with fighting concentrated in the Spanish-ruled duchies of Milan and Mantua duchies. The French troops were massed there with their ally, Victor Amadeus II of Savoy. In May 1701, the army of the Grand Alliance, led by Prince Eugene of Savoy, advanced into northern Italy and by early the following year had defeated Louis' forces, driving them behind the Adda River. After the defeat of the French campaign in Italy, Louis XIV dismissed Victor Amadeus as field commander and appointed the Duke of Vendome, Louis Joseph I, as his replacement. Shortly after taking command, the duke launched a counter-attack to recover the losses of the previous year. Under the leadership of Vendome, the French and their Italian allies advanced against the forces of the Grand Alliance, overwhelming them and compelling them to withdraw. In 1703, while the French continued to occupy most of the north of Italy, Victor Amadeus abandoned Louis XIV and declared war on France. Despite the loss of the Duke of Savoy's soldiers, Vendome resumed his offensive, defeating his enemies at Cassanot and Calcinato, and by 1706 had occupied all of Savoy with the exception of the city of Turin and the southern Piedmont region. In May 1706, Louis XIV's army besieged Turin to consolidate its hold in the region. While the French continued their investment of Turin, the Duke of Vendome and a large part of the army were sent from Italy by the king in July 1706 to reinforce France's northern frontier against the threat of an allied attack. Following the withdrawal of the French forces, on

7 September 1707 Prince Eugene, reinforced with German troops and 7,000 cavalry from Victor Amadeus, moved against the French south of Turin. After an exchange of artillery fire, Prince Eugene sent his infantry against the French defences, breaking through on the left flank and, after repeated attacks, compelling them to retreat. French casualties were over 3,200 killed or wounded, while the allies lost some 4,000 men. The French army then withdrew from Turin, allowing Victor Amadeus to enter the city in triumph the following day. The French were compelled to fall back from northern Italy, leaving most of Piedmont under the rule of Victor Amadeus. With the forces of the Grand Alliance now occupying much of Italy, representatives of Louis XIV signed the Convention of Milan, agreeing to surrender Milan and the other occupied towns in Lombardy to the allies, thereby ending the war in Italy.

While the French and their Italian allies were fighting for control of northern Italy, Philip V of Spain was contributing little to Louis XIV's war effort and had been forced to call on his grandfather for additional financial and military support. After his coronation as Spanish king, Philip V soon made himself unpopular with his nobles when they were excluded from his government, and they now gave little assistance to the royal regime. When the Portuguese abandoned Louis XIV's coalition and united with the Grand Alliance, Philip's hold on the Spanish throne became threatened. The Portuguese soon joined an Anglo-Dutch invasion force under the command of Archduke Charles of the Austrian Habsburgs. Charles was the second son of Leopold I, and as a claimant to the Spanish throne was seeking to impose his rule. With his kingdom under attack, Philip V issued a call to his subjects to defend their homeland against the foreigners. The Spaniards rallied to the king's summons and his army repulsed the invading troops of the Grand Alliance.

In the wake of his failed invasion, Archduke Charles boarded his troops on ships in 1705 and sailed to Barcelona, where the city declared its allegiance to him and opened the port to the allies. Following the victory of the Anglo-Dutch forces at Barcelona, the war effort of King Philip V was rejuvenated in Spain. He advanced his army against the allied powers and, with his men augmented by French troops led by the experienced and skilled Philip II of Orleans, was slowly able to force the allies from his lands. By 1711, the combined Franco-Spanish had driven the league's army from all of Spain. The king's military victories against the Protestant Anglo-Dutch army won him widespread support among his Spanish subjects, which consolidated and secured his monarchy. During his campaigns for the Spanish throne, Archduke Charles II had taken the title of King Charles III of Spain, which offended the Spanish nobility and population, who disliked being ruled by an Austrian Habsburg and preferred the Bourbons.

With Louis XIV no longer campaigning with his army in the field, he largely remained at Versailles, where life at the palace revolved around his unchanging daily schedule. In the morning, he held his levee, which was the time when his courtiers could speak to him without a formal audience. The traditional rising ritual began around 8.30 am, when the first valet woke Louis, and following a visit by the doctors the ceremony began. While Louis was washed and shaved, selected friends entered the bedchamber to watch. The grand ceremony followed, where the king was dressed in his morning clothes and drank soup for breakfast. The number of spectators allowed to attend the ritual was usually around 100. At mid-morning, a procession gathered in the Hall of Mirrors and followed Louis to the Royal Chapel for Mass, which lasted for half an hour. The religious service was celebrated with the queen and members of the court. The royal choir sang a new piece of music every day, written by the king's chosen composers. After the religious observance, Louis returned to his chambers and held meetings with his council members. The four councils gathered on different days during the week to deal with international, financial, religious and national affairs. The king ate his midday meal alone in his bedchamber but routinely admitted courtiers to his rooms to carry on wide-ranging conservations. In the afternoons, he frequently went on walks in his gardens or decided to go hunting in the surrounding forest. At six o'clock, Louis would sign letters prepared by his secretary and worked on important documents with his four state secretaries. After spending several hours with his ministers, he walked to the Antechamber to have dinner at the Royal Table with the queen and members of his family. Louis had a large appetite and routinely had four different soups, a whole pheasant and duck, two slices of ham and dishes of pastry, raw fruit and preserves. Following the dinner, he entered the salon of the court ladies to converse with them before returning to his personal cabinet to talk with family members and friends. Near midnight, Louis returned to his bedchamber, where the retiring ceremony was performed to end the day.

Although the War of the Spanish Succession included clashes in Spain and Italy, the outcome of the conflict was to be decided along the Rhine and in the Spanish Netherlands. The first three years of fighting were inconclusive in Germany, with the French resigned to maintaining their occupied lands. In 1703, Louis XIV devised a bold plan for the combined French and Bavarian armies to launch an attack against Vienna and inflict a deadly blow to the Habsburg war effort, jeopardizing the continuation of the Grand Alliance. As preparations for the Vienna campaign continued, the two local field commanders failed to coordinate their operations and resolve personal problems, dooming the incursion to failure. While the French and their allies had failed to take the initiative, in 1704 the allied powers unleashed a massive two-pronged attack, with the Anglo-Dutch forces of John Churchill, Duke of Marlborough, advancing from the north and Prince Eugene of Savoy leading his imperial troops up from Italy. The allied armies were to converge in Bavaria and force the remaining ally of the French, Maximilian II Emmanuel of Bavaria, to desert King Louis. On 13 August 1704, the rival armies clashed at the Battle of Blenheim. The Franco-Bavarian army of 56,000 men was led by Marshal Camille d'Hostun, Duke of Tallard, while Churchill and Prince Eugene commanded a combined force of 52,000 English, German and Dutch soldiers. After making contact with the allies, Tallard deployed his soldiers along a line with his right flank anchored on the Danube and his left protected by dense forest. The bulk of his army occupied three fortified villages in the centre. Marlborough positioned Prince Eugene to his right and began the battle by sending his infantry against the village of Blenheim, while Eugene attacked the Bavarian front. Tallard then ordered his infantry and horsemen from his centre to support his troops on the flanks, weakening the middle of his position. Marlborough, sensing the opportunity, sent his soldiers to attack the centre of the Franco-Bavarian line with superior numbers, forcing Tallard to retreat after fierce and bloody fighting. The collapse of the middle of Tallard's position left the French right vulnerable, and despite continuing to fight, they were overwhelmed and compelled to surrender. The Battle of Blenheim was a devasting defeat for Louis' war effort in Germany, forcing him to abandon operations in the eastern theatre.

Following the failure of the French campaign in Germany, the allies shifted their offensive operations to the Spanish Netherlands. In the wake of his victory at Blenheim, the Duke of Marlborough moved his army back to Flanders, fighting the French in a series of small skirmishes in 1705. After a year of limited engagements, Louis XIV's army of Marshal Francis of Neufville, Duke of Villeroy, was attacked by the combined Anglo-Dutch-German forces of Churchill at Ramillies on 23 May 1706. The initial assault of the allies was repelled by Villeroy's men, but while the French were driving the enemy back on the left, Churchill's troops rallied on the right flank, rushing forward and forcing the enemy to retreat in disarray. After the decisive victory of the allies at Ramillies, the French king was compelled to abandon his territorial gains in the Spanish Netherlands. During the next two years, Louis' troops were steadily pushed back by the allies and were compelled to defend their border fortifications. In 1708, Prince Eugene of Savoy transferred his army from Italy, again joining forces with Marlborough in Flanders. As the French military position continued to deteriorate, the king opened peace negotiations with the members of the Grand League, but the talks ended without any agreement.

With the campaigning season for 1709 approaching, Louis XIV prepared for the worst. The royal French treasury had been depleted, the kingdom was beset with widespread famine, crop failures, internal revolt and poverty, and France's armies had been repeatedly defeated.

In 1709, Louis appointed Claude Louis, Duke of Villars, as his new commander for the severely demoralized French troops in Flanders. The duke was a resourceful and skilled leader who had successfully led the cavalry forces of the royal regime. Louis succeeded in raising enough money to purchase armaments and supplies for the next year to field an army for the defence of the French border.

The Duke of Villars refused to give battle to Marlborough and Prince Eugene, only attacking the allies in small skirmishes or harassing their lines of communications to keep them in check. As the French continued to avoid attacking them, the Grand Alliance became convinced Louis XIV's regime was on the verge of collapse and ordered Marlborough to assault the fortress at Tournai. The garrison held out until early September before surrendering. Churchill soon resumed his campaign, advancing to besiege the stronghold at Mons. As the allied troops approached the great Mons citadel, Villars manoeuvred his army to prevent them from attacking the fortification. On 9 September, the French army finally made contact with the allies near Malplaquet, constructing a fortified line reinforced with trenches and breastworks in the centre and earthworks and entrenchments on the flanks, protected by woodland. Early on the morning of 11 September, Marlborough sent his English troops into the French left flank, and shortly after the Dutch moved against the enemy's right. Despite heavy casualties, the Dutch troops under Prince Eugene continued to press forward until Marlborough ordered their withdrawal. With his right side under heavy assault, Villars repositioned troops from his centre to reinforce the flank. As the French continued to strengthen their right with soldiers from the centre, their lines began to crumble, the allies securing victory when their cavalry overran the fortified French position. During the fighting, the army of Villars – who was wounded by a musket ball – suffered over 11,500 casualties, but allied losses totalled more than 20,000 wounded and killed. With victory for the Grand Alliance having proved so costly, it meant there could be no invasion of the Kingdom of France until those losses were made good. Louis expressed his gratitude to Villars for his efforts at Malplaquet by making him a Peer of France.

At the beginning of 1710, Louis XIV's realm remained impoverished, with the economy in shambles and the armies ill-prepared to fight a prolonged campaign. Hard-pressed to continue the war, the French needed to reach a peace agreement with the allies, and Louis sent envoys to open talks in Utrecht. To press their position when the discussions began, the armies of Marlborough and Prince Eugene advanced to besiege the French strongholds protecting the border. The allies, unwilling to risk another costly battle with Louis, were satisfied with a prolonged campaign of sieges. Believing they held the stronger position, members of the Grand Alliance escalated their demands for larger concessions. The French king refused to accept the allies' proposal and the war continued, with Churchill and Prince Eugene capturing several French border fortifications before the end of the campaigning season. Louis' outlook for the coming year was bleak, with an invasion of the kingdom seemingly imminent.

Despite the unfavourable circumstances for the French king in 1711, events would surprisingly turn to his advantage and make possible a negotiated peace agreement. In Spain, Philip V rallied his subjects and forced the allied troops out of Barcelona, this victory strengthening his hold on the throne. Meanwhile, in England, the parliament changed hands to the Tories and the new government dismissed Marlborough from command of the army, losing interest in pursuing the French war. The English administration instead manoeuvred to resolve the War of the Spanish Succession with a negotiated peace settlement. The European political climate changed further in Louis' favour when Emperor Joseph I died and was succeeded on the Habsburg throne by Archduke Charles II. Charles had earlier aggressively sought the Spanish crown, but no European power was now willing to pursue a war that could produce the unification of the German and Spanish kingdoms under the Habsburg emperor. To preserve the two independent realms, peace talks were renewed at Utrecht in the spring with a new spirit of collaboration.

The Utrecht negotiations dragged on through the year, with the Germans stubbornly refusing to reach a settlement. The German princes – Charles VI, Holy Roman Emperor; Prince Eugene of Savoy; Louis William, Margrave of Baden-Baden; Guido Wald Rudiger, Count of Starhemberg and chief Austrian army commander; and Leopold II, Prince of Anhalt-Dessau – wanted to resume the war and invade France to dictate terms. As talks continued inconclusively, fighting resumed and Marshal Villars defeated an Anglo-Dutch army led by Prince Eugene on 24 July 1712 at Denain. The battle began with a bombardment from Villars' artillery, then his infantry moved forward in close order to the beat of 500 drums, shouting 'Long live the King!'. As the French approached the allied line, they were hit by volleys of musketry. The front line wavered under the heavy fire, but pressed forward. When the Dutch saw the French continuing to advance into their musket fire, they deserted their position and retreated through the town of Denain, handing the victory to Villars.

In the aftermath of Villars' victory at Denain, the French continued their offensive against the allied forces. Over the next few months, the allies were driven out of several towns they had seized in recent years. Shortly after the clash at Denain, the French overran the enemy's supply depot at Marchiennes, capturing large stores of supplies and armament. Villars resumed the campaign by occupying the towns of Douai and Quesnay in present-day north-western France after short sieges. When the French retook Bouchain on 19 October 1712 following an eighteen-day siege, most of the pre-war lands occupied by Louis XIV in the southern Netherlands had been regained. Meanwhile, as the French king's army had reoccupied Flanders, his troops along the Rhine were also again moving successfully against the enemy. The resurgent French forces in Flanders and Germany convinced the allies that Louis XIV still retained the resolve and ability to fight them, resulting in a dramatic shift in their willingness to continue the conflict. A peace treaty was finally signed at Utrecht in 1714, ending the fourteen-year war. Under the terms of the treaty, Philip V retained the Spanish throne but renounced his and future heirs' rights to the French monarchy. The Habsburgs received the Spanish Netherlands and England was granted Gibraltar and several French colonies in North America. Louis XIV was ceded the Principality of Orange from Prussia.

During these wars of the French, Louis XIV, while not campaigning with his armies, had remained involved from Versailles, maintaining absolute control over all decisions and war strategies. Despite his advancing years, he regularly attended his council meetings and continued with the daily court rituals. Following the settlement of the War of the Spanish Succession, the king's health steadily deteriorated from the stresses of nearly twenty-five years of wars, an impoverished economic system and a series of personal family tragedies. The grand dauphin, Louis, had died in 1711. and all of his grandchildren – with the exception of King Philip V of Spain – were also dead, while Queen Maria Theresa had passed away back in 1683. Yet in spite of his age and periodic bouts of illness, Louis remained in charge of the governing of his kingdom. Each morning, he routinely met with his councils, and after lunch went hunting, then spending his early evenings with his ministers. After dinner, he talked to members of his family before retiring shortly after midnight. The first sign of serious illness occurred on 10 August 1715 with a burning discomfort in his stomach. In spite of treatment from his doctors, the aching remained, then black marks began to appear, indicating gangrene. The king continued to carry out his daily routines, despite the pain, until 25 August, when he was confined to his bed. During the following days, Louis' health steadily declined, the pain in his left leg growing worse. Louis made plans for his death, and on the afternoon of 31 August spoke his last words: 'Help oh God, help me quickly.' The king remained unconscious through that night and died on the morning of 1 September 1715 at the age of 77 following a reign of seventy-two years. During the early evening of 9 October, six black horses set out with the body of Louis XIV for the Basilica of St Denis on the outskirts of Paris for the entombment of the king. The royal cortege reached the basilica the following morning and the coffin was placed on a draped platform. The next day, a High Mass was sung and Louis' body was lowered into the Bourbon vault, where it remained among his ancestors until revolutionary mobs desecrated the royal tombs some eighty years later.

In the aftermath of the death of Louis XIV, the throne of France was occupied for fifty-nine years by his great-grandson, Louis XV. The new king was aged just 5 when he was acknowledged as the successor to the French crown, and for the next twenty-five years the kingdom was poorly governed by several regents, whose policies involved France in costly wars, ineffective economic policies and the return of parliamentary unrest. In 1743, Louis announced his assumption of the government but continued to leave his appointed ministers in charge, while he spent his time occupied with pleasurable pursuits. Beginning in 1749, the realm's stability and financial condition deteriorated further, while the Age of Enlightenment began to exert its influence on the French nobles and citizens with new critical philosophies. In 1756, Louis XV took his kingdom into the Seven Years' War, which resulted in the loss of most of France's colonial empire. The end of his reign was marked by further unrest with parliament, where the deputies moved to employ their powers over the monarchy. Upon his death in May 1774, Louis XV left France with a greatly weakened government and a restless population seeking a greater voice in the ruling of the country.

Louis XVI, the grandson of Louis XV, was recognized as the successor to the French throne. He inherited a deteriorating financial situation and a badly impaired image of the monarchy. Taking the reins of power, he attempted to reform the French government but was too easily influenced by self-serving noblemen and lacked a decisive personality, producing disastrous results. The king's decision to support the rebellious American colonists in their war of independence against England further weakened the realm financially. With the nobles and commoners increasingly demanding changes, Louis XVI was forced to convene the States General in 1788, which failed to make reforms, pushing the kingdom deeper into distress. A National Assembly was formed and swiftly gave itself constitutional powers without the approval of the king. As France moved closer to anarchy, the citizens of Paris revolted against the king's rule on 14 July 1789, ending the Age of Absolutism and establishing a constitutional government. In September 1792, the constitutional regime was revoked and Louis XVI was deposed and imprisoned in the Temple. He was put on trial and declared guilty of treason. On 21 January 1793, the king was guillotined, decisively ending the French monarchy. The succeeding governments – the Committee of Public Safety and then the Directory – failed to effectively govern the country, and in December 1799 Napoleon Bonaparte organized a coup d'etat, seizing control of France as First Consul.

Selected Sources

Bernier, Olivier, *Louis XIV – A Royal Life*
Boulenger, Jacques, *The Seventeenth Century*
Briggs, Robin, *Early Modern France 1560–1715*
Castries, Duc de, *The Lives of the Kings and Queens of France*
Cronin, Vincent, *Louis XIV*
Dunlop, Ian, *Louis XIV*
Erlanger, Philippe, *Louis XIV*
Laffin, John, *Brassey's Dictionary of Battles*
Lynn, John A., *The Wars of Louis XIV 1667–1714*
Norwich, John Julius, *A History of France*
Seward, Desmond, *The Bourbon Kings of France*
Volkmann, Jean-Charles, *The Family Trees of the Kings of France*
Wolf, John B., *Louis XIV*

Napoleon

In August 1805, Napoleon Bonaparte abandoned his planned invasion of England and relocated his Grand Army to the east to confront the newly formed hostile Grand Alliance of Austria and Russia. On 2 December, the French army of 70,000 men, commanded by Napoleon, collided with an 85,000-strong Russian and Austrian force near the small village of Austerlitz in the present-day Czech Republic. Early in the morning, the allies opened the battle by attacking the French right flank with soldiers transferred from their defensive position on the Pratzen Heights, driving their opponents back. Sensing the allied centre had now been weakened by the Austro-Russian assaults on his right, Napoleon ordered a counter-attack against the heights, telling Marshal Jean de Dieu Soult: 'One sharp blow and the war is over.' While the Austro-Russians continued to throw their soldiers into the battle, the French emperor's IV Corps, led by Soult, charged up the Pratzen Heights, seizing the high ground in violent and brutal fighting. As the marshal pressed his onslaught, his men cut the Austro-Russian army in two. With the allied centre now destroyed, the French swept through the flanks of the Austro-Russians, who as their lines started to collapse all along the front, began to flee the battlefield. In the wake of the battle, Emperor Napoleon told his men: 'Soldiers I am pleased with you. You have decorated your eagles with an immortal glory.' The French defeat of the Austro-Russians at Austerlitz is widely considered as Napoleon's greatest victory.

Napoleon was born on 15 August 1769 in the Corsican town of Ajaccio, the third son of the eight surviving children born to Carlo Maria Bonaparte, who was descended from Tuscan nobility, and Letizia Bonaparte. The island of Corsica had been ceded to France during the year before Napoleon's birth by the Republic of Genoa, to the disapproval of the residents, who rose up in a war of independence led by their national hero, Pasquale Paoli. Carlo Bonaparte supported the uprising and joined the resistance, serving as a commander in the rebel army and leading his troops against the French invaders. When the rebellion was suppressed by the French army several

184

months before Napoleon's birth, Carlo submitted and accepted the victors, while Paoli and his followers fled into the mountains to continue their resistance.

The young Napoleon grew up in the household of a passionate Corsican patriot and acquired a hatred of the French occupiers. The Bonapartes had emigrated to Corsica in the middle of the sixteenth century from Tuscany, establishing successful law and farming businesses. Following the suppression of Paoli's insurgency, the Bonaparte family returned to their home in the seaport of Ajaccio, where Carlo resumed his practice of law. In Ajaccio, Carlo earned a substantial income from his law practice and farmlands, and was considered among the island's nobility

Napoleon was raised in a loving and secure family environment, which was dominated by his mother. When Napoleon reached the age of 5, he was sent to a church school run by nuns to begin his education. Two years later, he was enrolled in a Jesuit school, where he learned to read and write in Italian while studying Latin, mathematics and ancient history. In the informal environment of Ajaccio, the young Bonaparte children had many friends and led a happy and active childhood as members of the Corsican nobility. Among his brothers and sisters, Napoleon was noted as the child with the most uncompromising and energetic personality.

The French occupation of Corsica brought many changes to the island's population and government. Under the new regime, a parliament was established to advise the king's appointed commissioner, and all who could provide proof of their noble birth were permitted to participate in the Corsican administration. When Carlo Bonaparte met with the French authorities and gave evidence of his royal ancestry, he was declared a member of the French nobility and appointed as a representative to the Corsican parliament. Participating in the island's assembly, Napoleon's father came into contact with the French-appointed governor, developing a friendship with him. Carlo utilized his relationship with the chief administrator to acquire scholarships for Napoleon to the military academy at Brienne and for his eldest son, Joseph, to attend the church-sponsored school at Autun. Before departing for France, Letizia took her two eldest sons to be blessed by the Father Superior, following the Corsican custom. On 12 December 1778, the two boys bid farewell to their family and set out on horseback to the port of Bastia for the sea voyage to France. During the winter of 1779, the 9-year-old Napoleon set foot in France for the first time.

When the ship carrying the Bonaparte brothers landed in France, they were met by their father, who was representing the interests of Corsica at the French court in Versailles. Carlo escorted Napoleon and Joseph to the town of Autun, where they were to learn the French language at the local college. In early January 1779, Carlo left his sons and made his way to Paris to secure Napoleon's certificate of noble birth. Napoleon spent four months at the school, slowly learning to speak and write in French. He had limited linguistic skills and spoke French with a strong Italian accent. After the royal heraldist issued Napoleon's documents certifying his noble birth, he was taken to the military school at Brienne, south-east of Paris, to begin his training as a French army officer, while Joseph attended college in Autun to prepare for the priesthood.

Napoleon arrived at Brienne in May 1779. Brienne Military School had been established two years earlier to train officers to fill the ranks of the army in France's wars against England, and was administered by monks from the Minimes religious order. Arriving at the academy, Napoleon was taken to a barrack with ten small cubicles, each furnished with a bed, mattress, blankets, chair and table. Each day began for Napoleon at 6.00 am, when the students were awakened and quickly dressed in their blue uniforms. After attending a briefing session with the other boys on the benefits of good behaviour, he went to Mass and then ate breakfast. School started at 8.00 am, and the cadets were instructed in the established subjects of mathematics, physics, Latin and history. At ten o'clock, lessons in fortification building were held, followed by map drawing. The main meal of the day was served at noon, followed by an hour of free time. The students returned to their courses in the afternoon, and later practiced dancing, fencing, music or gymnastics depending on the day of the week. The next two hours were devoted to homework, then at eight o'clock supper was served. A second hour of recreation was held after eating, and at 10.00 pm the lights were extinguished, ending the day's training. Coming from Corsica and speaking with a strong Italian accent, Napoleon stood out from the other cadets. He was considered a foreigner from a lower class of nobility, and was not readily accepted by his classmates, who routinely bullied him for his place of birth, accent and short stature. Feeling like a refugee, he became withdrawn and restrained. In Corsica, he had been at the top of the social scale; now he was near the bottom. Despite suffering discrimination from his fellow students, Napoleon excelled in his maths, geography and history courses, spending his free times reading about the great military leaders of the past.

After spending five years at Brienne, the 15-year-old Napoleon was accepted for admission to France's elite military school at the Ecole Militaire in Paris in October 1784. His high grades in mathematics at Brienne had earned the Corsican cadet a position in the artillery classes. He left Brienne on 17 October and travelled to Paris by coach and river barge. Napoleon began his military education at the school on a gentleman cadet scholarship awarded by King Louis XVI. The academy had been built thirteen years earlier and was one of the great sights of Paris. Napoleon found the building lavish, with the walls in the classrooms covered with blue and gold fleur de lys and curtains hanging from the windows and doors. The elaborate cadet rooms were larger and better furnished than the young Corsican had been assigned at Brienne, and the school provided delicious meals with wider choices. Cadet Bonaparte now wore a blue uniform with a red collar and silver braid. He was awoken in the morning by the sounds of drums, the school's atmosphere mimicking life with an army garrison. The military school had been established to provide an education to the sons of the court's nobles prior to their entry into the king's officer corps. Life was more comfortable for Napoleon at the lavishly appointed royal academy, where great attention was paid to learning the required social graces and proper etiquette of the crown's officers.

While Napoleon continued his studies, in late February 1785 his father died of stomach cancer. He was greatly saddened by his father's death, experiencing a deep sense of loss. When Napoleon was asked by the school's chaplain if he wished to have a few hours of solitude in the infirmary, the cadet replied that he was strong enough to bear the news. He soon resumed his studies and life as a military cadet. Napoleon remained a serious student; his best grades were in mathematics and geography, but he did poorly in drawing. After only one year at the Ecole Militaire, Napoleon had achieved high-enough grades in his examinations to receive an early graduation. At the age of 16, Napoleon Bonaparte was appointed a second lieutenant in the king's artillery. While most of his classmates had taken two years or more to graduate, he was commissioned after just one year, ranked forty-second out of fifty-eight. He was assigned to his first duty station in the south of France at Valence with the La Fere Regiment.

Lieutenant Bonaparte reported for duty with his regiment on 3 November 1785, dressed in his uniform of blue pants and royal blue coat with red facings and gold and silver epaulettes. He was assigned to a bombardier company and spent his initial ten weeks in basic training, first drilling as a private, then a corporal and finally as a sergeant. As a bombardier, he tended the vents in the breeches of the cannon and placed the ammunition in the muzzle for the gunner to fire. In mid-January 1786, he completed his orientation and began service as an artillery officer. In the mornings, the young second lieutenant practiced manoeuvring, sighting and firing his artillery pieces, while in the afternoons he attended lectures on ballistics, trajectories and firepower. During his free time, Napoleon became an obsessive reader of politics, history, military memoirs, science and political theory.

Napoleon returned to Corsica during 1786 for a brief visit with his mother and family, returning to the island again two years later, when he witnessed the effects of the now hostile and oppressive policies of the French regime. The throne's appointed governor had died and was replaced by a cabinet of administrators in Paris, who instituted a series of harsh economic and tax programmes against the island's residents. As a direct result of the repressive measures, the Bonaparte family's income from farming was greatly diminished. They now depended on Napoleon's military salary for their only regular source of funds. From his wide reading and witnessing the harsh life of his family and friends in Corsica, he developed a belief that it was the responsibility and duty of those in power to act in the best interest of those who gave them their authority. He now opposed the rule of an absolute king and favoured a constitutional monarchy. With the people of Corsica suffering under the administration of the government in Paris, Napoleon orchestrated several attempts to rectify their broken promises by making contact with the king's representatives, but no satisfactory resolution was forthcoming.

While Napoleon was involved in his period of self-discovery and political change, France was increasingly falling into financial crisis from the many years of wars, lavish and unrestrained court spending and a series of failed economic policies. As the kingdom entered bankruptcy, King Louis XVI was compelled to summon the Estates General to find new measures to increase the tax revenue. The assembled deputies rapidly turned away from the monarchy and came under the dominance of the Third Estate – comprising everyone apart from the clergy and nobility, the First and Second Estates – which quickly exerted its powers and in 1791 declared a constitutional regime.

In October 1791, Napoleon was granted an extended leave of absence from the army and returned to Corsica, where he became involved in the island's politics. Still considering himself a Corsican, he supported the islanders' acceptance of the 1791 constitution. The French Revolution had resulted in the creation of a new government and the establishment of a National Guard. While in France, Napoleon had aggressively campaigned for the new military unit's approval and became a candidate for one of its positions of command. During the establishment of the National Guard, Lieutenant Bonaparte was appointed lieutenant colonel for one of the Guard's two battalions.

Extending his leave in Corsica, Napoleon was given command of the National Guardsmen stationed at Ajaccio. When the National Assembly passed new religious laws involving the rights of the priests, Napoleon soon became involved in the conflict between the supporters of the decree and the dissenters. An armed dispute soon erupted, and Lieutenant Colonel Bonaparte intervened with his soldiers to restore order. As the conflict continued to escalate, Napoleon was compelled to call upon the local French commander for his mediation. When the request was denied, Napoleon ordered his men to attack the French-held citadel to force the garrison's colonel to order his soldiers to support his National Guardsmen. The assault was quickly repelled and civilian officials became involved to restore peace. The French governor sent an official report to Paris demanding the arrest of Napoleon for taking up arms against a military unit of the regime.

In May 1792, Napoleon was forced to return to Paris to explain and defend his actions and to justify his extended leave of absence. He spoke with War Ministry representatives, and following a series of meetings was successful in having the charges dropped. He was soon ordered to report back to his artillery unit by the army department, with the rank of captain. During the period of Napoleon's stay in Paris, the kings and nobles of Europe openly opposed the creation of the new French government. The Habsburg emperor of Austria and the King of Prussia declared war, sending their armies into France promising to restore the old regime. Louis XVI was suspected of plotting with them and encouraging their armed support. As the Corsican captain remained in Paris, a large mob of protesters marched to the Tuileries Palace on 20 June to confront the king. Napoleon followed the loud and boisterous protesters, who shouted insulting slogans against the king in the palace. They broke into Louis XVI's apartment and spent over two hours with him, complaining about the monarchy, before slowly dispersing. The unrest in Paris grew, and on 10 August the rebellious protesters again attacked the Tuileries, Napoleon watching from the window of a nearby shop. When the crowd grew more hostile, King Louis appeared outside the palace to calm them, but was greeted with repeated insults and forced to return to his apartment. He shortly thereafter departed from the palace and made his way to the safety of the Assembly. The anarchy spread throughout France, the extremists demanding the end of the monarchy and nobility. On 13 August 1792, the king was arrested and sent to the Temple prison. France was declared a republic on 21 September and the reign of the king abolished. Louis remained the prisoner of the Republic, and on 21 January 1793 was beheaded by the guillotine, beginning the era of the Terror

Napoleon Bonaparte returned to his native Corsica in October 1792, intent on bringing the spirit of the rebellion to his homeland. After arriving in Corsica, he was reappointed by the government as lieutenant colonel for a battalion of National Guardsmen. In his absence, Pasquale Paoli had returned to Corsica from his exile in England and had been named governor by the French Republic. Lieutenant Colonel Bonaparte pressed Paoli to carry the French revolt to its enemies by attacking nearby islands held by the Kingdom of Sardinia. Paoli reluctantly approved the operation and Bonaparte planned a detailed campaign, while the nephew of Paoli, Colonna Cesari, was appointed to lead the expedition. Napoleon and the invasion force were carried to the island on board the naval corvette *Fauvette*. In the late afternoon of 22 February 1793, he led his men in the assault against the island of San Stefano, located in the Tyrrhenian Sea off the west coast of Italy. The Corsicans landing on the beach were supported by the guns from the *Fauvette*. Under Napoleon's leadership, the Corsicans quickly overwhelmed the Sardinians and occupied the island, while Cesari prepared to lead the attack against a second island, Maddaleno. The incursion against Maddaleno was planned for 25 February, but the Corsican volunteers and regular troops led by Colonna Cesari refused to fight and the attack was cancelled. Unknown to Napoleon, Cesari was following Paoli's secret orders to disrupt the campaign. The French abandoned San Stefano and returned to Corsica to a greatly disappointed Napoleon, who sent reports to the War Ministry in Paris and Paoli, describing the lack of courage and ineptness of the soldiers in the second attack.

When Napoleon returned to Corsica from France, he had enthusiastically supported the island's participation in the French Revolution, while Paoli favoured the island's independence. The struggle between the opposing political parties quickly reached breaking point when Napoleon's younger brother, Lucien, addressed the Toulon Jacobin Club denouncing Paoli as a traitor of the revolution. A Corsican civil war erupted between the factions of Paoli and the Bonapartes, with the governor outmanoeuvring Napoleon and his supporters. The Bonapartes' house was ransacked and the island parliament, acting under instructions from the Corsican governor, declared the family traitors and outlaws. In June 1793, Napoleon – along his mother, three sisters and three brothers – was forced to flee from Corsica to France, settling in Marseille.

While Napoleon was occupied with the adoption of revolutionary beliefs in Corsica, the Terror had erupted in his newly adopted country. The ultra-extremist Jacobins, under the domination of Maximilien Robespierre, had seized control of the National Convention and initiated a reign of oppression against the opposition. The Jacobins were united by the belief that goodness was republicanism and everything else must be eliminated. As Robespierre's repressive measures multiplied, numerous provincial towns defied the regime's Committee of Public Safety and enthusiastically participated in the civil war in support of the restoration of the Bourbon monarchy. Many Frenchmen refused to accept the new government's radical beliefs, with much of the nation up in arms.

Following his departure from Corsica, Napoleon left his family in Marseille and soon rejoined his regiment at Pontet, north-east of Avignon. Before his arrival, the National Guard had seized Avignon, and Captain Bonaparte was now ordered to retake the town. On 14 July, he led his regiment in the attack and drove out the Jacobite supporters, reoccupying Avignon for the Republic. During the fierce fighting, Bonaparte witnessed the brutality of civil war as French soldiers shot French soldiers and civilians killed fellow civilians. Deeply disturbed by the butchery, he wrote to the War Ministry asking for a transfer to the army in the east to avoid fighting other Frenchmen. Instead of a posting to the Army of the Rhine, however, Captain Bonaparte was ordered to report to Toulon and take part in the siege against the royalist-occupied city.

After reaching the army at Toulon, Napoleon was appointed commander of the artillery besieging the city. The Mediterranean port had revolted against the Republican government and opened its harbour to English and Spanish ships. Toulon was occupied by 18,000 foreign troops, who had been transferred to the city to enforce the restoration of the monarchy and the succession to the throne by Louis XVII. Taking charge of the siege guns, Captain Bonaparte had only five artillery pieces and a few untested men. His commanding officers were inexperienced and incompetent, and the attacks against the city faltered. Napoleon spent three months building an effective artillery unit of 194 guns and mortars manned by 1,600 artillerymen. In November, a competent general, Jacques Coquille Dugommier, finally took command and Bonaparte convinced him to make an assault on the English-held fortresses protecting the harbour from the surrounding hills. The strongholds were the keys to the defence of Toulon, and Napoleon understood that once they had been neutralized, the English fleet could easily be bombarded and compelled to flee the port. He deployed a large artillery battery to shell the English forces in Fort Mulgrave and placed several smaller supporting units to fire on the other fortifications. During the night of 16 December, Bonaparte's guns began firing on the forts. The following morning, 5,000 Republican troops led by General Dugommier launched their attack, and after several hours of fighting drove off the defenders. Napoleon was then ordered to attack with his force of 2,000 men. He led his soldiers forward in the pouring rain. Approaching the fortification, Captain Bonaparte sent a detachment of infantrymen to assail the flanks, while he charged the fort's main defences. Following several hours of fierce fighting with bayonets, pikes and swords, the fort fell to the Republicans. Napoleon's cannons were then directed at the English and Spanish ships in the harbour. After ten vessels went up in flames, and still under heavy fire, the enemy naval forces were compelled to abandon Toulon, taking the garrison troops with them. The citizens of Toulon then opened the gates to the Republicans, crushing the spirit and enthusiasm for the civil war in southern France.

During the fighting, Napoleon was wounded in the thigh by a bayonet and was almost forced to have his leg amputated. He had displayed courage and leadership at Toulon, winning high praise from General Dugommier. For his outstanding performance in defence of the French Republic, he was promoted to brigadier general. The siege at Toulon had afforded Bonaparte an opportunity to demonstrate his military skills and professionalism, and he had seized it with both hands, sparking Napoleon's future rise to greatness.

Following Brigadier General Bonaparte's promotion, he was assigned a new post as inspector for the southern coastal defensive system. While performing his duties in southern France, he met and became friends with numerous members of Robespierre's government who ruled the nation during the Terror. In the early summer of 1794, he was sent on a secret mission to Genoa by the Robespierre administration to report on the strength of its army. In late July, however, the Jacobin political faction was overthrown and anyone who was associated with its members came under suspicion by the new regime. Due to Napoleon's involvement with the Jacobins, he was arrested in August. For several weeks his life was in danger, but no incriminating evidence was found and he was released. Despite the lack of proof, the charges against him left a stain on his reputation and career. General Bonaparte was now denied assignments in the eastern theatre of operations, and his continued service was in doubt. To further his career in the army, Bonaparte travelled to Paris, meeting with officials in the War Ministry in an attempt to persuade them to reassign him to a fighting unit, but to no avail. The only result of his meetings was a new assignment in the war and intelligence office. However, he only wanted to command a combat unit; anything else resulted in the frustration of his ambition.

As General Bonaparte languished in the War Ministry, France continued to be in turmoil, with widespread civil war and attacks against its borders by the First Coalition of Britain, Russia, Prussia, Spain, Holland and Austria.

The administration of the National Convention had proven incapable of governing the nation, and in August 1795 it was abolished. A bicameral legislature consisting of the Council of Ancients and Council of the Five Hundred was established as the central governing body, while the Directory of five elected officials served as the executive branch. The Council of Five Hundred drafted the laws, which were sent to the upper house for approval or rejection.

In Paris, the resurgent royalist party strongly opposed the new regime. On 4 October 1795, a rebellion was organized and an attack planned against the centre of the new constitutional government on the following day at the Tuileries Palace. To protect the newly authorized Directory, loyal Republican soldiers were hastily rushed to the city under the command of Paul Barras. Bonaparte had met Barras during the fighting at Toulon and impressed him with his military professionalism and resolve. Without hesitation, Barras gave Napoleon command of the artillery unit. He deployed his cannons to provide maximum protection to the Tuileries and inflict the greatest damage on the enemy. When the insurgent forces attacked on 5 October, they broke through the outer defensive line to face the massed guns of Bonaparte. As the royalists surged forward, General Bonaparte ordered his artillery to open fire. The first volley staggered the rebel advance, but they regrouped and moved ahead. Napoleon then fired his cannons again, and after repeated volleys the assault was repelled, swiftly ending the revolt. For the first time since the French Revolution had erupted, the Paris mob had failed to enforce its will on the ruling government. In a letter Napoleon wrote to his brother Joseph describing the mob's attack, he told him: 'We killed a great many of them and now all is quiet.' When future mobs attempted to seize control, they were met with a similar strong and determined response. Napoleon's decisive actions in defence of the Directory won the respect and admiration of the administration. Three weeks later he was appointed to the rank of full general and named second in command of the Army of the Interior under Barras. On 26 October, Barras was named to the Directory and Napoleon appointed to lead the army, which was reorganized to keep order in Paris and the surrounding region.

As commander of the Army of the Interior, General Bonaparte was stationed in Paris at the War Ministry, where he met many influential politicians and generals in the Republican government. Napoleon used these officials to gain access to many of Paris' fashionable salons and parties. He considered his relationships with these men as a means to further his army career by securing a posting to a combat command in Germany or Italy. Shortly after the defeat of the 5 October revolt, Napoleon was introduced to Marie Josephine Rose Beauharnais at a soiree. Josephine was born on the French-occupied island of Martinique in the eastern Caribbean on 23 June 1763 and spent the first fifteen years of her life on her father's sugarcane plantation. When a series of hurricanes destroyed the family's estate, she accompanied her father to Paris. In 1779, she married a wealthy aristocrat, Alexander de Beauharnais, with whom she had two children. She later received a separation from her husband for his continued verbal abuses and avoidance, returning to Martinique. In 1790, a slave uprising on the island compelled Rose to return to Paris, where she became part of the fashionable society in the capital. Her life became endangered when her husband was arrested as an aristocrat during the Terror. As the wife of a renowned nobleman, she was imprisoned. Josephine remained in the Carmes Prison until the leader of the Terror, Robespierre, was killed, and she was released by the new regime. As the wife of a notable, she had many influential friends and a refinement and sophistication that were useful in Parisian high society. At the time she met Napoleon, she was the mistress of Paul Barras, the most powerful and ranking member of the five-man Directory. Her relationship with Barras put Josephone at the centre of power, making her a person who could be useful to a young general seeking an assignment as commander of an army. As Napoleon spent more time with Josephine, he fell in love with her. Josephine did not return his feelings but with her looks fading and without a steady source of income to pay her large debts, she continued to meet with him.

While General Bonaparte carried on his relationship with Josephine, he actively pursued the command of an army on the war front. He had little success in gaining his appointment, but through the intervention of Barras his opportunities were now greatly improved. Barras, anxious to end his romantic affair with Josephine to pursue other women, offered Napoleon command of the Army of Italy as an inducement for his marriage to her. With an opportunity to lead the Italian campaign at stake, he pressed his marriage proposal more vigorously, and finally, in February 1796, Josephine agreed. The wedding ceremony was held on 9 March, and two days later General Bonaparte departed for his new Italian command. The relationship between Napoleon and Josephine quickly became strained, as she began a love affair with a handsome Hussar officer from the Directory's staff soon after he left for Italy. During their early years of marriage, Josephine continued to take lovers, but after Napoleon began an affair during his Egyptian expedition she remained faithful to her husband.

The French Republic had been at war with the members of the First Coalition since 1792, and the Directory ordered Napoleon to cross the Alps into northern Italy and defeat two of its enemies, Emperor Francis II of Austria and Victor Amadeus III, King of Piedmont. Francis II was born on 12 February 1768 in Florence, the eldest son of Holy Roman Emperor Leopold II and Empress Luisa of Spain. He was educated at the imperial court in Vienna in preparation for his assumption of the Austrian throne. After the death of his father on 1 March 1792, Francis II was acknowledged as emperor of the Holy Roman Empire. During the wars of the French Revolution and after Napoleon's seizure of power, Francis II led the Austrian war effort in defence of his homeland. He reigned as Holy Roman Emperor until August 1806, when he abdicated the title in response to Napoleon's creation of the Confederation of the Rhine. He then assumed the Austrian throne, ruling as Emperor Francis I.

After arriving at Nice, Napoleon established his headquarters and took command of the Army of Italy. The French soldiers had languished in Italy for more than two years and were now undisciplined and poorly motivated. On 27 March 1796, the general assembled his troops and told them: 'Soldiers of France you are naked, ill fed and I have come to take you into the most fertile plains in the world. Wealthy provinces and great cities will be in your power. I will lead you to glory, honour and great riches.'

To improve morale and discipline, General Bonaparte borrowed money and arranged for the purchase of food and clothing, while making preparations for his campaign against the forces of the First Coalition. He planned to first move against the weaker Piedmontese and drive Victor Amadeus' troops out of the war. After reequipping and provisioning his men, on 10 April 1796 Napoleon sent his army of 38,000 against the 25,000 soldiers of Piedmont. In less than two weeks, he outfought and outmanoeuvred his enemy, winning five battles in a lightning campaign. The French general continued to press his offensive against Victor Amadeus, and on 19 April launched a frontal attack at San Michelle, but when his flanking assault from the north failed the French were beaten back with heavy casualties. Two days later, Bonaparte's army attacked again near Mondovi, winning a decisive victory. Napoleon was now on the plain of Piedmont and ordered his cavalry, led by Joachim Murat, to pursue the retreating Piedmontese. Soon after the defeat of the Piedmont army at Mondovi, the king sent envoys to meet Bonaparte at Cherasco to discuss surrender terms. Under the resulting treaty, Piedmont agreed to withdraw from the First Coalition and pay a large indemnity in silver and gold.

Following the elimination of nearly half of the allied forces in Italy, Napoleon was free to concentrate his war effort on the Austrians. He directed his army to move against Milan. Bonaparte skilfully manoeuvred his troops past the main Austrian defensive line centred on the fortifications at Pavia and marched directly toward Milan. As the French soldiers approached the outskirts of the city, the Austrian commander, John Pierre Beaulieu, ordered his army to withdraw. At the Adda River crossing near the town of Lodi, Beaulieu deployed a reinforced rearguard to protect his retirement. The Austrian occupation of the fortified bridge at Lodi blocked the French approach to Milan, compelling Bonaparte to alter his plan of attack. He now ordered a frontal assault against the Austrians defending the bridge, while Murat's cavalry was sent upriver to attack the enemy's right flank.

On the afternoon of 10 May, the first French soldiers reached the wooden bridge, but were not strong enough to attack the Austrians. After additional troops arrived with artillery support, the guns began firing volleys on the enemy deployment. After several hours of bombardment, the light infantry was ordered by Napoleon to advance against the Austrians. Napoleon was at the front during the fighting, sighting his artillery pieces and deploying his men. When the French were partway across the bridge, the Austrian gunners fired a salvo that caused the column of troops to waver and stop. Bonaparte's men soon rallied, however, and charged across the bridge. The enemy now panicked and fled. While victory at Lodi was not decisive in the Italian war, it was where Napoleon first began to create his legend as a national hero through the use of propaganda presented in newspapers, pamphlets and paintings. The ambitious young general began to believe he had been chosen by destiny to achieve great feats.

Five days after his victory at Lodi, General Bonaparte entered Milan unchallenged. A Milanese delegation met Napoleon and presented him with the keys to the city, as the citizens wildly cheered his arrival. While in Milan, the general received instructions from the Directory to renew the war against the Austrians, while also undertaking a new offensive against Tuscany and the Papal States, who were allied with Emperor Francis II. He decided to first move south and attack the weaker Tuscan and papal forces, sending two divisions to seize the wealthy cities of Bologna and Ferrara. When the French army overwhelmed the papal forces near Bologna, which was allied with the Vatican, Pope Pius VI agreed to negotiate a peace settlement. Under the terms of the treaty, the pope pledged to pay a large indemnity in gold and silver, withdraw from the First Coalition and transfer numerous art treasures from the Vatican to Paris. After the surrender of Pius VI, Tuscany soon submitted, while Florence and Ferrara opened their gates to the conquerors. As Napoleon solidified his hold over his conquests, a riot erupted in Rome in late December in opposition to the presence of the two French envoys sent by Bonaparte to meet with the pope. When one of the representatives was killed, Napoleon responded by dispatching General Louis Alexander Berthier to Rome with an army to reimpose the French presence. Berthier entered the city unopposed and later, in February 1798, announced the creation of Rome as a republic under the French model. Pius VI was later deposed and died while still a prisoner of the French.

Meanwhile, in Milan, General Bonaparte established his headquarters in the ducal palace and published a series of proclamations assuring the Italians of the French Republic's friendship and protection. Once northern Italy was secured, he was given the freedom by the Directory to create the Cisalpine Republic, centred in Milan, and a second state in Genoa. The two new republics were allied with France and given representative-style constitutions.

In the summer of 1796, Emperor Francis II ordered the resumption of the war against the French in occupied northern Italy. Confronted by the advancing Austrians, Bonaparte assembled his army and moved east from Milan. During August, through a series of brilliant manoeuvres and counter-marches, combined with flanking assaults, the French won major battles at Castiglione, Bassano and Rovereto. As part of his campaign to drive the Austrians out of Italy, Napoleon had earlier sent troops to besiege the enemy fortress at Mantua. The Austrians, having made two previous unsuccessful attempts to raise the siege, launched a new offensive in mid-November 1796. Upon learning of the movement of the Austrians, Napoleon ordered his army of 20,000 to march from Verona on 14 November to oppose the enemy. He first made contact with the troops of Emperor Francis at the bridge over the Adige River, near the village of Arcole. The French unleashed several frontal attacks, but were beaten back by the infantry and artillery of the Habsburg emperor. Napoleon then grabbed a French flag and rushed forward over the bridge, leading his soldiers in a charge, but was compelled to withdraw after a fresh enemy division was thrown into the fight. On 17 November, Bonaparte finally forced his way across the Adige on hastily constructed pontoon bridges several miles downriver and quickly occupied Arcole. The Austrians then withdrew with over 7,000 casualties, ending their campaign to break the French siege at Mantua.

In early 1797, the Habsburg emperor resumed his offensive against the French with the objective of relieving Mantua. With the Austrian army again moving toward the besieged fortification, Napoleon led his forces to intercept them. In the early morning of 14 January, he attacked the Austrians at Rivoli, utilizing speed and flanking movements to crush the larger army. The retreating Austrians were pursued by the French and almost totally destroyed. In early February, the citadel at Mantua finally surrendered and all of northern Italy was now in French hands.

In the wake of the defeat of the Austrian forces in Italy, General Bonaparte began preparations for the invasion of Austria. He launched his campaign in early March, and by the middle of April was only 70 miles from Vienna. Unable to stop the French advance, Emperor Francis was compelled to begin peace discussions, Napoleon negotiating the agreement without instructions from the Directory. Under the Treaty of Campo Formio, signed by Napoleon and a representative from the emperor on 17 October 1797, the Austrians ceded most of present-day Belgium, the lands west of the Rhine and northern Italy to the French, and Francis II further pledged to abandon the First Coalition. With the signing of the treaty, Great Britain was the only remaining nation fighting against the French. In December 1797, General Bonaparte travelled to Paris and presented the Treaty of Campo Formio to the Directory. While in the city, he met with government officials and began campaigning for a new command that would enable him to gain additional glory and honours on the battlefield, while expanding his popularity with the French people.

With France now only at war with Britain, Napoleon was offered command of the Army of England, intended for an invasion across the Channel, but declined the position in favour of an expedition to Egypt. Meeting with the Directory, he proposed the conquest and occupation of Egypt as a means to weaken Britain's prosperous trade with India. The Egyptian campaign was approved by the Directors in March 1798, and Bonaparte began finalizing his preparations. By May, he had mustered an army of over 35,000 soldiers, along with several hundred civilians who were to conduct the first modern scientific study of the ancient Egyptian kingdom. On the morning of 18 May 1798, the Army of the Orient boarded its ships in Toulon and set sail for Egypt.

As the French fleet made its way across the Mediterranean, its ships anchored off Malta on 9 June. The island was occupied by the Order of the Knights of Saint John of Jerusalem, and Napoleon sent a small detachment of troops ashore to bribe the Order's French knights into rebelling against the Grand Master and seizing Malta. The 200 French knights joined Bonaparte's forces, and following token resistance captured the island. Napoleon then abolished the Order, deported the knights and turned Malta into a naval base to reinforce his lines of communication with France.

After remaining in Malta for ten days, the French fleet resumed its voyage, and by the end of June was off the coast of Egypt. General Bonaparte landed his army unopposed on 1 July near the port city of Alexandria.

The city was lightly garrisoned and the French quickly occupied it after overcoming brief resistance. On 3 July, Napoleon left a strong detachment of soldiers to hold Alexandria and began his advance to Cairo. During the trek across the desert, the French troops suffered greatly from heat, lack of water, dysentery, scorpions and flies. After a march of two weeks through the summer heat, the French were within sight of Cairo but their approach was opposed by the massed Mameluke cavalry and Egyptian soldiers, who were deployed in the shadows of the Great Pyramids of Giza. The Mamelukes were raised from birth as warriors and were renowned for their fierceness and cruelty. Confronted by 8,000 cavalry and 16,000 supporting infantry, Napoleon deployed his men into five large squares, with artillery on the corners, and awaited the charge of the enemy horsemen and their Egyptian infantry. Before the battle, Napoleon told his troops: 'Forty centuries of history look down upon you.' When the Mamelukes rushed forward in the mid-afternoon, Bonaparte's men held their fire until they were within fifty paces. The French close-range musket fire and cannon volleys repelled the horsemen and infantry with heavy casualties. Napoleon then ordered a counter-attack, which completed the rout of the army of the Turkish sultan. When reports of the Mamelukes' defeat at the Battle of the Pyramids reached Cairo, the Turkish forces there fled to Syria and the French entered the city unopposed on 24 July. Upon arriving at Cairo, Bonaparte said: 'I was full of dreams. I saw myself founding a new religion, marching into Asia riding an elephant, a turban on my head and in my hand the new Koran.' Napoleon's dreams of creating an empire in the Middle East were, however, short-lived, as British admiral Horatio Nelson intercepted the French fleet off the Egyptian coast at Aboukir Bay and destroyed it. The ships having been Napoleon's only link to his homeland, he would now have to provide for his needs from the local economy. He thus took command of the Egyptian government and, with the advice of local officials, became head of state.

While General Bonaparte was organizing the new government for Egypt, the scholars, archaeologists, map makers, engineers and artists who had travelled with the French army began work rediscovering the secrets of the ancient kingdom. To support the scientists, Napoleon founded the Institute of Egypt in Cairo, with its own buildings, libraries and scientific instruments. He led a party of archaeologists to investigate the remains of an ancient Suez Canal, while a geographical survey of Egypt was also made. The academicians surveyed the pyramids and Sphinx and navigated the Nile. They investigated ancient tombs and found the Rosetta Stone, which later led to the decoding of hieroglyphics.

Before the arrival of Bonaparte and his army, Egypt was part of the Ottoman Empire and ruled by Sultan Selim III. After Napoleon invaded and occupied the country, the Turks negotiated an alliance with Great Britain and Russia in opposition to the French. To regain his territory, in early 1799 Selim III began to assemble an army in Syria to attack the French in Egypt. When General Bonaparte was informed of the escalating threat from Syria, he prepared to strike first. Mustering a force of 900 cavalryn and 13,000 infantry, he set out across the Sinai Desert into southern Syria. On 25 February, the French seized the town of Gaza and captured over 2,000 Turks. Without adequate food for his men, Napoleon freed the prisoners on condition they would not fight against the French. He then renewed his advance, reaching the Turkish-held town of Jaffa on 7 March and quickly overrunning its defences. More than 3,000 of the sultan's troops surrendered, among whom were several hundred from the Gaza garrison who had broken their parole. Bonaparte was faced with a decision whether to release them and risk the captives fighting again or to order them shot. Rather than having to face the Turks again on the battlefield, he had them killed.

The French soon resumed their march up the coast to Acre, a seaport town heavily guarded by Ottoman soldiers and reinforced with artillery from a British naval flotilla. The French besieged Acre on 20 March, but the Turks under the command of Jezzar Pasha repeatedly repulsed their assaults. Jezzar's forces, with British aid, continued to beat back the French until early May, when a breach in the outer wall was made. As Napoleon's men rushed forward, a large detachment of British sailors landed on the beach and clashed with the French, driving them back. After more than nine weeks at Acre, Bonaparte realized he would not capture the city so he abandoned the siege and began the long march back to Alexandria. He led his battered forces down the coastline and into the Sinai Desert, finally reaching Egypt in early June.

After the French army returned to Alexandria, Napoleon immediately began preparations for the expected Ottoman counter-attack. On 11 July, the Turks duly came ashore near Alexandria and encamped on the Aboukir Peninsula. On 25 July, General Bonaparte launched an attack against the 9,000 Turks, who were deployed in two defensive lines across the peninsula with their backs to the sea. He ordered two divisions of infantry to assault the Ottoman centre, while Murat led the cavalry in charges on the flanks. The French horsemen pressed home their attack and swept the enemy troops into the sea. Napoleon's attacks destroyed the Ottoman army, with over 5,000 drowned, another 2,000 killed in the fighting and 2,000 taken prisoner.

As Bonaparte had been preparing for the attack of the Ottoman army, he received numerous reports from Paris indicating a dramatic deterioration in the power and popularity of the ruling Directory. The Directors were under increasing pressure from the combined effects of the civil war, the new and expanded Second Coalition and the growing danger of bankruptcy. The government was widely unpopular, having proven incapable of coping with the crisis. Napoleon was convinced that he had a role to play in a new regime and prepared to depart for Paris. He sailed from Egypt with a small cadre of supporters, arriving in France on 9 October. As Bonaparte made his way to Paris, he was enthusiastically welcomed by the citizens. The Egyptian expedition had become a potential quagmire for Napoleon's advancement, but he turned it into a political victory that would propel him to the heights of power.

When he arrived in Paris, Napoleon quickly realized the full extent of the Directory's unpopularity and ineffectiveness. He arranged to meet secretly with one of the Directors, Emmanuel Sieyes, and began to conspire with him against the regime. The two conspirators planned to force the remaining four Directors to resign and intimidate the legislature into authorizing a new provisional government, the Consulate, with three consuls serving as heads of state. On 8 November the coup was put into motion. To minimize the influence of the citizens of Paris, Bonaparte and Sieyes had the legislative bodies relocated to the Chateau Saint Cloud, and to control potential rioting mobs, the general was appointed commander of the capital's garrison. When the Council of Elders and the Five Hundred assembled the next day, the legislative bodies quickly became hostile to the conspiracy, refusing to approve the establishment of the Consulate. After Napoleon was told of the delegates' rejection of the revised government, he gathered a detachment of grenadiers and entered the legislative hall, with drums beating, to encourage a reversal of the vote. He was met with defiance and shouts of, 'He is trying to take over the government – outlaw him.' With the rebellion in danger of being crushed almost before it started, Sieyes proposed the use of the Paris garrison to impose their will on the assembled delegates. Napoleon appeared before the troops, convincing them to support the conspiracy. The grenadiers, led by Joachim Murat, then charged the legislative hall, forcing the deputies to flee. Later that evening, the Council of Elders reassembled and, under threat from the guardsmen, voted to approve the new regime. Almost 100 friendly deputies were convened in a rump session and voted in favour of the new triumvirate of Napoleon Bonaparte, Emmanuel Sieyes and Roger Ducos. Over the next five weeks, Napoleon outmanoeuvred the other two consuls and took control of the government. The new administration was readily and widely accepted by the French people, who had grown war weary, disillusioned by a series of weak and corrupt regimes and beset with oppressive financial sacrifices. The First Consul, Bonaparte, now resided at the Tuileries Palace and had become master of France.

While the newly approved constitution had created the mechanisms for an elective administration, Napoleon had in reality become the virtual dictator of France. He moved quickly to wipe out isolated areas of opposition and to solidify his authority. New economic reforms were adopted and a revised tax collection system was implemented, which helped stabilize the almost-bankrupt regime. The First Consul needed a period of peace and stability to regenerate France. To eliminate the threat against France from the Second Coalition of Britain, Austria, Russia and the Ottoman Empire, he spent the winter of 1800 reorganizing and refitting the army, preparing for a campaign against the principal enemy, Francis II of Austria.

The Austrian army had returned to northern Italy and was besieging the city of Genoa. General Bonaparte devised a bold plan to march his Army of the Reserves over the Alps through the Saint Bernard Pass and catch the enemy by surprise. On 14 May, some 25,000 French soldiers began the precarious crossing of the mountains, taking six days to reach the Piedmont plain to begin their pursuit of the Austrians. The French caught them near the small village of Marengo on the evening of 13 June. The following morning, the Austrian general, Michael von Melas, sent his 28,500 soldiers against the French, while his artillery pounded their prepared fortified lines. In the early afternoon, under the relentless assaults of Melas' forces, Bonaparte's defensive front began to waver and then break. The French were compelled to fall back 4 miles to the village of San Giuliano. Seemingly assured of victory, General von Melas left his army and retired to Alessandria, giving command of his troops to subordinates. The Austrians continued their attack against the French, and by late afternoon had driven them back over 5 miles. The French army was exhausted and nearly out of ammunition, when General Louis Desaix, who had been sent south to secure the road to Genoa, returned with his 5,300 men and counter-attacked alongside Napoleon's remaining forces, while a newly redeployed artillery battery of eighteen guns blasted the Austrians. Under the assault of the French infantry in the centre and cavalry on the flanks, the enemy fled the battlefield in total disarray. At the end of the fighting, the Austrians had lost over 9,500 soldiers, while almost 6,000 Frenchmen were either killed or wounded.

After the Austrian defeat at Marengo, General Melas was forced to come to terms with the French, agreeing to withdraw his forces east of the Minco

River and north of the Po, giving Napoleon possession of northern Italy. In 1801, Francis II agreed to sign a separate peace treaty giving France the old frontiers originally ceded by Julius Caesar to Gaul, extending the borders to the Rhine, Alps and Pyrenees. In the following year, with the Second Coalition in disarray, the British signed the Treaty of Amiens, which brought peace to France for the first time in ten years.

In the wake of the signing of the Treaty of Amiens, First Consul Bonaparte began the process of consolidating and expanding his consulship with a series of far-reaching reforms. With the approval of the newly revised legislature – composed of the Tribunate, Legislative Corps and Senate – the constitution was modified, making Napoleon First Consul for life. He was given complete power over the executive and legislative branches of government. Now having total supremacy, he initiated a succession of public works projects which expanded growth in employment and of the economy. Construction began on roads, canals, public buildings and schools, laying the foundation for a new France. The administration of the nation became highly centralized, with new legal, economic and political systems under the control of the First Consul. Loyal prefects were appointed to govern the provinces, which were closely monitored from Paris. In 1801, under Napoleon's instructions, negotiations were started with Pope Pius VII, resulting in the Concordat, which ended the schism that had lasted over ten years and re-established peaceful relations with the papacy. As part of his reforms, the First Consul issued a new Civil Code, which unified the laws of the nation under a single legal system based on the principals of the Revolution, while abolishing all feudal rights. Under the stability and security created by the new regime, the French economy continued to recover from years of mismanagement. The restructuring measures heightened the prestige of Napoleon across all of France and Europe, with the First Consul being considered the embodiment of revolutionary spirit.

While Napoleon was tightening his authority over France, relations with Britain grew increasingly tense due to its relentless efforts to minimize French expansion on the continent. The British made demands for the French to withdraw from occupied Netherlands and Switzerland, while ignoring Napoleon's call for the evacuation of Malta. An impasse developed between the two old rivals, which was broken on 18 May 1803, when the British declared war on France. The conflict quickly evolved into a stalemate, with Britain lacking a continental army to invade France and Napoleon's regime remaining landlocked without a powerful naval force.

First Consul Bonaparte ruled over the French with an iron hand but lacked a line of succession to ensure the gains of his administration would be preserved after his death. The movement to create a dynasty was given added impetus by numerous rumours of assassination plots against Bonaparte. In early 1804, a royalist faction under the pay of the British government was arrested in Paris and charged with conspiring to murder the First Consul and restore the monarchy. In the event of Napoleon's death, the government would be thrown into disarray and turmoil, with no designated heir and many parties vying for supremacy. An acknowledged dynasty would protect against the re-establishment of the royalists or the Jacobin regime, prevent the outbreak of civil war and protect the legal, social and territorial gains of the Revolution. The formation of a royal lineage would also place France on equal status with the European regimes and legitimize Napoleon's seizure of the French crown. By way of a Senate and plebiscite resolution, closely arranged by Bonaparte, the creation of a hereditary empire was approved in May 1804. The return to a monarchical form of administration, with Napoleon as emperor, carried with it an imperial court and nobility class.

On the cold morning of 2 December 1804, Napoleon and Josephine set out in an opulent coach drawn by eight horses for Notre Dame Cathedral to be enthroned in an elaborately staged coronation ceremony. They rode down streets lined with three rows of soldiers, with more than half-a-million spectators clustered behind them. As Napoleon and Josephine reached the church, cannons thundered, while two symphony orchestras played martial music. The couple entered Notre Dame, each under a canopy, and slowly moved up the nave to the waiting Pope Pius VII, as the congregation shouted: 'Long live the emperor!' After Pius VII anointed Napoleon and Josephine with holy oil, he sang the Mass. Napoleon now walked up the steps to the altar and took the golden crown, placing it on his head. Josephine then came forward and knelt before him, as the now Emperor Napoleon held her crown aloft and placed it on her head. The ceremony ended after Napoleon took the imperial oath, pledging to uphold the integrity of the Republic and to rule in the interest of the French people. Pope Pius had been invited to officiate at the coronation to further bond the new government to the papacy and give the assumption of imperial power the sanctions of the Church. As the three-hour ceremony ended, the herald announced: 'The most glorious and most august Napoleon, Emperor of the French, is consecrated and enthroned.' The emperor and Josephine exited the great cathedral and returned to the Tuileries Palace to celebrate their coronation.

The Treaty of Amiens between France and Great Britain had been dissolved in May 1803, the British declaring war on the French in opposition to Napoleon's continued expansion into Switzerland, the Low Countries and

Germany and his perceived intention to invade England. Austria and Russia later joined Britain in the Third Coalition to limit French encroachment into Eastern Europe. As the allies prepared to attack the French in 1805, the emperor accelerated his plans to invade England. The newly organized, equipped and trained Army of England, comprising some 200,000 soldiers, was assembled at Boulogne and Bruges and began preparations for the crossing of the English Channel. No crossing of the Channel could take place without the protection of the French fleet. Despite his attempts to put a formidable naval force in the sea lanes, by August 1805 the emperor realized his ships could not challenge the British in the Channel and ordered the Grand Army to abandon the invasion and instead march east to confront the forces of Russia and Emperor Francis II of Austria.

The potential union of the Russian and Habsburg armies was a formidable threat to the French, and to prevent their merger Napoleon moved quickly to attack Francis II. The Grand Army marched rapidly from the coast of northern France, across the Rhine and into Bavaria in less than a month. Napoleon first advanced against the Austrian Army of General Karl Mack, unleashing a lightning campaign of fourteen days in which he outmanoeuvred and outfought the Habsburg soldiers. The French corps of Marshal Michel Ney fought its way across the Danube at Elchingen on 14 October to complete the encirclement of the Habsburg forces, compelling Mack to surrender his 27,000 troops on 20 October at Ulm. With the submission of Mack's army, the approaches to Vienna were cleared and on 14 November the French army marched into the city unchallenged.

While the French were eliminating Mack's army, Francis II deployed a larger force of 70,000 soldiers to the north-east, awaiting the arrival of the Russian czar, Alexander I, and his troops. In late November, the Austrian and Russian armies united and aggressively pursued the Grand Army. On 1 December, they caught up with the French near the village of Austerlitz and prepared for battle. Napoleon held the Pratzen Heights, which was the dominating position on the battlefield, but abandoned it to lure the allies into occupying the Pratzen and assaulting his right flank. On the morning of 2 December, the Pratzen Heights was covered by a dense fog, and from his headquarters on the Heights, Alexander ordered his men to attack the French right flank, as Napoleon had anticipated. Bonaparte had placed two divisions of infantry below the Heights, and as the sun began to break through the fog, he sent them charging up the hill. Reaching the top of the plateau, the French swept across the battlefield, overwhelming the enemy in one sharp blow. By five o'clock, Emperor Napoleon had won his greatest victory. The French army had suffered 8,800 casualties, while the Russians and Austrians lost over 16,000 killed and wounded, plus 12,000 taken prisoner. Early the next morning, Emperor Francis II asked for an armistice, which Napoleon granted. On 27 December 1805, the French and Habsburgs signed the Treaty of Pressburg, with Francis ceding the Venetian region to France, agreeing to abandon the Third Coalition and pay a war indemnity, while the battered Russian army withdrew to the east.

After his defeat of the allied armies, Napoleon established the Confederation of the Rhine to consolidate and facilitate the rule of his territorial acquisitions in western Germany. The thousand-year-old Holy Roman Empire was dissolved, with sixteen satellite fiefdoms created under the protection of the French regime. The recent acquisitions of the emperor in Germany and the likelihood of the French seizing the Duchy of Hanover compelled King Frederick William III of Prussia to join the newly formed Fourth Coalition against Napoleon, along with Great Britain, Saxony, Russia and Sweden. On 7 October 1806, Frederick William ordered the French to evacuate the Rhineland states or Prussia would declare war. The emperor's reply was a six-day campaign which destroyed all Prussian resistance, ending with the crushing French victory at the Battle of Jena. The French army of 66,000 veterans clashed with the Prussians at Jena on 14 October 1806. Emperor Napoleon sent two corps of infantry to attack the centre of the Prussian line, but Ney's VI Corps was beaten back and left in a vulnerable position. With his assault in danger of failing, the emperor personally led a massed battery of artillery to rescue Ney with devasting cannon fire. Napoleon then instructed his soldiers on the flanks to advance against the enemy and drive them into the centre. The Prussians were encircled and forced to retire, the fleeing troops leaving over 10,000 casualties and 15,000 prisoners on the battlefield as they were pursued by Murat and the French cavalry. On the same day, a larger Prussian army was defeated at Auerstadt, several miles north of Jena, by a French force led by Marshal Davout. On 25 October, Emperor Napoleon entered Berlin unchallenged and Frederick William sued for peace.

With the Prussian threat to France eliminated for now, Emperor Napoleon marched his army east to confront Czar Alexander I. When the French entered Poland, Napoleon convinced the Poles to become allied with him with the enticement of independence. He established his winter quarters near Warsaw and sent troops to occupy Polish towns to await the spring campaigning season. During the winter, the czar sent an army led by General Levin Auguste Bennigsen to attack the French. The two armies collided at Eylau on 7 February 1807, where they fought to a stalemate over the following two days. The French withdrew to their winter quarters after losing over 20,000 men. During the next few months, Napoleon reinforced and re-equipped his army, while Czar Alexander negotiated unsuccessfully with the British for additional subsidies and soldiers.

In the spring, Napoleon renewed the war against the Russians, advancing to crush the czar's offensive against him. On 14 June, General Bennigsen moved his army across the Alle River and encountered the 10,000 troops of Marshal Jean Lannes, who repelled the Russian attacks with screens of well-deployed skirmishers, while messengers were dispatched to the emperor. Napoleon arrived with the main body of his army in the afternoon and sent Ney to attack the enemy from the right flank, driving them back toward the town of Friedland and away from the river. Using his artillery, Napoleon set fire to Friedland and the bridges across the river to trap the Russian soldiers. Unable to retreat, the troops were destroyed by the French, with over 25,000 killed, wounded or taken prisoner.

With his army annihilated at Friedland, Czar Alexander was compelled to sue for peace. Napoleon and the czar met on a raft in the Nieman River to settle the war. Talking with the emperor, Alexander developed a close friendship with him and was drawn into an acceptance of the new revolutionary spirit. During their prolonged discussions, they negotiated the Treaty of Tilsit in July 1807. Under the terms of the agreement, Alexander agreed to abandon the Third Coalition and join an alliance with the French regime. He promised to close his ports to English commerce and become a member of the continental blockade against Great Britain. Despite the pleas of the Polish nobles for independence, Napoleon created the Duchy of Warsaw under the regime of the King of Saxony, while the Kingdom of Westphalia was ruled by his brother, Jerome, with both fiefdoms becoming vassal states of the French Empire. During his talks with the czar, Napoleon revealed his grandiose plans for the partition of Continental Europe into western and eastern spheres, which would leave Russia free to intervene in Turkey, Sweden and Finland. The Treaty of Tilsit marked the summit of Napoleon's reign. At the end of 1807, he held power either by direct occupation or through negotiated alliances with most of Continental Europe, with the exception of the Iberian Peninsula.

In the aftermath of the signing of the Treaty of Tilsit, Napoleon was at peace with the European powers and ulilized this period to consolidate his recent territorial and sovereign gains. The French Civil Code was introduced into the vassal fiefdoms, and with it the ideals of the Enlightenment spread through Europe, which promoted the pursuit of knowledge and the aspirations of liberty, tolerance and brotherhood. The emperor was viewed as the protector of the revolutionary reforms, while his government's policies and directives were well received by the people.

In 1808, Napoleon opened a political campaign to conspire in the internal rule of Spain. The government of the Bourbon king, Charles IV, had become increasingly unpopular with the Spanish nobility and people. The emperor sent his agents to the Spanish court to plot the overthrow of the king, the French financing and sponsoring the revolt against Charles IV and forcing him to abdicate in March 1808. With control over the kingdom, Napoleon appointed his older brother, Joseph, as King of Spain. To secure his brother's hold on the crown, the emperor expanded the French military's presence in Spain. However, the Spanish people opposed the assumption of the throne by Joseph and their occupation by French troops. The exiled king's son, Ferdinand, was popular with the Spanish and became the symbol of their independence. On 2 May, the residents of Madrid rose up against the French garrison, which marked the beginning of a bloody partisan war that lasted the remainder of Napoleon's rule in the kingdom. As opposition to the French grew, the British supported the insurgency by sending financial aid, and in August an English army landed in Portugal to reinforce the Spanish war effort.

As the uprising spread through the kingdom and became stronger, Napoleon was pressed to send veteran French divisions from Germany to suppress the Spanish forces and the British invasion from Portugal. Despite these reinforcements, the rebels continued to press the French and reoccupied Madrid. In November, the emperor left France to personally intervene in the Spanish campaign in an attempt to bring peace and order. Arriving in Joseph's unruly kingdom, he took command and first moved against the insurgents, defeating them at the battles of Gamonal and Tudela, before marching on Madrid. The only barrier blocking the French from the capital was the Sierra de Guadarrama mountain range, which was crossable through two passes. Napoleon advanced against the Somosierra Pass to gain access to Madrid. The passageway was defended by the 12,000 soldiers of General Benito San Juan. On 30 November, the emperor began his attack by sending a division of infantry up the road toward the fortified enemy position, while a smaller force moved up the mountain side. Fighting erupted as the French made steady progress ascending the slopes. When the infantrymen on the roadway reached the summit, General San Juan's line began to waver. The emperor then ordered a detachment of volunteer Polish light cavalry and part of the Imperial Guard to launch a charge. As the horsemen struck, the Spanish broke and retreated, leaving behind their wounded and artillery. The road to Madrid was now open, and on 4 December Napoleon entered the city. As the French offensive gained momentum, the emperor was forced to return to Paris to cope with the renewal of the war with Austria. Marshal Nicholas Soult was put in command of the French war effort against the Spanish insurrectionists, as well as a British force under General John Moore, which he pushed back over the mountains of north-west Spain, forcing its evacuation from Corunna in January 1809.

Meanwhile, as the French struggled against the Spanish rebellion, the Austrian emperor, Francis II, became increasingly alarmed at his loss of power and influence in foreign affairs, the reduction of Austrian autonomy and the new prominence and sway of the French emperor. As the German patriots turned to Bonaparte as the leader and defender of their traditions, Francis was pressed to reassert his rights and authority. With the French military occupied with its war in Spain and the ensuing transfer of troops from Germany, a new wave of resistance to Napoleon swept across large parts of Eastern Europe. As the size and strength of the war party grew in the Habsburg government and among the people, Francis declared war on France on 9 April 1809.

To counter the new Austrian threat, Bonaparte ordered the return of veteran divisions previously sent to fight in Spain, while concentrating his local scattered forces. Once his army was assembled, he advanced against the Austrians and by a series of brilliantly executed manoeuvres and flanking attacks forced the enemy to retreat across the Danube and abandon Vienna. The French continued to pursue the Habsburg army of 100,000 soldiers, led by Archduke Charles Ludwig, younger brother of Francis. When Napoleon tried to force a crossing over the Danube using the single bridge at Essling, his troops were beaten back with large losses. Napoleon withdrew, built a fortified encampment on an island in the Danube and summoned reinforcements.

By early July, the French army had been augmented with additional divisions and supplies and Napoleon was ready to launch a fresh attack near the village of Wagram. The Habsburgs had constructed a fortified line of trenches and redoubts, and on 5 July Bonaparte sent two corps against the defences, but they were thrown back. He ordered a second assault, but the corps of Marshal John Bernadotte was also repelled. As night fell, Archduke Charles still held his position and had repulsed two major French attacks. The following morning, the archduke attacked the French left flank with two corps, nearly breaking through Napoleon's front. As the French wavered, the emperor shifted a corps to reinforce the gap in his line, saving the left wing from collapse. Meanwhile, on his right flank, the French punched a hole in the archduke's earthworks and swept down the rear of the Habsburgs, as Napoleon threw his reserves into the fray at Wagram, compelling the Austrians to slowly give way in a fighting retreat. After the bloody Battle of Wagram, over 32,000 Frenchmen lay dead or wounded, while the Austrians lost some 38,000 men. On 14 October, Napoleon and Emperor Francis signed the Treaty of Schonbrunn to end the war. Under the terms of the treaty, Francis ceded additional territories in Poland and along the Adriatic to the French, while the Duchy of Salzburg was transferred to Bavaria. Austria also acknowledged Joseph Bonaparte as the rightful King of Spain and pledged to pay France a sizable indemnity.

During the talks at Schonbrunn, Bonaparte barely escaped an assassination attempt on 12 October. As the emperor was leaving the palace with a large following to observe a military review, a 17-year-old German nationalist named Friedrich Staps was making his way toward him through the crowd with a large knife hidden in his coat. When Staps neared the emperor, he was seized and arrested. Under interrogation, he revealed his plans to murder Napoleon and was sentenced to death. On 17 October, standing before a firing squad, Staps shouted out: 'Long live freedom and Germany!' Following his death he became a martyr for the growing spirit of German nationalism.

The coronation of Napoleon as emperor in December 1804 had created a new hereditary empire. To ensure the continuance of his family's reign in France, Napoleon needed a son to firmly establish his dynasty, and Josephine, at the age of 41, was unlikely to ever produce the necessary male child. He had earlier taken measures to expand his authority over his conquests by naming members of his family as kings and queens of his vassal princedoms. Joseph had been appointed King of Naples and later of Spain, while his younger brothers, Louis and Jerome, were made kings of Holland and Westphalia respectively, and his sister, Caroline, along with her husband Joachim Murat, were given Naples. After the creation of his European empire, Napoleon began to consider the possibilities of a second wife. In 1809, still without a direct heir, he resolved to divorce Josephine and marry again. During his negotiations with Czar Alexander, the emperor had suggested a marriage to a Russian princess, but never received a reply. In late 1809, Bonaparte arranged his divorce from Josephine and began negotiations with the Austrian court for marriage to Francis's eldest daughter, Maria-Louise. An agreement was reached, and Emperor Napoleon was married to the Habsburg princess on 2 April 1810. Despite the political obstacles of the marital union, Napoleon and his new empress developed a close affection for each other over the following years, the emperor becoming a devoted husband and father. In the spring of 1811, Marie-Louise gave birth at the Tuileries Palace to the emperor's much-anticipated son, who was named Napoleon II and made King of Rome.

The 1807 Treaty of Tilsit had brought reconciliation and peace between France and Russia. During the following years, as Napoleon strengthened and expanded his powerbase in eastern Europe, relations between the two realms deteriorated. While the French were fighting the Austrians in 1809, the Russians failed to actively take part in the war, as had previously been agreed, and became openly hostile to the growing French presence. The repressive Russian court had objected to the czar's signing of the Treaty of Tilsit and the resulting importation of liberal revolutionary values from France. As part of the treaty, the czar had agreed to join the Continental System, which caused the financial ruin of many Russian nobles when trade became disrupted with Britain. Napoleon's friendship with Alexander weakened further when the emperor permitted the French Marshal John Bernadotte to accept the offer of the vacant Swedish crown. With indifference to the czar, the emperor continued to expand his presence into the east, adding Polish lands to his vassal Duchy of Warsaw. The czar considered such measures a direct barrier to his future quests for Russian expansion. In 1810, Alexander responded by slowly relaxing his support for the French economic blockade of Britain, opening his harbours to neutral ships. As Napoleon escalated his campaign to isolate the British, the czar grew progressively fearful of his Russian magnates and the possibility of their revolting in favour of his brother, Grand Duke Constantine. With the pressure against him mounting, Alexander issued an ultimatum to the French emperor demanding his withdrawal from Poland. As the threat of war with the czar deepened, Bonaparte attempted to negotiate a resolution, but there was no progress and armed conflict became inevitable,

The French War Ministry had begun preparations for war with Russia in 1811 by recalling infantry and cavalry divisions from Spain and Italy. To supplement his forces, Napoleon called upon the fiefdoms of the Confederation of the Rhine and his Austrian ally for reinforcements. During the late spring of 1812, the French Grand Army was assembled, and on 24 June over 600,000 predominantly French soldiers, but with 34,000 from Austria and smaller detachments from Germany, Poland, Holland, Italy, Spain and Prussia, crossed the border between Prussia and Russia at the Niemen River in current-day Lithuania to begin the invasion of Russia. The goal of Bonaparte's campaign was to force Alexander into a quick and decisive defeat and then to dictate terms to him. While the French and their allies advanced into Russia, Czar Alexander pulled his troops back, abandoning vast spans of barren territory and refusing to give battle. As the hot summer days dragged on, the czar withdrew his soldiers farther into the heart of Russia, losing Vilna and Smolensk without a fight and burning anything of value to the emperor's army. Napoleon's long lines of communication became increasingly exposed and were subjected to raids by Cossack horsemen and partisan forces. The ranks of the French army lost thousands from the summer heat, exhaustion and disease, while many others deserted. As his army deteriorated, the emperor made the decision to attack Russia's principal city of Moscow to entice Alexander into battle. When the French neared the city, Alexander removed his army commander and replaced him with the veteran Mikhail Kutuzov, ordering him to defend Moscow.

Taking command of the czar's forces, Kutuzov established a strong defensive position guarding the approaches to Moscow close to the village of Borodino. When French scouts reported the location of the massed Russians, Bonaparte rode forward to make a detailed reconnaissance of the battlefield and develop his plan of attack. Unlike most of his previous battle strategies, he ordered an unimaginative frontal assault into the enemy's centre, with only a small diversionary strike by his stepson, Prince Eugene de Beauharnais, who led his corps against the Russian left wing at the village of Borodino. Kutuzov built a formidable defensive system, with trenches, breastworks and redoubts over his 2½-mile front. Before the battle, the emperor sent an order to his soldiers telling them: 'Here is the battle you have so much wanted, let posterity say of you, he was present under the walls of Moscow.' Near 5.30 am on 7 September, as the sun slowly burnt away the morning mist, Napoleon's artillery opened the Battle of Borodino, with Kutuzov's cannons quickly replying. While the diversionary attack was made at Borodino by Prince Eugene, two French corps advanced against the Russian centre. They were met by a determined enemy, who would rather fight to the death than retreat. Marshal Michel Ney's corps broke through Kutuzov's front, but to the north the French were throw back with large numbers of casualties. Napoleon sent Ney reinforcements, but his attack stalled under heavy musket and cannon fire. The centre of the bloody and fierce fighting shifted to the Russian artillery emplacement called the Great Redoubt. In the late afternoon, the Great Redoubt was finally captured by the French infantry and Kutuzov's troops began falling back toward Moscow. However, Kutuzov maintained control over his retreating forces and withdrew in good order.

The Russians lost 42,000 soldiers killed or wounded at Borodino, while the French incurred casualties of more than 35,000 men. At the end of the fighting, the French emperor controlled the battlefield and could claim victory, but the Russian army had not been defeated and remained a threat to the French, isolated in an unfriendly country. Borodino was not the decisive victory Napoleon needed to bring Czar Alexander to the negotiating table. Nevertheless, the road to Moscow was now open, and late on 14 September Napoleon's battered army entered the mostly deserted city. In the evening, the city's mayor ordered the city put to the torch to deny the French any access to shelter from the looming cold weather. The blaze quickly spread through the abandoned streets, with countless shops and buildings burned to the ground. The savage firestorm was propelled by strong winds and lasted for four days before dying out during a rainstorm.

In the wake of the tattered Russian army's withdrawal from Borodino, Napoleon expected the czar would sue for peace, but Alexander remained worryingly silent. Over the next five weeks, the emperor waited in vain for a message requesting negotiations for a settlement. When a detachment of Murat's cavalry was attacked and defeated at Vinkovo, Bonaparte was forced to realize that Alexander was not going to negotiate, and with possible political and military dangers resulting from spending the winter in Moscow, the campaign had to be abandoned. On 19 October, a bright autumn day, the remaining 110,000 troops of the Grand Army evacuated the city and began the long retreat to safety in Poland. The march from Moscow started in good order, with the French soldiers and their allies heavily laden with the spoils of war but with limited supplies of provisions. By the end of the month, the mild sunny days had disappeared and on 6 November it began to snow. The French army was ill-prepared for the cold weather, and also suffered from a lack of food. As the troops advanced toward Poland, they were forced to abandon the warmer southern route that the Russians had effectively blocked, being compelled instead to use the same road they had taken for their advance on Moscow. Temperatures now fell well below zero, with snow falling heavily. The Grand Army began to slowly break up from the effects of starvation, exposure, disease and the harassing raids of the mounted Cossacks and local partisans. On 9 November, the French troops reached their first storehouse at Smolensk but found little food or supplies. Renewing their withdrawal, the cavalry scouts reported large Russian forces were approaching from both the north and south, while Kutuzov was closing from the rear. The emperor's army was in danger of being surrounded, and as the decimated French and their allies neared the bridge across the Beresina River, they found it destroyed. Napoleon sent his engineers to find an alternative crossing. A suitable location was found at Studianka and a passageway was quickly built. In mid-November, the emperor made his way over the bridge, just as the czar's army began to assault the French. Napoleon sent Marshal Ney with the remnants of his corps to check the enemy. While Ney held off the Russian assaults, the bulk of the French army was able to cross the river. As the czar's men intensified their attacks, Bonaparte was compelled to burn the bridge, leaving over 10,000 stragglers on the other side to the mercy of the Russians. Once the Beresina was crossed, the bulk of the Russian troops withdrew and the French struggled on to Vilna, harassed by the Cossacks and irregular forces.

On 6 December, Napoleon left the remnants of his shattered army after receiving reports of an attempted coup in Paris. Murat was named to lead the rest of the retreat as the emperor set off for France in a horse-drawn sleigh. He reached Paris twelve days later and immediately took control of the government. The emperor quickly reimposed his authority and began rebuilding the army, while preparing to deal with the political ramifications of the Moscow disaster. In late 1812, as the remnants of the Grand Army crossed the Niemen into Poland, with fewer than 95,000 soldiers remaining from the original invasion force of over 600,000.

In the aftermath of Napoleon's retreat from Russia, Czar Alexander continued his campaign against the French and crossed the Neimen with his army into Poland. He soon opened talks with Frederick William III of Prussia and formed an alliance against the French, with the objective of restoring the old order and expelling Napoleon from Central Europe. While his enemies were uniting against him, Bonaparte continued assembling his forces to defend France. As the adversaries organized for war, Emperor Francis remained neutral and honoured his agreement with Napoleon, while waiting on the outcome of the allies' 1813 spring offensive.

In April 1813, the Russians and their Prussian allies launched their campaign, advancing into eastern Germany. When Napoleon learned of the allies' movements, he rejoined his army on 28 April near Leipzig and planned to capture the city. The Prussians struck first, attacking Ney's corps at Lutzen, but were beaten back. On 20 May, the two armies clashed again at Bautzen, but the fighting there was indecisive. While the two armies remained in the field, Francis of Austria intervened, arranging peace talks between the two sides. In the ensuing negotiations, the allied powers demanded the evacuation of all French-occupied lands and the acknowledgement of the Rhine as their eastern border. Napoleon refused to accept the terms, and with the continuation of the war seeming certain, Austria finally joined forces with the allies.

When the truce expired in the autumn, France faced the Sixth Coalition, comprising Great Britain, Austria, Russia, Prussia and Sweden. Napoleon and his marshals continued to defend the French conquests in eastern Germany. As the emperor remained with his men, on 26 August the Austrians, under Prince Karl Philip of Schwarzenberg, collided with the French near Dresden. The Habsburgs were deployed in a semicircle around half of the city, anchored on the Elbe River. As the battle began, the French were steadily pushed back, but after Bonaparte arrived in the late afternoon, the Austrians and their allies were repulsed. On the following morning, Napoleon advanced his troops into the enemy, and with superior utilization of his artillery, the Austrians were compelled to abandon the battlefield with heavy losses. In the following months, the French fought a succession of inconclusive clashes that slowly depleted Napoleon's army. In mid-October, with the allies closing in, Napoleon ordered his men to withdraw to Leipzig, where he was resolved to stand and fight. He established his headquarters south of the city on a slight rise and issued his orders for battle. Napoleon planned to open the encounter with an attack against the Habsburgs to the south and a move to the north against the Prusso-Austrians of General Gebhard von Blucher.

On the morning of 16 October, the French army of 177,000 men clashed with the forces of Austria, while the Russians were still hurrying to Leipzig. The battle began with a massive French artillery barrage, over 2,000 cannons firing into the enemy lines for several hours. After the guns fell silent, the Austrians on the allied southern front moved forward, but were thrown back in savage fighting. Meanwhile, to the north, Blucher sent his soldiers against Napoleon's left wing, with the whole French line now drawn into the fighting. At nightfall, both sides continued to hold their positions after a day of charges and counter-charges. The following morning, the armies were too exhausted to renew the fierce struggle and engaged only in artillery exchanges. In the late afternoon, the Russians and Swedes finally began arriving at Leipzig, increasing the allied troop strength to over 380,000 soldiers. On 18 October, the Swedish troops unleashed an attack against the French front to the north, compelling Emperor Napoleon to send his elite Old Guard to repel them. During the fighting, Napoleon took command of a cavalry unit and personally led the charge into the Swedish lines. By the end of the day, the French had sustained severe casualties, with over 38,000 killed or wounded, and Bonaparte was forced to order his battered army to withdraw. In the wake of the French defeat at Leipzig, the Confederation of the Rhine broke apart and the remnants of the non-French forces retreated across the Rhine, leaving the border unprotected.

The emperor hurried back to Paris to prepare the defence of France against invasion by the allies, who attempted to negotiate an end to the war. To resolve the issue of France's border, the allies proposed the natural boundary of the Rhine, but Britain strongly opposed the suggestion and the border of 1792 was substituted. Napoleon rejected the proposed treaty, and in January 1814 he rejoined his army in eastern France to counter the allied attack. Fighting with significantly smaller forces, Napoleon led his men in a brilliant succession of battles against Blucher and the Austrian troops of Schwarzenberg, winning four minor encounters in nine days. Despite the determined resistance of the French, the combined strength of the allied armies, along with British financial assistance, compelled the surrender of Napoleon. On 31 March 1814, the troops of the allied powers marched into Paris, and six days later Emperor Napoleon signed his abdication, overwhelmed by the united military might of Britain, Austria, Russia, Prussia, Sweden and numerous German princedoms. The emperor had earlier offered to abdicate in favour of his young son, but the proposal was rejected and he was forced to accept the Treaty of Fontainebleau. Under the terms of the treaty, he was granted the title of emperor and the small island of Elba in the Mediterranean, off the coast of western Italy. The agreement stipulated that Elba was to be an independent principality ruled by Napoleon. Upon his death, the island – just 18 miles long and 11 miles across at its widest point, with a population of 12,000 residents at the time of Bonaparte's arrival – was to return to Tuscan control.

Napoleon sailed from France in late April 1814, landing on his new island home, to the welcome of its citizens, on 4 May. He quickly took possession of his new realm and established his government. After touring the poor and mountainous island, Napoleon ordered and oversaw a massive infrastructure improvements programme. After forming his imperial army of 1,100 soldiers and his administration, Bonaparte, showing his characteristic energy and enthusiasm, set about ruling his domain. Under the emperor's watchful eye, new roads were constructed, agriculture increased by draining marshlands, the schools overhauled and the legal system modernized. Napoleon remained in touch with events in France, where the allied forces had restored the Bourbon dynasty to power. King Louis XVIII was placed on the French throne, but became increasingly unpopular after restoring the ultra-royalist factions in his new government, who supported the return of the old regime. France was beset with an economic slowdown, the king's policies doing little to improve the hardships of the citizens. Reports from the emperor's agents in France began to suggest growing dissension was developing among the allies, as England and Austria united to fend off the expansionist policies of Alexander I. As the discord escalated, in February 1815 Napoleon decided to break his agreement with the allied powers and return to France. He sailed from Elba on 26 February, having remained on the island for ten months, landing in Cannes three days later, where his arrival was greeted with widespread enthusiasm and support. As Napoleon moved toward Paris, Louis XVIII fled to Ghent on 13 March; a week later, the emperor entered Paris. He established his headquarters in the Tuileries Palace and issued a new liberal constitution for the governing of his realm, while renouncing any desire to rebuild his fallen empire. Meanwhile, in Vienna, the allied powers quickly resolved their differences and reaffirmed their determination to march against France.

By June, the allied nations had devised a battle plan, sending a British army (containing Dutch and German elements) led by the Duke of Wellington, Arthur Wellesley, and the Prussian troops of Blucher to attack France from the north, while Austrian and Russian armies advanced to invade from the east. Napoleon needed a quick and decisive victory in the north to be free to counter the approaching armies from the east. He planned to first eliminate the Prussians and then move against Wellington, before swinging to the east. When the French clashed with Blucher at Ligny, they were unable to conclusively defeat him. Two days later, on 18 June, the emperor's army clashed with Wellington's forces at Waterloo. To save his regime, Bonaparte needed to defeat the British before the Prussians could unite with them. At Waterloo the French soldiers were deployed along a 2½-mile front and prepared to attack the British. Napoleon delayed the battle for five hours to allow the wet ground to dry after several hours of hard rain. He had an army of 72,000 soldiers against Wellington's 68,000, and planned to begin the battle by attacking the enemy's left centre after his artillery blew holes in the British defences. Near 11.30 am, the French cannons opened fire, pounding the British lines for over an hour before Napoleon ordered his infantrymen forward. Wellington had earlier moved his men back behind the slope of a hill, minimizing the effects of the bombardment. The French I Corps, under Jean-Baptiste Drouet, led the attack,but came under heavy musket and cannon fire when they approached the enemy's positions and were pushed back with heavy losses. Despite repeated assaults by the French infantry, and massed cavalry charges led by Marshal Ney, the British defensive front held firm. Late in the afternoon, the advance guard of the Prussian army began reaching the battlefield, and the allies slowly gained the advantage. In desperation, the emperor ordered the Imperial Guard into the onslaught, but when they too were driven back and Wellington countered-attacked, the Battle of Waterloo was lost for the emperor.

Following his devastating defeat at Waterloo, Napoleon travelled back to Paris and attempted to save his crown by rallying the French to his cause. Despite his appeals for support, he generated little enthusiasm. The emperor's position had become untenable, with both the French legislative body and people having turned against him. On 22 June, he abdicated for a second time in favour of his son, but the Chamber of Deputies refused to acknowledge Napoleon II and voted for the restoration of Louis XVIII. Napoleon was forced to leave Paris three days later, spending several days at Josephine's home at Malmaison before departing for the Atlantic port of Rochefort in the hope of fleeing to America. However, the harbour was blockaded by the British, and with escape impossible he surrendered on 5 July. Bonaparte crossed the English Channel on HMS *Bellerophon* and was compelled to remain on the ship while the allies decided his fate. In August, he was declared a British prisoner and exiled to the remote and rocky South Atlantic island of St Helena. The British stationed 1,400 soldiers on the island to ensure Napoleon could not escape again. When the deposed emperor landed on St Helena, he called his new home 'A disgraceful land, it is a prison',

Bonaparte was assigned Longwood, a converted wooden farmhouse, as his residence. Longwood contained five small rooms and a bedroom, where Napoleon spent most of his time. He followed a strict daily routine, being awoken at 6.00 am and having breakfast. If the weather was clear, he went for a ride before lunch. In the afternoons, Bonaparte occupied his time by writing a history of Napoleonic France and his military campaigns. His last offensive was launched through his memoirs, where he glorified and magnified his legend. He represented himself as the defender of the liberal spirit and gains of the Revolution against forces that wished to keep Europe under the old order's subjugation.

At the beginning of his stay on the island, the emperor's relations with the British were friendly, but when Hudson Lowe was transferred to St Helena as governor, they quickly became hostile. Under Lowe's instructions, attempts were made to isolate Bonaparte from outside visitors, while his correspondence was censored. The former emperor skilfully used Lowe's interventions to depict himself as an abused martyr in European public opinion. During his first years on St Helena, Napoleon maintained a generally robust physical condition, despite the harsh weather and his failing relations with the British. As time wore on, however, he began to suffer from a series of illnesses caused by the cold, damp weather, coupled with inactivity, boredom and despair. Under these unfavourable conditions, Bonaparte's physical state deteriorated, leaving him feeling weak and feeble. His once-robust health steadily declined, and at 5.49 pm on 5 May 1821, after five-and-a-half years on St Helena, Napoleon Bonaparte died in his bed at Longwood. Reportedly, his final words were 'France', 'army' and lastly 'Josephine.' He was buried on the island in an unmarked grave, where he remained for almost 20 years. In the years following his death, his legend grew across Europe, in large part due to the success of his propaganda campaign devised on St Helena. A movement began to sweep across France to return Bonaparte's remains to the heart of his former empire and bury him according to the wishes written in his will. In 1840, the regime of King Louis Philippe I approved the funeral arrangements for Napoleon's arrival in Paris, and he was buried at Les Invalides in a ceremony of great pomp and grandeur.

Selected Sources

Barnett, Correlli, *Bonaparte*
Brett-James, Antony, *The Hundred Days*
Cronin, Vincent, *Napoleon*
Delderfield, R.F., *Napoleon's Marshals*
Delderfield, R.F., *The Retreat from Moscow*
Herold, J. Christopher, *Bonaparte in Egypt*
Herold, J. Christopher, *The Age of Napoleon*
Markham, Felix, *Napoleon*
McLynn, Frank, *Napoleon – A Biography*
Norwich, John Julius, *A History of France*
Potter, Philip J., *Kings of the Seine*
Rothenberg, Gunther E., *The Napoleonic Wars*
Segur, Philippe-Paul de, *Napoleon's Russian Campaign*

Illustrations

Charles II – Image from the National Library of France, a reproduction by scanning of a bidimensional work from Saint Marin Abbey, Tours, France, considered in the public domain.

Philip II Augustus – Coronation of Philip II Augustus of France (British Library). The work is in the public domain in its country of origin and other countries and areas, where the copyright term is the author's life plus seventy years or less.

Louis XI – This work is in the public domain in its country of origin and other countries and areas, where the copyright term is the author's life plus 100 years or less.

Louis XII – This work is in the public domain in its country of origin and other countries and areas, where the copyright term is the author's life plus 100 years or less.

Francis I – This work is in the public domain in its country of origin and other countries and areas, where the copyright term is the author's life plus 100 years or less. This work is in the public domain in the United States because it was published or registered with the US Copyright Office before 1 January 1926.

Henry IV – This work is in the public fomain in its country of origin and other countries and areas, where the copyright term is the author's life plus 100 years or less. This work is in the public domain in the United States because it was published or registered with the US Copyright Office before 1 January 1926.

Louis XIV – This work is in the public domain in its country of origin and other countries and areas, where the copyright term is the author's life plus 100 years or less. This work is in the public domain in the United States because it was published or registered with the US Copyright Office before 1 January 1926.

Napoleon – This work is in the public domain in its country of origin and other countries and areas, where the copyright term is the author's life plus 100 years or less. This work is in the public domain in the United States because it was published or registered with the US Copyright Office before 1 January 1926.

Louis XII Leading his Army into Battle – This work is in the public domain in its country of origin and other countries, where the copyright term is the author's life plus 100 years or less. This work is in the public domain in the United States because it was published or registered with the US Copyright Office before 1 January 1926.

Francis I at the Battle of Marignano, 1515 – This work is in the public domain in its country of origin and other countries and areas, where the copyright term is the author's life plus 100 years or less. This work is in the public domain in the United States because it was published or registered with the US copyright Office before 1 January 1926.

Louis XIV at the Siege of Maastricht, 1673 – This work is in the public domain in its country of origin and other countries and areas, where the copyright term is the author's life plus 100 years or less. This work is in the public domain in the United States because it was published or registered with the US Copyright Office before 1 January 1926.

Napoleon at the Siege of Toulon, 1793 – This work is in the public domain in its country of origin and other countries and areas, where the copyright term is the author's life plus 100 years or less.

Napoleon at the Battle of Friedland, 1807 – This work is in the public domain in its country of origin and other countries and areas, where the copyright term is the author's life plus 100 years or less. This work is in the public domain in the United States because it was published or registered with the US Copyright Office before 1 January 1926.

Coronation Ceremony of Napoleon

This work is in the public domain in its country of origin and other countries and areas, where the copyright term is the author's life plus 100 years or less. This work is in the public domain in the United States because it was published or registered with the US Copyright Office before 1 January 1926. Painting by Jacques-Louis David, on display at the Louvre Museum in Paris.

Bibliography

Barnett, Correlli, *Bonaparte* (New York: Hill and Wang, 1978)

Baumgartner, Frederic J., *Louis XII* (New York: St Martin's Press, 1994)

Bernier, Olivier, *Louis XIV – A Royal Life* (New York/London: Doubleday, 1987)

Boulenger, Jacques, *The Seventeenth Century* (New York: G.P. Putman's Sons, 1920)

Bradbury, Jim, *Philip Augustus* (London: Addison Wesley Longman, 1998)

Bradbury, Jim, *The Capetians Kings of France 987–1328* (London/ New York: Hambledon Continuum, 2007)

Brett-James, Antony, *The Hundred Days* (New York: St Martin's Press, 1964)

Briggs, Robin, *Early Modern France* (Oxford/London/New York: Oxford University Press, 1977)

Butler, Mildred Allen, *Twice Queen of France* (New York: Funk and Wagnalls, 1967)

Castries, Duc de, *The Lives of the Kings and Queens of France* (New York: Alfred A. Knopf, 1979)

Champion, Pierre, *Louis XI* (New York: Dodd, Mead & Company, 1929)

Cleugh, James, *Chant Royal* (New York: Doubleday & Company, 1970)

Cronin, Vincent, *Louis XIV* (London: The Harvill Press, 1964)

Cronin, Vincent, *Napoleon* (London: Harper Collins Publishers, 1994)

Delderfield, R.F., *Napoleon's Marshalls* (New York: Stein and Day Publishers, 1962)

Delderfield, R.F., *The Retreat From Moscow* (New York: Atheneum, 1967)

Dunbabin, Jean, *France in the Making 843–1189* (Oxford/New York: Oxford University Press, 2000)

Dunlop, Ian, *Louis XIV* (New York: St Martin's Press, 1999)

Erlanger, Philippe, *Louis XIV* (New York: Praeger Publishers, 1970)

Fawtier, Robert, *The Capetian Kings of France* (London/Melbourne/ Toronto: MacMillan, 1968)

Frieda, Leonie, *Francis I – The Maker of Modern France* (New York: Harper Perennial, 2018)

Gisserot, Jean-Paul, *The Family Trees of the Kings of France* (Paris: Jean-Charles Volkmann, 2002)

Hackett, Francis, *Francis the First* (New York: The Literary Guild, 1935)

Hallam, Elizabeth M., *Capetian France 987–1328* (London/New York: Longman, 1980)

Herold, Christopher J., *Bonaparte in Egypt* (London: Hamish Hamilton, 1962)

Herold, Christopher J., *The Age of Napoleon* (New York: American Heritage Publishing Company, 1963)

Hutton, William Holden, *Philip Augustus* (London: Macmillan and Company, 1896)

James, Edward, *The Origins of France* (London: Macmillan Press Ltd, 1982)

Kendall, Paul Murray, *Louis XI* (New York: W.W. Norton & Company, 1971)

Knecht, R.J., *Renaissance Warrior and Patron* (Cambridge, UK: Cambridge University Press, 1994)

Knecht, R.J., *The Rise and Fall of Renaissance France 1483–1610* (Oxford: Blackwell Publishers, 2001)

Knecht, Robert, *The Valois – Kings of France 1328–1589* (London/New York: Hambledon and London, 2004)

Laffin, John, *Brassey's Dictionary of Battles* (New York: Barnes and Noble, 1998)

Law, Joy, *Fleur de Lys – The Kings & Queens of France* (New York: McGraw Hill Book Company, 1976)

Lynn, John A., *The Wars of Louis XIV* (Harlow, UK: Pearson Education Limited, 1999)

Markham, Felix, *Napoleon* (New York: New American Library, 1963)

Mass, Gustave, *Medieval France* (London: G.P. Putnam's Sons, 1901)

Maurois, Andre, *A History of France* (London: Minerva Press, 1968)

McKitterick, Rosamond, *The Frankish Kingdoms Under the Carolingians* (London: Longman Group Limited, 1983)

McLynn, Frank, *Napoleon* (New York: Arcade Publishing, 1997)

Norwich, John Julius, *A History of France* (New York: Grove Press, 2018)

Nelson, Janet, *Charles The Bald* (London: Longman Group Limited, 1996)

Pearson, Hesketh, *Henry of Navarre* (New York: Harper & Row Publishers, 1963)

Potter, David, *A History of France 1460–1560* (New York: St Martin's Press, 1995)

Potter, Philip J., *Kings of the Seine* (Baltimore, Maryland: Publish America, LLLP, 2005)

Riche, Pierre, *The Carolingians* (Philadelphia: University of Pennsylvania Press, 1994)

Romier, Lucien, *A History of France* (New York: St Martin's Press, 1953)

Rothenberg, Gunther E., *The Napoleonic Wars* (London: Cassell, 2001)

Russell, Lord of Liverpool, *Henry of Navarre* (New York: Praeger Publishers, 1969)

Sedgwick, Henry Dwight, *Henry of Navarre* (Indianapolis: The Bobbs-Merrill Company Publisher, 1930)

Segur, Count Philippe-Paul de, *Napoleon's Russian Campaign* (New York: Time Incorporated, 1965)

Seward, Desmond, *Prince of the Renaissance – The Life of Francis I* (London: Sphere Books Ltd, 1974)

Seward, Desmond, *The Bourbon Kings of France* (London: Constable and Company, 1976)

Seward, Desmond, *The First Bourbon* (Boston: Gambit, Inc, 1971)

Sumption, Jonathan, *The Albigensian Crusade* (London/New York: Faber and Faber, 1978)

Tilley, Arthur, *Medieval France* (New York/London: Hafner Publishing Company, 1964)

Wilkinson, Burke, *Francis in All His Glory* (New York: Farrar, Straus & Giroux, 1972)

Wolf, John B., *Louis IX* (New York: W.W. Norton & Company, 1969)

Index